Presence

Presence

Giving and Receiving God

J. Alexander Sider
and
Isaac S. Villegas

CASCADE *Books* · Eugene, Oregon

PRESENCE
Giving and Receiving God

Copyright © 2011 J. Alexander Sider and Isaac S. Villegas. All rights reserved. Except for brief quotations in critical publications or reviews, no part of this book may be reproduced in any manner without prior written permission from the publisher. Write: Permissions, Wipf and Stock Publishers, 199 W. 8th Ave., Suite 3, Eugene, OR 97401.

Cascade Books
An Imprint of Wipf and Stock Publishers
199 W. 8th Ave., Suite 3
Eugene, OR 97401

www.wipfandstock.com

ISBN 13: 978-1-60899-671-1

Cataloging-in-Publication data:

Sider, J. Alexander.

    Presence : giving and receiving God / J. Alexander Sider and Isaac S. Villegas.

    xii + 218 p. ; cm. Includes bibliographical references.

    ISBN 13: 978-1-60899-671-1

    1. Sermons, American. 2. Christian life—Sermons. I. Villegas, Isaac S. II. Title.

BV4241 .S54 2011

Manufactured in the U.S.A.

Contents

Introduction | vii

1 Hope | 1
Lament and Repent | 2
Gone Missing | 7
Silent Witnesses | 11
Waiting for a Promise | 17
Waiting with Mary | 22
Mater Ecclesia | 28
A Protest of Hope | 33

2 Communion | 35
Eucharist Means Gratitude | 36
Flesh and Blood | 40
Our Tortured King | 46
Bodies Matter | 50

3 Desire | 55
Heart's Desire | 56
Faith and Love | 62
Closer | 69
If Our Hearts Condemn Us | 74
You Shall Not Covet | 79

4 Power | 85

    Illusions of Peace | 86
    Paul's Politics | 91
    Power in Weakness | 99
    Preparing for Peace | 105
    Remembering Home | 112

5 Money | 117

    Caesar's Coin | 118
    Dirty Money | 125
    Irresponsible Stewards | 130
    Human Enough | 135

6 Salvation | 143

    Companions without Paychecks | 144
    Life on the Vine | 149
    Deliverance from Egypt | 155
    Salvation Is Created | 160

7 Strangers | 165

    Do You See This Woman? | 166
    Strangers | 173
    Who Are You? | 179
    The Risen Body | 186

8 Conclusion | 191

    Voices | 192
    What Is This? | 198

Notes | 205

Introduction

This book is about relaxing into God through and with the activity of preaching. The reflections we offer here began their life as sermons and meditations at Chapel Hill Mennonite Fellowship (CHMF) in Chapel Hill, NC. For both of us, life together at CHMF has been the most profoundly transformative, embracing, and intensive church experience of our lives. To go to church with people whom you like, and to trust them for God's care, is to welcome a grace that disarms your guardedness and makes room for you to fall into the love of God. Gratefulness and thankfulness seem like paltry words to describe the gift CHMF has been to us. We have experienced this church as nothing less than Christ's saving life for us. Salvation has happened to us through the companionship found at our church. The people there have changed our lives, and now we can't help but take them along with us wherever we go. It is a frank acknowledgement of CHMF's place in our lives to say that we would not know who we are and who we are meant to be had it not been for this congregation. The friendships we've found in church have infused us with God's presence. Our lives will be forever marked with the kindness and grace, tensions and anxieties, and patience and concern of the people who are CHMF. In many ways this book of sermons is a collection of sappy love letters to the people who taught us what God's love feels like. As you read them, we hope that you may hear echoes of this same love in your church and among your friends—and our hope is that you not merely hear the echoes, but that the echoes would draw you further into the places where God's love is made flesh.

To give you, as readers, a better sense of the community from which we are writing, we want to offer a series of snapshots of "how it all works" at CHMF. From our descriptions we hope that you will be able to sense something of what we find so life-giving in church, and that you will be able to read our sermons as invitations for you also to relax into God's presence.

As a Mennonite congregation, our worship is a display of what it means to be a priesthood of all believers. To be a church of priests means that *you* mediate God's life to *me*. The Holy Spirit offers a fresh word for you through each of the people gathered for worship. Christ comes to church with you and offers himself through you to me. Our conviction about the church as a priesthood of all believers is not merely a typically Protestant tenant of faith that is never liturgically displayed—or a Gnostic belief affirmed as an invisible, psychological reality that doesn't need to be enfleshed. At CHMF our priesthood is made liturgically real with our bodies by sharing leadership roles. The authority to re-present God is shared among those who gather for worship. Each worship gathering draws from the wealth of gifts in the community. Rotations of volunteers share the responsibilities of preaching, worship planning, praying, and leading our songs. No one person dominates the pulpit. Up to ten people occupy that position of authority throughout the service. They are our priests, speaking the Word of God for us.

The sermon prepares us for the high point of our worship, which is a time set aside for anyone to respond to what God's Spirit is saying to us. The preacher steps away from the pulpit and returns to her or his pew with the rest of the congregation. Someone else gets up from a pew, walks up to the pulpit, and leads the rest of us in a time of "discerning the Word"—or, as it is called in the Mennonite tradition, the "Zeugnis." The congregation is asked to discern whether or not the gospel was preached, and if it was indeed preached, then to discern what this gospel may mean for our lives. Because we believe that anyone can offer an inspired interpretation of the Bible, we provide time during worship for people to share their reflections on the Scriptures and the sermon. The last word belongs to the congregation, not to the preacher. We deliberately divest the preacher of control over the gospel. Because our church is an assembly of priests, the final authority to speak for God comes through the conversation (the Zeugnis) where we discern the Spirit together. The conversation after the sermon continues the proclamation of God's Word as it echoes through all of our voices.

Of course, preaching is exhausting. Becoming incandescent to God's Spirit in preaching is hard work, for it demands an utter openness that allows us (as preachers) to be transparent to Christ's gathered body so that we are in no way obstacles to the flow of grace. We move in registers of success and failure in this regard, and that too is exhausting. It feels risky to lay our lives bare in order to be received by others as grace, and to wait for their response and hope that God's Word did indeed make a connection between them and us. So, slumping down into a pew while the congregation takes up the word we have offered and tests it, tears it, enriches it, and transforms it is often profoundly unsettling. And yet, we have found that our vulnerability and riskedness as preachers has become a way of resting into God, because the dispossession of God's Word that happens through dialogue occurs in a context where the conversation is infused with love. We hope that in these sermons you can feel the pulse of that love.

Three quick notes as you read. First, worship with our sisters and brothers at CHMF has convinced us that the Word of God is not God's Word until it has been received as both *good* and *news*—thus the roots of the word "gospel." Sometimes the discernment of that Word takes time; sometimes one never knows if the Word of God has been spoken or not. So, secondly, pause as you read. CHMF is a place where we are silent much of the time and do not necessarily have a lot to say. Make that silence—as an opening into the stillness of God—part of your reading, too. And, thirdly, only a few of these sermons ask you to do something as a response to the gospel. As you read, if you are like us, you might well say, "This is all fine, but where do we go from here?" We have recognized this drive for productivity in our lives as one that steers us toward doing God's work in order to hide from how God's presence is gently and insistently molding and transforming us, as the apostle Paul says, "from glory unto glory." So read these sermons and reflect on this practice of preaching not so much as a call to do, but as an invitation to be who you are—impatient, driven, anguished, confused, despairing, enraptured, centered—in the presence of the One who is closer to you than you are to yourself, as Augustine of Hippo once wrote in his *Confessions*.

Suggestions for Reading

Our sermons are meditations on different passages from the Bible. The Worship Committee at CHMF asks us to preach from the Scriptures assigned from the Revised Common Lectionary. You will find the assigned passages listed at the beginning of each sermon. We would suggest that you meditate on the passages before and after reading the sermon. The best preaching doesn't provide a final reading of a passage that leaves the text behind once we find the "right" answer or the "correct" meaning; instead, sermons return us to the Scriptures again and again so that we may read, meditate, pray, and discuss the Word of God. In Scripture we encounter the Word as a companion, not a solution. The purpose of each sermon in this book is to offer another invitation to enter "the strange new world of the Bible," as Karl Barth once described our Holy Scriptures.

The sermons are arranged according to themes: Hope, Communion, Desire, Power, Money, Salvation, and Strangers; and the two sermons at the end of the book serve as an invitation to take up the task of discerning the Word in your own community. Feel free to read around in the book as meets your needs. If you want a sermon on money, by all means skip the preceding themes and get to the section on money. We also hope that some of you will use this book as a resource for small groups or as material for Sunday school.

Lastly, there are notes for each sermon at the back of the book. They are not exhaustive, but may help you dig deeper into the resources from which we've drawn. We list as many sources as we can remember using. But, as is the case for preaching, ideas come from everywhere during the week—a line from a newspaper article, a phrase from a television commercial, a feeling from a song on the radio, or a sentence in a book—and we didn't catalogue everything at the time of our preparation. So it's important to say that our best readings of Bible passages are probably not original to us; we're always dependent on others—whether they are biblical commentators, or the profound insights from the people at CHMF who ask tough questions, humbly offer important corrections, and outline new ways forward in our biblical faith. That's why you will find scattered throughout the sermons names of people at our church who have shared questions and comments during our liturgical time for discernment as well as in conversations during the week. For every name we mention, there are many others we've forgotten. This book is as much a book by them as it is by the two of us. In many respects, it's hard to parse out their thoughts from our "own," whatever that word means. For that reason, we gratefully dedicate this book to our sisters and brothers who have gathered and continue to gather for worship at Chapel Hill Mennonite Fellowship.

We are especially grateful to the following people from church who read sections of our manuscript and offered helpful criticisms and suggestions: Jen Coon, Jon Dueck, Catherine and Michael Lee, Tom Lehman, Nick Plummer, Matt Thiessen, and Katie Villegas.

Hope

Lament and Repent

Isaiah 11:1–10; Matthew 3:1–12

A shoot shall come out from the stump of Jesse,
and a branch shall grow out of his roots.
~ Isaiah 11:1

As soon as Katie and I moved into our house, I began to make some changes to the front yard. I became obsessed. I started to tear out all the plants the previous owners had planted or let overgrow. First I took out all the ivy. It was everywhere, even breaking its way into the crawl space below the house. It had to go. Once I had taken all of it out, I looked at the front yard and I still wasn't satisfied. There were three holly bushes that had turned into trees, very ugly trees. Katie didn't mind them so much, but I hated them. After much persistence she let me cut them down. I borrowed Bradley King's chainsaw. I woke up Monday morning, took the chainsaw out front, and got to work on those holly trees. I soon found out that this was a strange thing to do. I guess it's unusual to walk your dog down the street and see a crazed neighbor wandering around in the front yard with a chainsaw. But the worried looks from dog walkers didn't stop me. With only mangled stumps left from the holly trees, I got a load of compost and a load of mulch from the dump and filled in the area where the holly trees used to be. The space was now reclaimed for my own gardening. The holly was gone.

Or so I thought. The two smaller trees were done for; they couldn't survive the chainsaw trauma. But the other one wasn't so small. The tree was gone, but it left a large stump and an extensive root system. In late spring I discovered some strange shoots poking out from the middle of my newly planted verbena. What were they? It took me a week or so to figure it out. Sure enough, they were shoots from the submerged holly stump and roots. They came up everywhere. Almost everyday I found a new one. Even after such devastation something survived. Under all of the compost and mulch, life started to fight back.

This is also the story of Israel. It's the story the prophet Isaiah knows well, the story of God's people who suffer destruction at the hands of foreign armies. Babylon moves into the neighborhood with many armies and levels the southern kingdom of Israel, also called Judah. Just as I took a chainsaw to that large holly tree, so did Babylon use their armies to cut down the people of Judah. Nothing remained, only a stump—the humiliated remains of a people laid low to the ground. But Isaiah says that Israel resembles my holly stump: even though it's cut down and buried, there will be a shoot, a sprout, a sign of hope. "A shoot shall come out from the stump of Jesse, and a branch shall grow out of his roots" (Isa 11:1). When every reason for hope seems lost, Isaiah tells us to wait and watch and hope—*something is coming, something is stirring in the earth.*

When John the Baptist comes on the scene many years later, the people of Israel have been waiting a long time for this shoot of Jesse—another David, another king—to restore Israel to its splendor among the nations. John appears in the wilderness of Judea proclaiming, "Repent, for the kingdom of heaven has come near" (Matt 3:10), and the crowds flock to him. The people of Jerusalem leave the courts of the temple and go out into the wildernesses to be baptized. John becomes a threat to the religious establishment in Jerusalem. He's a figure on the margins who gathers crowds from Jerusalem and challenges the authority of the elite, the Pharisees and Sadducees. As one New Testament scholar puts it, John is a "counter-clerical prophet" (Wright, 161).

When I read about John the Baptist, I am drawn to him and frightened by him at the same time. For John, the advent of the Messiah means devastation and collapse. Advent means everything will be crushed, demolished, cut down. For John, the coming of the Messiah looks like me, running around my front yard with a chainsaw, chopping down trees. He says as much in Matthew's Gospel, "Even now the ax is lying at the root of the trees, every tree therefore that does not bear good fruit is cut down and thrown into the fire" (Matt 3:10). John goes on to talk about what the Messiah will do when he comes: "His winnowing fork is in his hand, and he will clear his threshing floor and will gather his wheat into the granary; but the chaff he will burn with unquenchable fire" (v. 12).

The season of Advent is a time for new beginnings, but this new life shoots out from piles of debris. The chainsaw comes first. Advent is a time for cleansing, for repentance, for lament. As Jay Forth said in his sermon last week, Advent is a season of hospitality—a season that teaches us how to receive the Messiah. And John tells us that we extend hospitality to the Messiah—we prepare for Advent—through repentance.

A few weeks ago Katie and I went to a talk by Chris and Phileena Heuertz. They lead an organization called Word Made Flesh. Phileena and Chris have teams throughout the world who locate themselves among the poorest of the poor; they live among the crushed and abused, and make friends. Through these friendships they learn what it means to serve Jesus in those places. At their talk, Chris and Phileena told lots of stories, stories about their friends—about AIDS-infected children who live in orphanages, about little boys and girls who've been sold into prostitution, and about mothers and fathers who have absolutely no way to provide bread or rice for their families. As they told stories about their friends, I sat in a cushy chair in a big, fancy church in Durham. The worlds Phileena and Chris described grated against the middle-class world in which I lived and moved and had my being. I thought to myself: *How can anyone, how can this couple, see and feel so much and not go crazy?* I kept on expecting them to overturn tables as Jesus did, or knock down pillars as Samson did. *How can they sit there and tolerate me and my half-hearted world?*

Finally, a woman asked a question and I hoped for some resolution: "What would you like us to tell our churches to do, what can we do, how can we reach out and make a difference?" As she spoke I thought to myself: *Yes, that's exactly what I want to know, that's what I need to know; I can't go on with all of these stories in my head without knowing that I'm doing something positive. I need someone to tell me my penance so I can get rid of the guilt that comes with my privileged life.*

Phileena was about to say something in response, and I slid to the edge of my seat. But, instead of words, she gave us tears and sobs. She cried for about thirty to forty-five seconds, which felt like an eternity. She just cried, and all of us sat there in silence, fidgeting in our seats, uncomfortably watching her or finding a spot on the ground to stare at. Finally, between tears and sobs she said two words, only two words: "Repent and lament." *Repent and lament!* That's all she had to say? Her words took me by surprise. I was baffled. I guess I'm used to the television commercials for humanitarian aid organizations that bombard me with pictures of suffering so that when the phone number or Web site flashes at the bottom of the screen, I will be ready to pay my penance. These agencies try to tap into my conscience and compel me to give them money and make a difference. But Phileena refused those tactics. That's not what she gave me—and I'm almost mad at her for it. She gave me something much more difficult. Her cries chopped down my prideful thoughts of quick and easy solutions—like a donation to ease my conscience. Nobody passed a plate so I could empty my pockets and empty my head from all of the stories. Instead, in the debris of our messianic solutions, she planted the words that lead to life, that lead to humility, that lead to John the Baptist in the wilderness: "Repent and lament," Phileena said. Those words did not map out the solution for which I had hoped. Phileena's cries marked a beginning. Her modest words silenced my ready-made answers and provoked new questions. For what must I repent? And what loss, whose death, should I lament? How can lamentation and repentance connect me with strangers across an ocean and across the street?

Those are the questions of our season of Advent, the questions that extend hospitality to the Messiah, the questions that prepare us for the coming of the Lord. John the Baptist says, "Repent, for the kingdom of heaven has come near." And Matthew adds, "This is the one of whom the prophet Isaiah spoke when he said, 'The voice of one crying out in the wilderness: Prepare the way of the Lord'" (Matt 3:3). But what exactly are we preparing for? Why did Phileena tell me to prepare for hope through repentance and lamentation? Why leave our lives behind and venture into the wilderness to repent and wash in the Jordan? Well, because we've heard the promises of a coming kingdom, a coming Messiah, and we want to be members of that humble people of God who are laid waste, chopped down, cut to the ground, in order to make room for the shoot of Jesse to break through the darkness, to break through our lives, and to make us a people fit for the Messiah. That's Advent hospitality. Lamentation and repentance are how we make way for the coming of the Lord.

Now, what exactly are we preparing for? What will the Messiah bring? Isaiah tells us. His vision exposes the shadows of our world and invites us to receive a different one, the world of the Messiah, the kingdom of heaven come to earth:

> with righteousness he shall judge the poor, and decide with equity for the meek of the earth; he shall strike the earth with the rod of his mouth, and with the breath of his lips he shall kill the wicked. . . . The wolf shall live with the lamb, the leopard shall lie down with the kid, the calf and the lion and the fatling together, and a little child shall lead them. The cow and the bear shall graze, their young shall lie down together; and the lion shall eat straw like the ox. . . . They will not hurt or destroy on all my holy mountain; for the earth will be full of the knowledge of the Lord. . . . On that day the root of Jesse shall stand as a signal to the peoples; the nations shall inquire of him, and his dwelling shall be glorious. (Isa 11:3–10)

Gone Missing

Job 23:1–9, 16–17; Psalm 22:1–15

Job is a righteous man, a pious man, a master of spirituality. And he enjoys all the pleasures of life: wealth, family, sons and daughters. But all of these gifts are taken suddenly from him and he is left in misery. Job's friends come along and try to help him make sense of the calamities. They try out their theories about evil and offer Job the comfort of an explanation for his suffering. They offer theories of sin and punishment. The friends try to fit Job into their well-crafted theologies—ideas about the way God uses evil to punish a sinful creation. Yet with every explanation Job's misery gets louder and louder. The words of his friends bring no comfort; they only prod Job's festering wounds, thus increasing the pain. At one point Job says to his friends: "I have heard many things like these; miserable comforters are you all! Will your long-winded speeches never end? What ails you that you keep on arguing?" (Job 16:1–2). And again, "How long will you torment me and crush me with words?" (19:2).

In our lectionary reading for today, we find Job in his darkest moment—a darkness that comes in spite of his friends and their miserable attempts at comfort. The world is dark for Job because God seems absent; God seems to have forsaken him: "But if I go to the east, he is not there; if I go to the west, I do not find him. When he is at work in the north, I do not see him; when he turns to the south, I catch no glimpse of him" (23:8–9). As a cloud of darkness settles over his life, Job can't find God. In the midst of so much suffering and misery, God doesn't seem to be around.

I am reminded of something Nick Plummer said a couple weeks ago in response to Fred Bahnson's sermon on Esther. Fred noted how the name of God is surprisingly absent in the book of Esther. God isn't an obvious actor in that story. Then Nick commented about how this is the way we experience God many times, perhaps all the time. God seems to be absent. And this is exactly what we hear from Job. God has gone missing. Job can only see darkness, empty and silent darkness. He struggles to feel God's presence, yet finds nothing: "God is not there. . . . I do not find him. . . . I do not see him. . . . I catch no glimpse of him" (vv. 8–9). Not even a glimpse, a sliver of light to give him hope. No flash of lightning to illumine a path of healing. Instead, darkness . . . stillness . . . silence . . .

Well, not exactly silence. The darkness echoes with Job's desperate and bitter cries: "Yet I am not silenced by the darkness, by the thick darkness that covers my face" (v. 17). In this passage where God is nowhere to be found and darkness settles over the face of the earth, Job's bitter cries are all we can hear. And in our world where God seems to have gone missing, Job is our only guide. His cries still echo through the voices of misery and suffering all around us.

The way of Jesus takes us into the darkness of those who experience abandonment, because Jesus himself is among those who, like Job, intimately know the empty silence of God. From the cross he remembers the desperate words of the Psalmist: "My God, my God, why have you forsaken me? Why are you so far from saving me, so far from the words of my groaning? O my God, I cry out by day, but you do not answer, by night, and am not silent" (Ps 22:1–2). Those are the last words of Jesus in Mark's Gospel. As he gasps a last breath on the cross, Jesus prays the first verse from Psalm 22:

> At the sixth hour darkness came over the whole land until the ninth hour. And at the ninth hour Jesus cried out in a loud voice, "Eloi, Eloi, lama sabachthani?"—which means, "My God, my God, why have you forsaken me?" (Mark 15:33–34)

This is Jesus in his darkest moment. God seems to have gone missing at the point when Jesus needs God the most. "My God, my God, why have you forsaken me?" But like Job, Jesus will not be silenced by the darkness. He cries out to God the same sort of question Job asks: *Why has God disappeared?*

The temptation is to add a little light, a little hope, at the end in order to make those haunting voices go away—Job's bitter cries, and Jesus' cry of abandonment. That's apparently what some scribes did to Mark's story. If you flip to the last page of Mark's Gospel (chapter 16), you'll see what I mean. The original story ends without Jesus' resurrected appearance. Women go to the tomb and see it empty, and "a young man dressed in a white robe" tells them that Jesus is risen. But the book ends with fear and bewilderment: "Trembling and bewildered, the women went out and fled from the tomb. They said nothing to anyone, because they were afraid" (Mark 16:8). End of story. Unlike the other Gospel accounts, the resurrected Jesus doesn't return to enjoy the company of his disciples. Mark's ending of the story is so troubling that good and pious scribes added a "better" ending to the story later on—you can read it in chapter 16, verses 9–20.

Like the scribes who edited Mark's Gospel, Job's friends also try to moderate Job's cries of abandonment. They hear the profound despair in what Job is saying, and as a response his friends try to witness to a distant hope. Here's one example, one of the worst. This is what Bildad says to Job: "But if you will look to God and plead with the Almighty, if you are pure and upright, even now he will rouse himself on your behalf and restore you to your rightful place. Your beginnings will seem humble, so prosperous will your future be" (Job 8:5–7). Job's friend is basically saying, *Don't let this stuff get you down; I see a bright future ahead*. But they are empty words, platitudes. This is a man who doesn't know what to do with a suffering friend. Bildad is a friend who can't bear the darkness, who can't sit still and listen, who can't offer the comfort of silent solidarity—the gift of presence, the sympathy of a quiet moment.

Job teaches us the importance of taking suffering people seriously, so seriously that we refuse to offer them cheap hope, escapist hope, hope that can't bear the darkness. Instead, we let ourselves be drawn into their pain and darkness and wait with them so we—*together*—might come into the presence of Jesus who also cries out: "Eloi, Eloi, lama sabacthani," "My God, My God, why have you forsaken me."

The skies grow dark. As we read in Mark's story of the crucifixion, "At the sixth hour darkness came over the whole land" (Mark 15:33). There's a fog of darkness and God seems to have gone missing. We can't see enough stars to discern the right path through the wilderness of this world. But we do hear something . . . cries in the distance. Those voices are our compass. We learn the way of Jesus as we listen carefully for whispers of abandonment. And we walk toward those voices—even though we may not be able to see where our lives will end up—because those are the places where we may find Job; and with him we may find Jesus, who was last heard saying, "My God, my God, why have you forsaken me."

Although this message may not be too hopeful for some of us, I imagine that it is hopeful to those who are suffering, those who are in misery, those who feel the abandonment of God. It's a hopeful word for them because they can know that the One we worship was also abandoned by God. Jesus experienced that same darkness. They are not alone. But, to those of us who may not hear this message as hopeful, perhaps it means that we need to learn how to share our lives with those who know only darkness, those who know the darkened land where we last saw our Savior, on the cross, when the last word was abandonment.

Let me close with a comment on an experience during one of our worship services that witnessed to this kind of darkened hope. Last week during our time of sharing and prayer, Rebecca Rich shared the pain and tears of her friend's miscarriage. You listened to that pain. And we joined Dirk Tysmans in a prayer that took those tears seriously. He didn't rush past the suffering to get to cheap hope and suffocating platitudes. He didn't offer a comfortable ending to the story. Instead, Dirk's prayer made space for voices of pain to echo in our midst. In our prayer we remembered those tears and asked God to remember them with us—and to do something about it, because we didn't know what to do. That's our witness of hope—a hope that we don't possess, a hope that we can't muster-up with our imaginations; yet a hope nonetheless that waits for God to answer Jesus' question on the cross, a hope that waits for God to answer Job's bitter cries.

Silent Witnesses

Ephesians 1:3–14; Mark 6:14–29

Another absurd murder. Escalating violence. Unceasing suffering. This is the world of this past week just as much as it was the world of Mark's Gospel. John the Baptist's beheading wasn't necessarily a unique event during the Roman occupation of Palestine—and it's hard to see how it wouldn't fit in our world today, except that we use more sophisticated methods. For the sake of the stability of Palestine, Herod and others in the Roman administration had to douse the wild-fires of revolution spreading across the countryside by silencing the voices of protestors—and, sometimes, as in the case of Jesus' comrade John, the best way to silence a tongue was to cut off a head.

But we don't remember this story in the Gospel of Mark as simply another example of the violence empires deem necessary to stay afloat in a sea of anarchic terror. For some reason, Mark thinks this murder is an important piece in the story of Jesus. Yet he doesn't come right out and explain why this episode in the drama is important. Mark doesn't tell us why John's death is significant for the life of Jesus. He doesn't explain why this bit of information fits in the plot development. Right after the story of John's beheading, Mark returns to the disciples' adventures as if the past sixteen verses didn't even happen. What's Mark up to? Why does he take the time to include this gruesome story?

Here's the question I think Mark forces us to think about: How is John's death meaningful to us and to our understanding of the story of Jesus? Let's keep that question in the back of our minds as we work our way through the text like detectives at the scene of a murder.

We can be sure of one thing: Mark wants to make sure we don't forget John's beheading. In fact, Mark doesn't spend nearly this much time on any other scene in his drama—except, of course, on the passion of Jesus at the end. When comparing Mark's Gospel to the others, commentators will point out how Mark tells the story of Jesus' ministry in fast-forward so he can get to the important part, which is Jesus' death. That's why Mark's favorite word is "immediately"—Jesus performs miracles in a town, then *immediately* gets on a boat and gets on with the story. That's the typical flow of the narrative. Jesus is the focal character, and Mark wants to get Jesus to Jerusalem quickly so he can start telling us about the passion of Christ. Yet, for some strange reason, Mark interrupts the story he's telling. He makes us slow down and shift our attention from Jesus to John, that strange man from the desert. As our eyes try to keep up with Mark's fast-paced story, we get caught on a rough edge—the camera abruptly cuts away from the film's leading man and fixes our gaze on another character, someone we thought had his five minutes of fame in the first scene (at the baptism of Jesus).

Surprisingly, the main character in this episode isn't very interested in Jesus; Herod doesn't give Jesus a second thought. He's too busy worrying about John: "But when Herod heard of it [that is, the news about Jesus' growing popularity], he said, 'John, whom I beheaded, has been raised'" (6:16). News about Jesus makes Herod think about John. And you can almost feel the camera zoom in on Herod's wide eyes as he turns his head and stares off into the distance as his memory replays a traumatic experience. . . . Then, in a flashback, Mark gives us all the juicy details of Herodias' scheme to have John killed on the night of Herod's birthday party.

There is a banquet. Food everywhere. Bottomless glasses of drink. The party lasts well into the night. Then a seductive dance and Herod makes an oath that he must keep in order to save face with his important guests. And the story ends with John's head on a platter for all the people at the party to see. Herodias finally succeeds in silencing John's protest. And, strangely, *silence* is all we get from John as well. John's death sentence unfolds without a word from him. He has no chance to argue his case. John's fate is decided in his absence, as he sits in prison. The passage ends with John's disciples taking the body and laying it to rest in a tomb. Then John fades out of the story, and so does Herod. In Mark's account of Jesus' trial and death, Herod does not appear. That's an important difference from the other Gospels. The chief priests and Pilate—not Herod—execute Jesus. So we know that Mark doesn't tell us this story in chapter six to warn us about Herod, to give us a peak into the psychology of Jesus' nemesis, a preview of the killer who will send him to the cross. Not at all. King Herod is not important for the rest of the story, and neither is John. So why does Mark spill so much ink over this, at best, seemingly tangential event—John's beheading?

Here's the point I want to make: John's death is pointless and senseless. King Herod cuts off John's head for no significant reason. This episode doesn't really strike us as important to the story of Jesus. Yet isn't that also the case when we hear about more death and more violence around the world? There's been so much death this past week, and it seems so senseless—somebody killed over a grudge, like Herodias' grudge. Countless victims of war, of crime, of murder. But it's hard to see how the names mean anything to us. Those people don't play a role in the story of our lives, at least we don't live and act like they do. They don't really fit. Their deaths are senseless. Meaningless violence. Victims of someone else's madness. And that's what Mark gives us in the middle of his story about Jesus—a senseless beheading, the product of a drunken oath.

I can only imagine what many of you might be thinking at this point: "Isaac, what a depressing message! We don't need any help noticing the terrible violence around us. Now you're telling us that this is just the way things go, and even Mark has to admit that! And that's what he's doing with the story of John the Baptist!" Well, before you throw hymnals at me, give me a chance to bring it all together. I want to return to the question I asked at the beginning: *How* is this death significant to us? We have to ask that question when we consider John's beheading and when we hear and see the victims of the violence in our world. To get to Mark's answer we have to look at the end of the story. John's death is significant because Jesus takes into himself the wounds of all victims as he breathes his last on the cross. Jesus' crucifixion gives John's beheading significance, and in turn makes every death significant. When Mark includes John's beheading in the middle of Jesus' story even when it doesn't contribute anything to the unfolding drama, Mark shows us that senseless deaths find a place in Jesus' story. The killing belongs in Jesus' story even when we can't figure out why or how, even when we fail at making connections. John's beheading shows us that victims of violence, even when senseless, belong to the story of Jesus. Mark knows that the story of Jesus must include senseless deaths like John's because Jesus himself is the victim of pointless violence.

When telling the story of the trial, Mark makes it clear that the enemies of Jesus have no legitimate reason to kill him. Mark turns the trial into a joke, a complete fabrication. If it wasn't so tragic, it would be humorous—a comedy of errors. Here's the account from Mark 14:55–61 (my italics):

> The chief priests and the whole Sanhedrin were looking for evidence against Jesus so that they could put him to death, *but they didn't find any*. Many testified falsely against him, *but their statements did not agree*. Then some stood up and gave false testimony against him: "We heard him say, 'I will destroy this man-made temple and in three days will build another, not made by man.'" *Yet even then their testimony did not agree.* Then the high priest stood up before them and asked Jesus, "Are you not going to answer? What is this testimony that these men are bringing against you?" *But Jesus remained silent and gave no answer.*

Not only does Mark display the absurdity of the fabricated reasons for the killing of Jesus, Mark also emphasizes Jesus' *silence* before those who have already decided his fate. The passage I just read ends with the silence of Jesus before the chief priests and Sanhedrin. The next day Jesus gives the same silence to Pilate. Here's the account from Mark 15:1–5 (again, my italics):

> Very early in the morning, the chief priests, with the elders, the teachers of the law and the whole Sanhedrin, reached a decision. They bound Jesus, led him away and handed him over to Pilate. "Are you the king of the Jews?" asked Pilate. "Yes, it is as you say," Jesus replied. The chief priests accused him of many things. So again Pilate asked him, "Aren't you going to answer? See how many things they are accusing you of." *But Jesus still made no reply*, and Pilate was amazed.

You see, there is no legitimate reason why Pilate and all the others should kill Jesus. Therefore, there is no reason Jesus can give to change their minds. So Jesus dies *in silence*. He is a silent victim like John. And the silence of John and Jesus reveal the madness of those who want to kill them. There was no good reason for anyone to kill Jesus. It was absurd, the product of a world drunk on power. Do you hear how John's beheading and Jesus' death resonate with each other? The trial and death of

Jesus echo back into the story of John. And John's beheading—in all its absurdity, in all its senselessness—points us to the death of Jesus. Now, from the perspective of the cross, we can look back and see the light of Christ through John's death.

God's light, the hope of the gospel, is here even though it's hard to see. Who wants to look at death? Who wants to gaze into the darkness? But that's exactly what Mark teaches us to do with John's beheading: we have to look at this death without shifting our gaze, because that's how Christ died, too. Once we see that Christ died like that, we can begin to learn the mystery of the Savior who comes to us with open wounds. The light of the good news is here, in this story, even in the darkness. "The light shines in the darkness, and the darkness cannot overcome it." The cross of Christ calls us into a gospel that doesn't run away from darkness, but instead asks us to find our suffering Jesus in the victims of our world's violence. Let me say that again: the victims of this world's violence draw us into the sufferings of Jesus. Jesus shares in the pain and death of all victims of senseless violence.

We cannot forget the scars of Jesus. It's important to remember that the resurrected Jesus comes to his disciples with wounds; his body still bears the marks of suffering. The hope of Christ's everlasting life poured out for the world flows in the blood that came down from the cross, from Jesus' side as soldiers pierced his body. Jesus bears the marks of death. He takes human suffering into his body, and those marks are not erased, they are not forgotten. His body remembers with scars.

We are this body. That's what our passage from Ephesians tells us: "you are also included in Christ" (Eph 1:13). And as Christ's body we cannot separate our remembrance of Jesus' senseless sufferings from the suffering of all the victims of a world gone mad with violence. The body of Jesus is linked in its fibers to the bodies of all silent victims. Broken bodies show us again the body of Christ broken for us, the blood of Christ shed for us. When we turn our gaze into the suffering of this world—the victims who die in silence, without a voice—we see again the agony of Jesus' brokenness. Those sufferings give us new eyes to look upon our wounded Savior, the slain lamb.

I am asking us to learn the painful stories, to listen carefully to the silent victims, to learn the absurdity of their deaths, the senselessness of the violence that sent them to their graves—for, like John, their senseless deaths witness to Christ's death. These moments of darkness shed new light on the cross—a cross that lies in the shadow of two thousand years, hidden from view by history, dead to our senses. John's beheading turns us to the cross of Christ, and that cross points us to all of the death in this world—for Christ also shares in those deaths and pains. Throughout history the mysteries of the cross continue to flow from each episode of senseless violence.

This sermon is quite different from the recent trend of my preaching. Usually I find some way to call us to turn to the fellow worshiper next to you and learn the gift of God's love from one another. I usually talk about our church as the site of God's revelation, the place where God speaks his Word of hope. But our text from Mark's Gospel won't let me say that. Instead, this message is a call to look outside of ourselves and move toward the victims of our world's senseless violence so that we may find God's broken body in their suffering. Remember, in Mark's story John is not a disciple of Jesus; he is not part of the community that gathered together to follow Jesus. John actually has his own disciples. A turn to John to see how Christ's cross echoes in his story is a turn to a victim who suffers outside the community of Jesus' disciples.

The gospel isn't an escape route from the pain, suffering, and darkness we see in the world. That line of Karl Marx should always haunt us as we attempt to live out our faith: he said, "religion is the opiate of the masses" (Marx, 171). Christianity should not be an escape route from the darkness, a drug to kill the pain, a hallucinogenic to cloud our eyes from disturbing violence. If our religion is any different from the host of others, if our faith is at all unique, part of it has to be that we worship a defenseless, silent victim. Yes, he is resurrected. But his wounds are not bandaged, covered over, or hidden from sight. They are open and they pulse with the blood of all victims. All that I'm trying to say is found in a quote from Blaise Pascal, writing in the seventeenth century: he said, "Jesus will be in agony until the end of the world. There must be no sleeping during that time" (Pascal, 289).

Here are my questions for us tonight. Linger with them for the next week or two: How do we stay awake? How do we resist the temptation to slumber and escape to pleasant dreams when darkness settles over the earth?

Waiting for a Promise

Psalm 122; Isaiah 2:1–5; Romans 13:11–14;
Matthew 24:36–44

Every year for the first Sunday of Advent the Revised Common Lectionary appoints texts having to do with waiting. Waiting is really an ugly word for us. I mean, you don't have to be a very savvy cultural analyst to figure out that our culture doesn't like waiting. Just look at some of the commercials on TV. Take, for example, a commercial for The Olive Garden Italian Restaurant. The images in those commercials are always of timeless abundance. There is never any waiting whatsoever. No waiting in the lobby with the after-church crowd, no waiting for the server to take your drink order, no waiting for the salad or breadsticks, no waiting for your entrée, no waiting for others to finish their meals, and no waiting for your check and the nice mints that come with it. The message is that you can have what you want, and you can have it now. The Olive Garden is a place of timeless and delicious bliss. Of course, we know this isn't true. We know that any restaurant experience necessarily involves a good amount of waiting—waiting for good things eventually to come for us.

Consider a more serious cultural association with waiting: a visit to the hospital. Unless we are in the health care professions, our overriding experience of hospitals likely involves a lot of waiting. You wait for the experts to do what they do. Even our hospital architecture reinforces this experience. When you are a patient in the doctor's office, or accompany a friend or loved one to the hospital, you will likely spend most of your time segregated from where the action occurs. You will spend most of your time in the waiting room, in fact, surrounded by icons of idleness (*People Magazine*, for instance, and gentle landscape photography on the wall), waiting for someone else to make something happen. In such contexts, waiting makes us feel useless. We feel ignorant and ineffective, even though we know that what we're waiting for is actually very good, perhaps even vital, for us.

But it seems to me that we must enjoy waiting in some respects. How else can you explain the shopping binge that happens annually the day after Thanksgiving? Every "Black Friday" millions of Americans go shopping, expecting to wait in long lines, not just in stores, but in parking lots and access roads to the malls. We pretend that the alleged bargain prices on Black Friday make waiting in lines worthwhile, but we all know that this is a farce. The sales will run through the week and the items we really want are never on sale. At some level, it seems to me that we secretly enjoy the long lines of Black Friday—we wouldn't shop then if we didn't. Perhaps, if you're like me, what you enjoy most about waiting in shopping lines is getting to complain about all the waiting involved. We enjoy our affliction and do it repeatedly year after year!

These three examples of waiting—The Olive Garden, hospitals, and shopping lines—display how waiting is a normal part of our lives. Most of the time we're more or less grumpy about it, but there are certain rituals (like shopping) where we find out that our attitude toward waiting is tempered. I think this helps explain a lot of the pageantry surrounding the Advent and Christmas season in American culture. At this time of the year, we collectively engage in a massive cultural enjoyment of waiting. This is a season in which we celebrate waiting.

Obviously, a lot of our perception of waiting depends on what we're waiting for. Waiting for your fettuccine alfredo to be served is a lot different than waiting for the results of a biopsy. And both of these experiences of waiting are different than standing in line to buy a DVD at Best Buy. A lot of this has to do with whether or not we know what we're going to get when the waiting is over. We expect to be delighted by the food we wait for at a restaurant, but we might well expect to be terrified by the results of a biopsy. I think in our culture we treat Advent a lot more like the wait in a restaurant than like the wait in a hospital: we think we know what we should expect when we're finished waiting. But, our texts this morning suggest that we might do well to spend a good deal more time thinking about the nature of waiting during Advent. When Advent is over, what should we expect to happen?

We read in Isa 2:5 the prophet's invitation to wait expectantly: "O house of Jacob, come, let us walk in the light of the Lord." We hear the urgency in Paul's voice in Rom 13:11, "now is the moment for you to wake from sleep," and in Jesus' exhortation in Matt 24:42, "Keep awake . . . for you do not know on what day your Lord is coming." The theme, quite obviously, has to do with waiting as a time of preparation. Yet these texts are not about preparation in any general sense: they aren't telling Christians to be Boy Scouts. Rather, these Scriptures describe waiting with the expectant and prayerful attentiveness appropriate for the disclosure of God's promise among us. Each of them suggests that there is an ethic appropriate to waiting for God—or, rather, they suggest that Christians are to have a spirituality of waiting.

In 1984 the German biblical scholar Ernst Käsemann wrote a theological commentary on the Epistle to the Hebrews called *The Wandering People of God*. In the book Käsemann put forth a startlingly forthright thesis: the gospel, he claimed, is a promise. The very form God's good news to the world takes *is* a promise. The good news of Jesus Christ is necessarily future-oriented. It is not just about what God has done, but it is also about what God is doing and what God will do. Christianity often gets a bad rap in popular culture for its vision of what God will do, of what we can expect for the outcome of history given Christ's lordship. Either we tend to be hopelessly vague, invoking some blurry bliss about streets paved in gold with angels on clouds. Or we're altogether too specific, as William Miller was when he predicted the end of the world on October 22, 1844, and led fifty to one hundred thousand of his followers into what became known as The Great Disappointment.

But this isn't necessarily our fault. It's hard to know what the gospel promises. I mean, some of it is God's fault because God is keeping God's mouth shut. That's the point, in part, of our texts today. Here we have texts that tell us to be prepared, but they tell us to be prepared precisely for the advent of a promise, which we're told we can't anticipate: "About that day and hour no one knows" (Matt 24:36). How do we wait for a promise that we can't expect? Do we wait like we wait for our food at The Olive Garden? Do we wait like we wait for the results of a medical test? Do we wait like we wait to rip into the presents under the tree on Christmas morning? Those are the very real questions our texts ask us.

I'm tempted to leave us at the threshold of these questions about waiting. I'm tempted to stop and let the anxiety of these questions about how to wait for God's promise fire our Advent imagination.

But I can't stop here because we notice another theme in these Scriptures, especially in Psalm 122 and Isa 2:1–5—the theme of peace. "Pray for the peace of Jerusalem: 'May they prosper who love you.'" "Nation shall not life up sword against nation, neither shall they learn war any more." The connection between waiting and God's peace goes some distance toward fleshing out the point I started to make about a spirituality of waiting.

Israel used Psalm 122 in exile. Scattered among the nations, with their best and brightest shipped off to Babylon, Israel began to read the prayers of the Psalms as its promise for the future coming of God. The idea of going up to the house of the Lord in Jerusalem—as described in Psalm 122—wasn't something Israel should bring about by its own strength, wait around to see happen, or plan for. Instead, Israel's hope for Jerusalem came to function as a metaphor for the promise that God will renew the life of faith anywhere. And that promise required the patience and faithful obedience of not being in charge, of not making sure history comes out right. The promise of Psalm 122 meant that the exiled people of Israel had to live their lives as prayer—a prayer for the peace of Jerusalem, yet unable to anticipate how God would answer that prayer.

The case is similar in Isa 2:1–5. The prophet Isaiah proclaimed his message to Judah and Jerusalem from 742 until 701 BCE, that critical period in which the Northern Kingdom was annexed to the Assyrian empire while Judah lived uneasily in its shadow as a tributary. It was a period during which Isaiah undertook a massive theological reorientation project, attempting to steer the gaze of Israel away from the period of monarchy, replete with military and political disasters. Isaiah had to put an end to Israel's paralyzing nostalgia for the security of its own political identity, and the only way he could do this was to point to a future for Judah and Jerusalem on the other side of judgment. He had to give his people hope in God's promise; for where there was no hope of newness, there was no hope for a living future. But note: this future was not one that either Judah or Jerusalem could bring about. Instead, the people of God were largely passive in Isaiah's vision; the "house of the God of Jacob" follows the nations to the "mountain of the Lord's house." In other words, this vision of peace is sure only under the conditions of

God's gracious activity. The Lord's work alone will give Israel the gift of its future. The hope that the peoples of many nations "shall beat their swords into plowshares, and their spears into pruning hooks," is one that Israel cannot secure on its own terms. The people must learn to live in the uncertainty of accepting its fulfillment from beyond itself, and the people must learn that life in that uncertainty is itself the material of obedience.

That sense of uncertainty, as we have already noticed, is front and center in our Gospel text for this morning. Matthew 24:36–44 comes hard on the heels of Jesus' apocalyptic oracle. Here, too, Jesus speaks about the future, the contours of which we cannot know. In this chapter of Matthew, Jesus says both that the world and his disciples have been made part of God's story and that the plot of that story—how history is being worked out—is up to God. The task of Jesus' disciples is not to make history come out right, but to be alert and prepared, so that when history does come out right and the kingdom of God is established, they will find that they have become the kind of people who fit in.

Now, what does all of this have to do with Advent? What does all this have to do with waiting, and with cultivating a spirituality of waiting? We—like the Psalmist, like Isaiah, like the hearers of Jesus' gospel—do not know everything about what the future will bring. But we do know that the gospel is a promise, and that God is discovered, not in a theory about the future, but in and as a community of love and worship held together by that promise. This brings our impatience with waiting to judgment; for in this community of love, we are taught how to wait—not simply as we wait for a delicious meal to be served, or as we wait in fear for the doctor to tell us the tests have shown that we are sick, or as we wait to open the present under the tree. In God's church we are taught to wait as we serve God—as we feed the hungry, minister to the sick, and enrich the poor. The work of the church is our reception of God's grace.

Waiting with Mary

Luke 1:26–38, 47–55

For the past few weeks, each of our preachers has reminded us that Advent is a time for waiting. This is a season when we take time to remember how to wait. Today we turn to Mary and learn from her waiting. I will tell you two stories to help shed light on how Mary waited for the Messiah.

Story #1

It was a few weeks before my sixteenth birthday. I came home from soccer practice one evening and my mom asked me what I wanted to do for a party; your sixteenth birthday is a big deal, after all. "Well, mom," I said with a smile on my face, "I've always wanted a surprise birthday party." I thought I was making a joke since it doesn't make much sense to suggest for someone to throw you a surprise birthday party. Obviously it wouldn't be much of a surprise if I knew about it. But my mom took me at my word. "Okay, let's plan a surprise birthday party." She was completely serious. We sat at the kitchen table; she pulled out her calendar and checked some dates; then she grabbed a notepad and asked me whom I wanted to invite. I sat there with my mom and planned my own surprise birthday party.

When the day came my mom told me to go out for a couple hours with my sister so we wouldn't be around when the guests arrived. We wouldn't want to ruin the surprise. I drove to a coffee shop, hung out with my sister, and came back two hours later. We parked in the driveway and walked up to the front door. As I opened the door everyone yelled out, "Surprise!" I did my best to look shocked. Little did they know that I had planned everything.

This kind of waiting is the opposite of Advent waiting. I knew the party was coming. I knew the day and the hour. I even knew who would be there and what we were going to eat. Everything happened according to plan. I knew what I was waiting for.

That is not the case for Mary in our story from Luke's Gospel. The angel Gabriel shows up out of the blue and completely surprises Mary. The Greek word Luke uses to describe her reaction means something like profoundly unsettled, agitated, disturbed, or terrified. She is, basically, completely freaked out. And we can't blame her. Angels aren't cuddly creatures with glowing halos who play the harp all day. No. Angels are terrifying and powerful, wielding swords and ready to smite the enemies of God. It's not necessarily a good thing to be visited by angels. They can bring good news or bad news. Mary is not sure what the appearance of this angel means. That's why Gabriel's word of reassurance is so important. He says, "Do not be afraid, Mary, for you have found favor with God" (Luke 1:30). *Don't be afraid, Mary, I won't strike you dead.*

All this to say: Mary doesn't wait for Advent in the same way that I waited for my sixteenth birthday party. I knew what was coming when I opened the front door. I planned my surprise, which meant that the party wasn't really a surprise. But Mary—she had no idea. She was caught off guard and terrified, trembling and confused. Mary had no idea that she was supposed to be waiting for something. Advent just happened, without warning, like a thief in the night.

Story #2

When I was three years old, my mom was pregnant with my sister Cynthia. The way my parents prepared me for Cynthia's birth was to tell me that from my mom's belly would appear a friend for me. I was excited. Now I would have a friend to play with and I wouldn't even have to leave my house. When my mom and dad brought my sister back from the hospital, they put her in a crib and I went to work getting ready for hours of endless play. I brought out all of my Hot Wheels (those little toy cars) and lined them up along the edge of the crib. I was prepared for my new friend to play with me. But nothing happened. She just lay there.

Nothing. She wouldn't respond to my attempts at friendship. Completely rude! So I took my cars and went across the street to my friend Matt's house. Obviously I didn't understand my parents' announcement, nor did I understand how to prepare for Cynthia's advent.

Now that is Advent—waiting for something that we don't know how to receive, waiting for a guest for whom we know not how to prepare, waiting for a savior who arrives in the most unexpected place: the womb of a young, poor, unprepared, and terrified girl. Mary doesn't believe the news at first. She doubts; confusion and doubt come first: "How can this be, since I am a virgin?" (v. 35). Mary makes a good point. She knows her biology. Sex comes first. Gabriel's announcement is absurd. The Messiah isn't supposed to come from her belly. Not her. She comes from the wrong side of town—that slum called Nazareth—and everyone knows that nothing good comes from Nazareth. It is one of those dumps that doesn't even make the history books. Mary exemplifies insignificance and weakness. She is a replaceable part in the machine, from a village of disposable people. But that's exactly the sort of place where God shows up. That's where the Messiah comes from, where salvation is born, where good news begins.

Now, what does this mean for us? It means that as hard as we try, we don't know how to prepare for God to show up. God happens in ways that we least expect and at times when we feel unprepared. During Advent you are like me at the age of three, waiting to welcome my sister but not knowing how to prepare. Despite my failed attempts at understanding what was going on, she came anyway. That's the way God works. Jesus comes anyway, despite our preparations. Jesus comes anyway—and that's called grace. So, here's a question for us: How do we go on when we know that God will arrive at any moment?

Grace means that Jesus comes anyway, even if you don't want him to, even if you don't think you are ready. Jesus comes anyway, even if you don't think it makes any sense, even if you doubt. Jesus comes anyway, even if you are terrified, even if you can't muster up the courage to believe. Mary doesn't believe at first: "How can this be, since I am a virgin?" She doubts that Gabriel's news can really come true in her life. She isn't ready. She has not met the prerequisites for this news to become reality. But the messenger from God doesn't ask for Mary's permission—which, I think, is one of the more scandalous details of this story. The angel doesn't ask, "Will you do this, Mary?" No. Gabriel simply announces this wonderful and terrifying news: *This will happen*. And what is Mary's response? She says something incredible. She's terrified, completely surprised—this is the strangest news ever heard—and she says: "Here am I, the servant of the Lord, be it done to me according to your word" (v. 37). *Let it be done to me.* Mary surrenders control—she welcomes the mysterious workings of God. She embraces God's plan for the world, even though she doesn't know how it will turn out. It's a risk. And she says *yes* to God.

Mary's story is now our story. We are like Mary: we've heard the good news of the Messiah's coming. And our response is like Mary's: we aren't sure how this good news can take shape in our lives. With Mary we have our excuses: *How can this be since . . .* you can fill in the blank. Perhaps we'll be ready next year. Once we figure out our lives, then we can start learning how to welcome what God is doing—once we finish school, once the rush at work settles down, once we fix that relationship, once we conquer this sin, once we find the right job, once we start a family, once we become more spiritual, once we find a place to call home, and so on. But that's not how God operates. This is where Advent sounds a little offensive: God didn't ask Mary's permission, nor does God ask for ours. God doesn't wait until we think we are ready. Why? Because God knows that we always already have all that we need. That's what grace means: God has already given us all that we need to welcome God's new life. So God announces and waits with us.

Yes, God *waits with us*—that's an important part of the good news. Advent is also about the way God waits *with* us. Advent shows us the patience of God. Think through the story of Mary. Pretend that you are God—which is usually a bad idea, but try it with me this one time. If you are God and you're trying to save the world, nine months of gestation in a poor, young girl might seem like a bad idea. I mean, the situation in the world is pretty bad, and God thinks it's important to wait in Mary's womb for a while! Sounds like a bad plan, even a bit irresponsible. The whole story seems like a bad way to save the world—not simply because God waits, but because God waits in such a risky place. After Gabriel's visit, Mary doesn't get to drive around in the protection of Benedict XVI's bullet-proof pope mobile, nor does she get president Obama's secret service agents to make sure she makes it to the big day. No. Mary doesn't receive any of that kind of security. Gabriel doesn't stick around or call for back up angels. The last line of our passage from Luke has an ominous ring to it: "Then the angel departed from her" (v. 55). The angel leaves! Now what? She has the savior of the world in her belly and she has to fend for herself in a land occupied by enemies! Abandoned by God, yet God in her womb. Isn't it so strange? In our waiting, God waits with us.

To have faith is to recognize that our waiting is a time of pregnancy. Mary teaches us how our waiting becomes the labor of the gospel in our lives. It's not that God only comes to those who have faith. That's not it at all. Our faith isn't the permission God needs to get involved with us. God doesn't wait for our faith. God doesn't ask for permission. Instead, to have faith is to know that God waits *with* you. To have faith is to recognize that this laborious waiting is the coming of God. Your travail is the coming of God. You are overflowing with God, whether you believe it or not. God's new life is always about to happen, even when it seems impossible.

We can believe this good news because our God creates new life from chaos. The waters of Mary's womb echo the first chapters of the Bible, the very beginning of the Messiah's story: "The earth was a formless void and darkness covered the face of the deep, while the Spirit of God hovered over the waters" (Gen 1:2). The same Holy Spirit that hovered over the waters at the beginning of creation hovers over the waters of Mary's womb. In the beginning, with God's word, formless chaos became the site of new life. And here, at the beginning of God's new creation in Jesus Christ, God forms life out of the waters of Mary's womb.

This is also our story. We entered those same waters at our baptism. And when we emerged, we entered into God's new life. But there's more to baptism than that one event. I think it was Martin Luther who talked about how all of life is baptism. We are always submerged in the waters of meaninglessness, and we are always being created anew. Thus, all of life is our baptism into new life. We are tossed here and there, floating bubbles of foam on a stormy sea (William James, 408)—and God forms new life from these waters. Our life is travail, the labor pains of new life—which is our baptism.

Where does Christ arrive? Where does Advent take place? Where does God's new life happen? God comes to us in the mess and waits with us. And what exactly is God waiting for? God is waiting for us to pray with Mary, "Be it done to me according to your word." Then we can begin to see how God is already at work transforming chaos into new life. God comes to us in the mess and gives us a chance to receive new life—profound life, mysterious life, re-created life, eternal life. The trouble for us is that we have a hard time believing that the messes in our lives are the places where God's new life happens. It seems impossible. That is why we must listen, with Mary, to Gabriel's last words just before he abandons her. He says, "For nothing is impossible with God" (v. 37). *Nothing is impossible with God.*

Christ is always coming to us, whether or not we think we are ready. Christ is always re-forming our lives into the kingdom of eternal love, whether we believe it or not. And so, in our travail, we pray the words of Mary: "Behold, I am the servant of the Lord; be it done to me according to your word." That is the prayer of Advent, which takes a lifetime to learn.

All of life is birth. All of life is baptism. Behold, all things are made new.

Mater Ecclesia

Proverbs 31:10–31; Mark 9:30–37

If Jesus doesn't make any sense to you, you are in good company. The disciples don't understand Jesus either. When he discusses his death and resurrection with them, the disciples misunderstand. Jesus says, "The Son of Man is going to be handed over into human hands. They will kill him, and after three days he will arise" (Mark 9:31). Jesus couldn't be clearer. He tells his followers about the way of the Messiah—that the Christ will journey into the darkness of the cross and await the resurrection. Yet the disciples are confused: "But they did not understand what he meant and were afraid to ask him about it" (v. 32). Instead of wrestling with Jesus' strange and disturbing words, the disciples rush on to the issue they consider most pressing: who among their band is greatest, the most important, the most significant to Jesus' movement? Which disciple is second-in-command? Who will be Jesus' right-hand man in this new kingdom of God? Jesus overhears his disciples' argument. So he sits them down and says, "If anyone wants to be first, he must be the very last, and the servant of all" (v. 35).

We must learn to be the servant of all. We've heard this message plenty of times: the Christian is called to a life of self-giving servanthood, like that of Jesus. It's a good message, and I know I need to be reminded of it. But I want to take us in a different direction today.

A couple weeks ago Katie and I were in California with my mom's side of the family—uncles, aunts, and cousins. A few of my cousins had little, squirmy kids. Some were around ten, another was six, and two others were toddlers. Their imaginations were incredible—in one moment they were sailing on the high seas while swinging in a hammock, and in the next they were having a tea party in the African wilderness with a giraffe as their guest of honor, right in the middle of the living room. The adults spent their time sitting and talking—enjoying their time of reunion. But the kids, they were explosions of energy, outbreaks of life. Sometimes they'd run through the grownup area with screams and squeals. And other times a conversation would end when a parent heard her or his kid crying or yelling in the other room. But whatever the children were doing, I couldn't help but see and hear *life*—wiggly and whiney, screaming and squirming, joyful and inconvenient *life*. So much life surged from those little bodies.

It's the same life I see in Tristan Plummer's smile as he walks into church, steadying himself with Nick's hand. It's the same life I see and hear in Carsten Bahnson's tireless body. They are so excited to be alive. They can't stop smiling or moving because everything is so new, there's so much to explore, so much to discover, so many interesting things to look at and taste and feel. In our passage from Mark's Gospel, Jesus turns the disciples' attention to children: "Jesus took a little child and had him stand in their midst. Talking him in his arms, he said to them, 'Whoever welcomes one of these little children in my name welcomes me; and whoever welcomes me does not welcome me but the one who sent me" (vv. 36–37).

The disciples argue about important things; they argue about the kingdom. But Jesus tells them that the way of the kingdom is about servanthood, and it's a servanthood that looks like Jesus welcoming a little child: wiggly and whiney, screaming and squirming, joyful and inconvenient. Welcoming life is what it means to be a servant of all. Jesus wants his disciples to join his mission of creating places of hospitality for life—every kind of life, even inconvenient life. Of course this means children, but it should also include all of the other lives that disrupt our order of things. Being a servant of all means welcoming new life, like Jesus does. He invites a little child into the disciples' midst. The church is a band of followers that continues to offer this invitation from Jesus. He wants to turn us into people who can welcome new life. Church shapes our lives into spaces that invite others to join us, even if they will mess with our usual ways of being church.

At the end of our worship service today, the Virginia Mennonite Conference and Chapel Hill Mennonite Fellowship will install me as a licensed minister in Mennonite Church USA. Let me read one of the questions you will be asked as part of this installation service: "Sisters and Brothers of Chapel Hill Mennonite Fellowship, you have heard the commitment to ministry and to this congregation made by Isaac. Do you receive him as your pastor? If so, answer 'we do.'" In many ways you have already affirmed my calling to be your pastor. But, nonetheless, I think it's fair for you to hear what you're getting into. So, let me tell you how I envision my pastoral ministry with you.

The first thing I want to say, although it's quite obvious, is that I'm not Jesus. If you have spent enough time with me, then you know for certain that I'm not Jesus. But I also know that you aren't either. None of us are. We are disciples, followers of Jesus, not a bunch of wannabe messiahs. And unlike our story from Mark's Gospel, becoming a pastor is not the result of an argument about who is the greatest in God's kingdom. Jesus doesn't need hierarchies of authority—he doesn't need a second-in-command. Instead, Jesus calls us—all of us, not just the pastor—into a life of servanthood. We are called to be servants of all, and that involves creating a community of hospitality. We are called to be a people who offer the gospel of peace to all who live in this world of death and destruction. And that takes work. It takes the hard work of confrontation, forgiveness, and reconciliation. Through the labor of the gospel, we are becoming a place for all to come and be sustained by God's peace, as we ourselves learn to live at peace with one another. As a congregation of Jesus' followers, we are called to be servants of Christ's peace. And I am called to serve you as we patiently discern the path of God's peaceable kingdom in our community.

But you probably expected me to say that I won't be an authoritarian pastor. I mean, what kind of *Mennonite* minister isn't going to talk about being a servant-leader and not a priest? And what kind of Mennonite pastor isn't going to talk about the call to the gospel of peace? Hopefully I've proven my orthodoxy. But there's something else I want to commit to as your pastor. There's something else I want you to know about me, something about the church that makes me think it's worthwhile to give my life to proclaiming the gospel with you. It's related to what I've been saying in this sermon: we are called to be a community that provides a place of peace for those who know pain, suffering, and violence. When

I consider the life of the church for the world, I have an image in mind that is familiar among Roman Catholics. The Catholics call the church their "mother"—or, as they say in Latin, *mater ecclesia*. "No one can have God as her or his Father who does not have the church as her or his mother," they say. Irenaeus, writing in the second century, makes the image quite clear: "one must cling to the Church, be brought up within her womb, and feed there on the Lord's Scripture."

To picture the church as mother returns us to our passage from Proverbs 31 about the wise or virtuous woman. In order to understand the challenge this passage poses to all of us, we must reach back to Proverbs 9, where God's wisdom (God's *logos*) is personified in this character called "woman wisdom." Let me read several verses from the beginning of chapter 9: "Wisdom has built her house . . . she has prepared meat and wine; she has also set her table. She has sent out her maids, and she calls from the highest point of the city . . . 'Come, eat my food and drink my wine'" (Prov 9:1–5). The description of a wise woman at the end of Proverbs displays the life of those who live according to God's wisdom mentioned toward the beginning of the book. The one who decides to follow God's wisdom calling out "from the highest point of the city" becomes the virtuous women mentioned in chapter 31. In one sense, the church is this woman, and her husband is Christ. We are committed to a relationship of fidelity with Jesus. It's no mistake that in the book of Revelation the church is also identified as a woman; John the Seer calls her the bride of Christ: "Come, I will show you the bride, the wife of the Lamb" (Rev 21:9).

According to one Catholic tradition, the church is described as a mother who gathers all peoples into her womb. This is an image of evangelism and growth in holiness—what some these days call "the missional church." But, if we aren't careful with that image, the church can easily cultivate a culture of possession, of accumulation, of obsessive gathering. Evangelism can become a form of conquest and colonization. Yet, when I think of the church as mother, I see a different reality. I see people the Holy Spirit gathers together and forms into Christ's body, whose life is ready to be born again in the world. A mother not only gathers and protects, but also births new life. A mother gives herself for the sake of the life growing in her womb. And that fragile life soon grows into its own life. Mothering also involves learning how to let life become something other than the mother; and that's what Mennonites know how to do. We are schooled in the way of non-violence and non-coercion, which also entails dis-possession. We don't hold onto the grace God has given us with our greedy and tight-fisted hands; rather, we receive in order to give. We live in the way of Jesus, a way that finds life as we give ourselves for the sake of others. We abide in Christ's life as we learn to be the servant of all.

As your pastor, you call me to be your servant as we discern together how to be a servant to all, how to be a mother who forms new life and lets go of that precious life. The church as mother is a dispossesive church. We gather in order to receive the life of Christ in our midst, which is how we become the womb of God. My hope is that the Spirit of God may overshadow our humble body and birth something unspeakably new—something that eye has not seen, nor any ear has heard: new wine that will quench our thirsty souls and bread of life to satisfy the hunger of a world starved of God's love.

What will emerge from our womb? What new life will God birth in our midst? What kind of life can we offer for the sake of the world? As your pastor, those are the questions I will help us ask.

Let me close with Prov 31:20, a passage that may show us how to open ourselves to receive new life. This Scripture is about woman wisdom, which means it's about our church. It's a simple verse, yet one that takes a lifetime to learn how to embody. Receive it as a description of who we are as a *mater ecclesia*, a mothering church. It reads: "She opens her arms to the poor and extends her hands to the needy."

A Protest of Hope

John 13:1–17, 31b–35

The people of Jerusalem welcome Jesus as their king: "Blessed is the king of Israel" (John 12:13). A few days later, on Maundy Thursday, Jesus is in the valley of darkness. Later in the night he will be arrested and his procession to the cross will begin.

The disciples and Jesus meet in secrecy: we are told in chapter 12 that Jesus is in hiding—"Jesus left and hid himself" (v. 36). At the end of the meal, Judas Iscariot wanders into the night to reveal Jesus' hiding place to the Roman and Jewish authorities. As Jesus sits at the table with his disciples, he's at the edge of death.

It is night. Darkness surrounds Jesus and his followers. Actually, with Judas at the table the night has already pierced the center of Jesus' kingdom of light. It will be only a matter of time before the last bit of hope flickers and dies.

Jesus could have saved himself. He could have retreated from Jerusalem to safer territory. He could have returned to a village and strategized new plans, away from Jerusalem's forces of death. Feeling the encroaching darkness, Jesus could have discerned that now wasn't the right time— better to go back to where he came from and start all over, find more followers, amass more supporters. Instead, Jesus waits: he sits there and eats. Then, John says, "Jesus got up from the table, took off his outer robe, and tied a towel around himself. Then he poured water into a basin and began to wash the disciples' feet and wipe them with the towel" (13:3–5). Jesus offers no strategies for success, no escape plans, no rallying cries for a last stand, no solutions. Jesus instead interrupts the meal, strips down to servant's clothes, takes a basin and pitcher, and circles the table. Bowing down to the ground, he takes each of his disciple's feet in his hands, pours water, and dries them. When night falls, when evil is about to triumph, Jesus washes feet. Jesus pours out his love with a pitcher. He even washes the feet of Judas, who uses those same feet to run into the night and hand Jesus over to his killers. Jesus loves even the betrayer, his enemy.

Night has fallen also upon us. It's in our neighborhoods, even the "safe" ones around here where the student from the University of North Carolina was killed last week. If the triumph of evil hasn't happened already in our communities, it feels like it will happen tomorrow. What are we supposed to do?

Well, if Jesus is our model, we wash feet. We learn the movements of a servant, of a slave. We kneel and bow our bodies before one another. We learn what it feels like to pour out our lives in love, with a pitcher—generously flowing water. When the last bit of hope is about to die, what do we do? Well, we let someone wash our feet. We don't *do* anything. We sit there and undergo a seemingly useless activity. We can easily wash our own feet—some of us probably already did before we came. But here we wash feet in order to give and receive God's love. We learn how to let go of ourselves, to let someone take our bare feet—dirty, vulnerable, maybe even funny-looking in our own eyes. Being loved, receiving love, takes work. Pausing, waiting, letting go—it's hard work. Yet it's holy work because with those hands, with this water, with that bowed body, comes the love of God—Christ's love poured out for the world, poured out for you.

When the night comes, when hope dies out, we practice footwashing. We create spaces where the love of God may flow into our worlds—into our feet and through our hands. Footwashing is our protest of hope—that Christ's love is still here, available, where we walk with our feet and where we serve with our hands. What we are doing tonight, and the way this worshipful activity overflows into the rest of our lives, is how we proclaim the good news of John's Gospel: "the light shines in the darkness, and the darkness did not overcome it" (1:5).

Jesus said, "I give you a new commandment, that you love one another. Just as I have loved you, you also should love one another. By this everyone will know that you are my disciples, if you have love for one another" (13:34–35). So, let us love one another, that we may receive the love of Christ.

Communion

Eucharist Means Gratitude

Psalm 100; Ephesians 1:15–23; Matthew 25:31–46

The lectionary texts today are about gratitude. The Psalmist exclaims, "Enter his gates with thanksgiving, and his courts with praise. Give thanks to him, bless his name" (Ps 100:4). The Scripture resounds with thanksgiving to God. In our passage from Ephesians, the apostle Paul reveals a personal source of gratitude: "I do not cease to give thanks for you as I remember you in my prayers" (Eph 1:16). He is thankful for people.

Gratitude is especially central to our worship service today because we will celebrate the Lord's Supper together. The oldest name given to this practice—*Eucharist*—is taken from the Greek word *eucharisteo* (meaning "I give thanks"), which occurs in the New Testament. Thus Eucharist means "thanksgiving." The apostle Paul uses this word in the passage from 1 Corinthians 11 that we use for our Words of Institution, which we recite every time we celebrate Communion: "the Lord Jesus on the night when he was betrayed took a loaf of bread, and when he had *given thanks*, he broke it and said . . ." Jesus hands out the bread after he gives thanks. Communion is about gratitude; the Lord's Supper is our Eucharist.

Gratitude is the life-giving pulse of our faith. Christians are people who let thankfulness run through every fiber of our bodies. We are people who say that our very lives are testimonies of gratitude to the One who gives us life. We come together every Sunday to say thank you to God—thank you for life, for gifts, for each other, for grace, for forgiveness, even for trials. We say *thank you* because we believe that we are held in existence—that all of creation is held in existence—by God's merciful hands.

Our lives are constantly formed and re-formed through God's grace. The Holy Spirit is always breathing new life into our lives. The Word that proceeds from the mouth of God is always creating and re-creating us, drawing us out from darkness and chaos. We are people who confess that all of the randomness—the chance occurrences that brought us into existence—is the work of God. The Holy Spirit breathes through all of it and holds us within the life-giving heart of God.

As the first line of the ancient Christian confession, the Apostle's Creed, reads: "I believe in God, the Father almighty, creator of heaven and earth." This confession isn't only a statement about the primordial past. God's work of creation did not end at the beginning of time. To believe that God is our creator is to experience all of life as flowing from the gracious hands of God. This is the substance of our faith. We are led astray by the way some talk about creation—the creation of the world—as an event that happened a long time ago. Many talk as if the doctrine of creation has only to do with what happened at the beginning of time: *How did life emerge? How many days or years did it take?* And so on. But those ponderings only scratch the surface of what it means to believe that God is the creator of heaven and earth. As Rowan Williams, the Archbishop of Canterbury, writes, "Creation isn't a theory about how things started; as St Thomas Aquinas said, it's a way of seeing everything in relation to God" (Williams, 37). In other words, life and love happen all around us because God is the eternal overflow of life and love. Some get this truth from important theologians like Thomas Aquinas; others get the same truth from a simple song: "He's got the whole world in His hands..."

All of this would be clearer to us if we took the Psalms more seriously. We don't always and immediately have to turn to the first few chapters of Genesis for our doctrine of creation. There are passages throughout our Scriptures that help us get to know the God who is our creator. Our Psalm for today, Psalm 100, is a wonderful place to start. Let me read verse 3: "Know that the Lord is God. It is he that made us, and we are his; we are his people, and the sheep of his pasture." *God made us,* the Psalmist declares. God creates us. We are God's people. God sustains us as a shepherd cares for his or her sheep. This passage resounds with the depths of God's creative and intimate presence in our lives. To believe that God is the creator is not simply a statement about the beginning of the world, it also means that God is at work in the random messiness of life, breathing forth new life, light in the midst of darkness, love in the midst of destruction, hope in the midst of misery.

Christians are people who grow more and more intimate with the grace of God that sustains our lives. We are on a life-long pilgrimage of thanksgiving, of learning how to say *thank you* to God. All that we are comes from God. There is nothing in us that is not already a gift. Our very being proclaims God's gracious provision with every heartbeat and every breath. We are always in need *and* always recipients of God's grace at the same time. The more we consider the extent of our need, the more we discover the radical depths of God's loving grace.

But we don't like to pay much attention to our need. It is foreign in our time and place to confess our profound needs. No one wants to appear desperate. Everyone wants to be able to care for herself. I've talked with some who are afraid of growing old because they don't want their needs to be exposed: "We don't want to be a burden," they say. It's hard to confess that we need other people to help sustain us. We hide our weaknesses from each other. In a world where only the fit survive, we don't want to appear vulnerable.

And then Jesus comes and breaks all the rules. How dare he appear so weak and vulnerable? He is our king, after all! How dare he expose his needs and frailty? I want a God to reassure me with power, not to come as a weak peasant. Herein lies the scandal of the passage we heard today from Matthew 25: Our king Jesus is weak, utterly dependent, completely in need. I'll read verse 34:

> Then the king will say . . . "I was hungry and you gave me food, I was thirsty and you gave me something to drink, I was a stranger and you welcomed me, I was naked and you gave me clothing, I was sick and you took care of me, I was in prison and you visited me."

The Creator has a face, the face of Christ, which appears in weakness— among the least of these, among the ones who are intimately familiar with their need. Jesus shows us that neediness is not shameful. Dependency is not to be hidden. In the weakness of the "least of these," Jesus offers us an example for our lives. Christians are people who do not run from our weakness. We instead confess that we are nothing but bundles of need, utterly dependent on the gracious care of our Creator.

You may be wondering: *Why is this good news?* Well, the good news is that our *need* is also our *gift*. Sometimes the greatest gift you can give someone is to say, "I can't do it on my own; I need you." With these words, we offer the gift of showing how someone is desired, is necessary, is needed. When we confess our weakness, we become spaces of need where others can discover their necessary gifts. Then we, like Paul in our passage from Ephesians, can say to someone, "I do not cease to give thanks for you"—*I am grateful from the depths of my being for you, for the grace of God that you are, for the gift of God that you are, for the love of God that you are . . . I thank God for you.*

In a moment we will celebrate Communion, the Lord's Supper, Eucharist, our thanksgiving feast. When we eat the bread and drink the wine, our neediness is exposed for all to see. Notice how no one can serve herself or himself the elements. At the Lord's Table, we all become *beggars*. We hold out our hands and wait for a handout. We stand and wait as people do in bread lines, desperately looking forward to the generosity of others. Even Laura Nickel and Matt Thiessen who will serve us the bread and wine have to wait until everyone else has eaten. And notice how they serve one another when their turn comes at the end. Laura and Matt do not break off the piece of bread they want. No. They must instead receive from the hand of another. Everyone is dependent on another if they want to eat the Eucharist. In this meal, our *thank you* to God and our *thank you* to each other are spoken in unison, thus our union with Christ and neighbor.

And, most of all, Communion is our thanksgiving; it is our Eucharist. From the Lord's Table we eat spiritual food for our nourishment. We receive the gift of God's sacrifice of love for us—that, in Jesus, God gave his life that we may have life. Communion is where we discover the depths of our need, the depths of God's love for us, and the depths of our gratitude. Like Paul, we come to say, "I do not cease to give thanks for you." For God in Christ feeds us. We are his beloved sheep.

Flesh and Blood

John 6:51–58

We're in Capernaum again tonight, and Jesus is still talking about bread. It all began some time ago, you'll recall, when he stirred things up by feeding over five thousand people with a few loaves and a couple fish. And ever since then, people keep on asking Jesus why he's doing all this stuff. Last Sunday we saw the stakes raised a bit. Jesus didn't just account for the things he'd done, but he also began to account for himself. And in the course of that conversation, he started to refer to himself as bread, bread that came down from heaven. It seems like Jesus, rather than calming people's nerves—giving them reliable explanations, assuring them that everything will be all right—is intent on whipping them into a frenzy. I mean, what better way to convince people that you're a quack than to say, "I'm bread from heaven"? Well, maybe I spoke too soon, because tonight Jesus has found an even more outlandish claim to make: "The bread that I will give for the life of the world is my flesh" (John 6:51).

"Eww, Jesus. That's just gross!" He's like that guy who always takes his jokes one step past the limits of cultural acceptability, then the laughter dies and people wave their hands in front of them, desperately trying to ward off the mental images. What's Jesus contemplating here? Pulling out a carving knife and roasting up a human drumstick? Whatever the answer, it seems unlikely to be something I'm going to be interested in. So it isn't very hard to be sympathetic with the Jews who protest in the middle of this story, asking, "How can this man give us his flesh to eat?" (v. 52).

For the Jews in Capernaum, there are bound to be other problems than grossness. When they hear of eating someone's flesh, they think of Ps 27:2: "When evildoers assail me to devour my flesh—my adversaries and foes—they shall stumble and fall." Or perhaps they think of Zech 11:9, where the prophet refuses to guide the nations: "I will not be your shepherd. What is to die, let it die; what is to be destroyed, let it be destroyed; and let those that are left devour the flesh of one another!" For these Jews, eating someone's flesh connotes hostility and violence. So now Jesus hasn't just pushed the limits of what you say in polite company; he might actually be belittling his hearers. He might be suggesting that those hearing him are going to kill him. But it's hard to tell, so you can imagine these Jews standing around nudging each other: "Did he just say what I think he said?"

It gets worse when Jesus adds drinking his blood to the picture. It isn't enough for him to be crass; it isn't enough that he might be insulting people's dignity. But now he's going after Scripture. The Jews are thinking of God's covenant with Noah in Genesis 9: "Every moving thing that lives shall be food for you. . . . Only, you shall not eat flesh with its life, that is, its blood." They're thinking of Lev 3:17: "It shall be a perpetual statute throughout your generations, in all your settlements; you must not eat any fat or any blood." And they're thinking of Deut 12:23: "Be sure that you do not eat the blood; for the blood is the life, and you shall not eat the life with the meat." The list of passages goes on. Since blood is linked to life, which is God's to give and to take, drinking blood is simply out of the question for those interested in obeying God's law. So, Jesus, just for the record, let's make sure we're all on the same page: You're making a disgusting suggestion that may implicate us in violence, and you're compounding that with a clear violation of Torah?

How *indeed* can this man give us his flesh to eat? Flesh is what we live in—warm, mobile, and frail. Flesh is how we learn—through the bits of flesh called eyes and ears and vocal chords. Flesh is how we communicate—with hand and eyes, lips and tongues. But flesh is not something we eat, at least not if it is flesh like ours.

The temptation, I think, is to assume that Jesus is speaking metaphorically. That "flesh" is really a stand in for something else, probably something a whole lot less fleshy than flesh. Perhaps, for instance, Jesus means by "flesh" the words of Scripture (finding the Word with a big "W" in the words, small "w"), like we mean when we speak of someone who has studied the Scriptures long and hard as having digested them. Or, perhaps he's talking as he did in last week's reading, about believing in him, only now he's substituted "eating my flesh and drinking my blood" for "believing in me." Either of those interpretations would be theologically suggestive, though also a little weird, *but* they at least would alleviate our anxieties about the cannibalism Jesus seems to be recommending.

John's Jesus, however, doesn't seem to want us to make those moves: *Don't intellectualize this. Don't "spiritualize" it. Keep it fleshy.* Indeed, one of my favorite word-study nuances in the New Testament comes up at precisely this point. We don't see it in our translations, but it's in verse 54 when Jesus says, "Those who eat my flesh and drink my blood have eternal life, and I will raise them up on the last day" (John 6:54). Just like in English, there are lots of Greek words for eating, and some of them, just like in English, invite "spiritual" interpretations. So, instead of using the regular word for "eat," which is *esthiein* (we could say "eat," or "consume," or "ingest") John's Jesus says *trogein*—chew, gnaw, munch. John's wording seems chosen precisely to ward off nice, clean, intellectualized or spiritualized interpretations of this passage. Whatever Jesus has in mind here, John's telling us, you'll need a napkin. It's going to be messy.

Even though these verses we're looking at tonight are remarkably similar to—and in places repeat almost verbatim—the ones we studied last week, John wants us to sit up and take notice of this new vocabulary running through them: "eat," "feed," "drink," "flesh," "blood." John wants us to ask what's going on here that's so powerfully important that he needs to repeat this entire discourse about bread from heaven. So let's put it as plainly as we can: changed lives, eternal lives, remaining in Christ and Christ remaining in us—these are not just (perhaps not even primarily) matters of the mind. Belief in Christ is meaty, fleshy. That, I would say, is the primary point of this text.

But, even if that's the case—even if this whole bit about heavenly bread and flesh and blood is a way for John to remind us that God wants our bodies, that Christianity doesn't favor the "spiritual" over the "material," but rather disciplines and trains us in the very materialities and fleshiness of our lives—even if all that is the case, why does Jesus have to say, "Those who eat my flesh and drink my blood have eternal life"? Wouldn't a simple reminder have done the trick just as well? Couldn't Jesus have just said, like James says, like Matthew says, "Look, you need to believe in me with your bodies, with your actions"? Why does Jesus have to be so graphic, with all this talk of eating flesh and drinking blood?

I want to suggest that there are two things going on here. They won't exactly make it easier to understand what Jesus is up to—after all, it's a "difficult teaching" that drives many of his followers away (6:60, 66)—but they might set a context in which our struggle to understand can take place.

The first thing, as I've already suggested, is that being in Christ is physical and material: it's about flesh and blood, it's about bodies. Christ's sacrifice, Christ's self-gift is "no bloodless myth," and so discipleship isn't spiritual, at least not if spiritual is the opposite of material.

We're very close tonight (maybe as close as John ever gets) to eucharistic themes, close to language about the Lord's Supper: flesh and blood, food and drink, living bread. Indeed, traditionally, when Christians reflect on these verses, they're thinking about Communion. And it's understandable that this is one of the main texts for discussions of transubstantiation, where the bread and wine in the Great Thanksgiving are changed substantially into the body and blood of Christ. Now, this is something a lot of us find terribly easy to disparage. I always thought Richard Dawkins' comments a decade ago were very clever: "it takes a real, red-blooded Catholic to believe in something as daft as the transubstantiation" (Dawkins, 23). I am inclined to agree, and I imagine you are, too. But Dawkins prefaced that remark by saying, "Any wimp in religion could believe that bread *symbolically* represents the body of Christ." Any wimp like me, because, to be truthful, I don't want the threat of God showing up materially (physically, bodily) in the bread and wine. Better if God is just spiritually present in the life of the congregation. I know all of you—I know how you act and react; so, if there's something fishy and God-ish going on in our Communion service, I can suss it out and monitor it. I'll be able to keep it at arms' length, to make sure it doesn't change me unless I want to let it.

But, if God gives Godself to us as body and blood to eat . . . what then? How would I ever get a handle on that? God in my gut? Oh Jesus, I'm not sure I want you to get *that* close to me. But that's the first thing here: the realism of John's language in this passage reminds us that if God gives us *living* bread, we aren't likely to have control over the difference it makes in our lives In a word, by giving us his body, Jesus commandeers ours.

Yet, and this is the second thing, eating flesh and drinking blood also reminds us that the context in which we come to Christ and remain in him is one of betrayal. Remember how I said that the Jews hearing Jesus' words would have associated eating flesh and drinking blood with violent, unspeakable acts? Well, they hadn't misinterpreted him; they "got" what he was saying. The context in which Christ gives himself to us and to the world is one in which he dies at *our* hands, in which *each* of us has already denied him, where we have *all* turned our backs on him. Each of us has already refused Christ's self-giving love for the world. Each of us demands his crucifixion, each of us hates him and reviles him—we do it in our flesh every day—and he takes that very demand and changes it into the gift of eternal life. But the form that gift takes is his flesh to eat and his blood to drink. That is difficult to hear; it's hard to swallow—flesh to eat and blood to drink: what kind of gift is *that*?

Contrast it perhaps with the gift of wisdom to Solomon. All of us would say that wisdom is a good thing to have, a good thing to be given. Indeed, Solomon has to recognize wisdom's goodness in order to ask for it. Solomon knows that in order to be a good king, he'll need wisdom. He isn't a skilled warrior or leader; he's not a consummate politician; he's just a boy who is in over his head. What he needs is wisdom, the power of discernment, and so that's what he asks for. God gives him what he needs, and more besides—all the things Solomon could have asked for but didn't.

I bet this is the kind of gift we can get our heads around. It computes: we say, "Yes. Wisdom will make Solomon a good king. Would that our own rulers asked for wisdom." But, just because wisdom computes, just because it fits with our expectations, I wonder whether Solomon's gift is really, at bottom, radically a gift.

Of course, at some level it is. Solomon doesn't have wisdom, he knows he needs it, and God provides it. Again, that fits most of our assumptions about gifts. For example, at Christmas we make lists of gifts. Our friends and family give us what's on the list, and we do the same for them. But what happens when we get something that isn't on the list? Take the bumbling idiot husband on umpteen different sitcoms each week. You know, the one who gives his wife a vacuum cleaner. Maybe she needed it, but she definitely didn't want it; it wasn't on the list. What she probably wanted (and needs) is for *him* to buy *himself* a vacuum! It's hard to see stuff that doesn't show up on the list as a good gift, but it still computes, doesn't it? At least we can get our heads around why giving your spouse a vacuum is a bad idea.

Sometimes, however, and more often than we would like to admit, we get caught up in our self-inflated perceptions that we know better than others what would be good for them to receive as gifts. Perhaps your sister is way too materialistic. Her list goes like this: gift certificate to the Gap, gift certificate to Pottery Barn, gift certificate to Bath and Body, J. Crew rollneck cable sweater (color: pumpkin, size M, p. 17 of the fall-winter 2003 catalog). And you think, "No way. She's getting a donation to the Heifer Project in her name." What's going on there? Is that donation a good gift? Probably not if you're interested in hearing your sister's voice, if you're interested in her perception of who she is and what she needs or wants. Probably not, also, in the sense that you've turned gift-giving into an occasion for psychological warfare, for your perception of who she ought to be to triumph over hers.

Jesus' self-gift of flesh and blood isn't like any of this. It doesn't show up on the list. Why? Because this gift arises at the point where you are most alienated from the giver. While in the depths of your sin and betrayal and rebellion, you wouldn't recognize Christ's gift by looking at it. You have to be told, you have to be instructed, you have to be led—and even then the gift often doesn't seem like much. It doesn't make you beautiful or successful or more fun. It doesn't even help you clean the house. But Jesus' gift of flesh and blood also isn't a browbeating gift. It isn't a gift given without regard to who you are, where you're at, who you think you ought to be. You might find out—no, you're going to find out—that this gift calls your life into question, this gift asks for transformation. But here is the really astounding thing, and I'll end on this note: *your ability and desire to change isn't a condition for the gift to be given.* Flesh to eat and blood to drink is blood like your blood and flesh like your flesh, reminding you gently but insistently that the Maker became the made, that now and forever God is closer to you than you are to yourself—even when you pull away from God as violently as you can.

Our Tortured King

Colossians 1:11–20, Luke 23:33–43

Hanging on the cross, tortured, nearing death, a convicted rebel asks Jesus to remember him: *Don't forget me.*

While we are usually very good at running away from death, our passage from Luke's Gospel won't let us look the other way. As we wrestle with this story from the Bible, our attention must focus on three people on crosses, painfully awaiting their last bit of life to drip to the ground.

Crucifixion isn't a mode of punishment for a typical thief or criminal. Only special people get killed on crosses. To crucify someone takes a lot work and it's costly. It's a torturous death reserved for people whom the Roman authorities consider subversives or revolutionaries, enemies of the state, threats to national security, sectarian radicals, or freedom fighters.

Sometimes the stories from the Bible sounds like they come from a distant planet or another world, separated from ours by thousands of years. But not this time, as we read the story of crucifixion and hear the former U.S. president George W. Bush speak, without regret, of his authorization of torture during his war on terror. "Damn right," he said in response to questions about whether he authorized the torture of Khalid Sheik Mohammed.

With this news in mind, we don't need to do much work to make this passage from Luke relevant. It's about three guys from the Middle East who are tortured to death because they are for some reason deemed a threat to society. In today's language, they would be called "terrorists."

Jesus, though wrongfully accused, dies hanging between two convicted terrorists. For the people passing by, Jesus would appear to be just one more radical, sectarian freedom fighter.

The torture and killing of Jesus is a public humiliation. Rome has done it before, and they'll do it again. They try to make an example out of him, as they did to other Jews who claimed to be messiahs, liberators of Israel. The Romans put a sign on his cross: "This is the king of the Jews" (Luke 23:38). In other words, the sign says, *this is what happens to messiahs*. It's a public deterrent. All of the other wannabe radicals hear the news of crucifixion and learn what happens when Jewish peasants talk too much about the promise of a kingdom other than Caesar's, the hope of a different dominion or empire. Too much kingdom-talk will get you killed on a cross.

But this man Jesus is different from the other radicals. As we enter the crucifixion scene, if we want to know more about this messiah we'll have to trust the guy hanging on the cross next to him—one of the guilty terrorists. He's the one who gets Jesus right; he's the one who calls Jesus a king: "this man has done nothing wrong," he says in verse 41. Jesus is innocent. He is a casualty of people who are drunk on power.

In this story the guilty man who hangs beside Jesus is the one who speaks the truth. After speaking the truth that no one else is willing to utter, the convicted rebel says, "Jesus, remember me when you enter into your kingdom" (v. 42). Jesus answers his companion on the cross: "Truly I tell you, today you will be with me in Paradise" (v. 43).

There's something very strange about reading the crucifixion story today. The church calls this day "Christ the King" or "Reign of Christ" Sunday—a day for us to focus on the reign of Jesus and our service in his kingdom. So, how strange is it that we read about his humiliating death, not his coronation? We read about a cross on a deserted hill, not a throne in a beautiful palace. We read about the tortured death of two terrorists and a falsely accused one, not an extravagant banquet and celebration. What can any of this mean?

What is completely unnerving about this passage, at least for me, is that Jesus invites one of *them* into paradise, to be his companion forever. "Truly I tell you," Jesus says, "today you will be with me in Paradise."

It's crazy enough for this tortured Jesus, with the thorns of death digging into his soul, to forgive his torturers and killers: "Father, forgive them," he prays from the cross, "for they know not what they do" (v. 34). That prayer for grace is shocking enough. Can you imagine a power of forgiveness that would enable you to forgive your killers as they are torturing you? But at this point in the life of Jesus, the plot of the story has prepared us for such a profound display of grace. Jesus has been extending God's forgiveness to people throughout his ministry, so it makes sense for him to forgive as he is being tortured. Nonetheless, that Jesus accepts a *terrorist* into God's kingdom, into paradise, is completely disturbing. It's unsettling because that place is our hope, too. It's like being invited to a party and discovering that someone you hate is going to be there. You can't stand him; he disgusts you. The last thing in the world you want is to be stuck in the same room with *him* for an evening. So you make up an excuse and apologize to the host for having to miss the party. Similarly, Jesus invites the violent rebel next to him to the same party he promised for us. Are we sure we want to party with an enemy like *him* in the paradise of God for eternity? Why does Jesus have to invite *him* to *our* heavenly party?

The conversation Jesus has with the two other crucified people reveals to us the profound mysteries of God's peace, which is something quite different from how our world talks about peace. The apostle Paul discusses this mystery of peace in the passage we heard from Colossians: "Through Christ, God was pleased to reconcile to himself *all* things, whether on earth or in heaven, by making peace through the blood of his cross" (Col 1:20). It's that little word *all* that disturbs me. At the cross, Jesus invites a convicted criminal into paradise—to be with him for eternity, to live at peace with him and with those whom he has wronged. Yes, Jesus shows us that peace is possible. But it is a peace that takes work; it's a reality we receive as we enter into God's power of forgiveness. To participate in that power is to forgive the ones who have hurt you, and to be forgiven by those whom you have hurt. The peace of Christ is not only about making all of the guns and bombs go away. The reign of God's peace is not accomplished at the moment when wars cease. No, the peace of Christ is a much more difficult promise. It's about being drawn into the power of forgiveness, the power of asking for forgiveness from someone you have wronged and the power of forgiving someone who has wronged you. As we let that power flow through our lives, we may find the hope of companionship, of being invited to eat at a table with friends and enemies, with people we like and with people we would rather never see again.

Communion is that table. As we eat the bread and drink from the cup, we are eating at the table of our tortured savior—the one the powers of this world wanted to make go away. At the Lord's Table we gather our lives around the wounded one and learn that in God's kingdom the dead will come back to life, the tortured will be able to speak the truth. As we celebrate the death and resurrection of Jesus through this holy meal, we are being drawn into what Johann Metz calls "a dangerous memory." We remember what the powers of violence want us to forget: that, in Jesus, the tortured one comes back, and with him comes all of the others. In paradise the tortured come back and are invited to eat. Thus, Luke's crucifixion story poses a question for us: Do we want to be part of that party, of that heavenly banquet? Or, will we have to excuse ourselves because we can't bare the thought of sitting at the same table not only with the enemies of society we see on the news, but also with the people who have hurt us and the people we have wounded?

At this table, with this bread and this cup, we open ourselves to God's forgiveness, which is a flow of love and grace that dissolves the hostility of this world—the rivalry that organizes our reality in terms of friend and enemy, the rivalry that organizes our lives according to the hatred and grudges that run deep within us. For as Paul says in our passage from Colossians: "Through Christ, God was pleased to reconcile to himself *all* things, whether on earth or in heaven, by making peace through the blood of his cross."

Bodies Matter

John 13:1–17, 31b–35

Part 1

> *In a quiet office park off Evans Road sits a two-story red brick building with tinted glass windows and shades. There's no sign outside; no U.S. flag nearby. But some forty protesters bearing wooden crosses drove there Thursday morning to inform its tenants they know what goes on inside, and they're outraged. The building, at 140 Centrewest Court, is one of many unmarked Immigration and Customs Enforcement field offices where illegal immigrants are detained. . . . Using familiar civil rights tactics, the protesters sought to bring attention to the building and demand transparency, including a list of the people being detained and access to attorneys and family members for those arrested. . . . The timing of the protest came during Holy Week on the day Jesus washed the feet of his disciples, prior to his crucifixion . . . .*
>
> ~ Yonat Shimron, *The News & Observer*, April 1, 2010

Footwashing is about bodies. Jesus strips down to servant's clothes, takes a basin and pitcher, and bowing down to the ground he takes each of his followers' feet in his hands, pours water, and dries them. Jesus pours out his love for human beings with a pitcher, with the water. For Jesus, bodies matter. He shows his love for us by washing feet, by taking our bodies into his hands. And he commands us to go and do likewise: "I give you a new commandment, that you love one another. Just as I have loved you, you also should love one another. By this everyone will know that you are my disciples, if you have love for one another" (John 13:34–35).

That's why we are here this morning, gathered outside this detention center, witnessing to the love of Christ. "For God so loved the world . . ." and that means everybody. We are here to proclaim God's love, and to show that love through this worship service. The church, the body of Christ, is brought together through this intimate and holy act of footwashing, where God's love flows with this water. Footwashing binds us together as the body of Christ. Footwashing is about bodies—about the way the love of Jesus makes us care for bodies.

As you can see, there are two chairs behind me. If you want your feet washed, please come forward and sit in this chair and I will wash your feet. But this other chair up here will remain empty as a sign of all the bodies that the U.S. Immigration and Customs Enforcement agency has hidden from us, the bodies that law enforcement officers have torn from our communities and our families in the middle of the night, the bodies that they have ripped away from our churches. By refusing to let us wash the feet of the people hidden in these detention centers, the federal government has dismembered the body of Christ, it has torn apart the church, it has pierced and severed the body of Jesus.

May this service of holy footwashing be a sign of God's love for the people who have been torn from us, leaving us wounded, with holes in our sides and in our hands, the dismembered body of Christ.

> *The protesters, many of whom are Christians, came with a washbasin and several gallons of water. As people chanted psalms and read Scripture passages, the Rev. Isaac Villegas managed to wash about five people's feet before an unmarked white van rolled in dispersing the protesters. A handcuffed Hispanic-looking man was then let out of the car and escorted into the building. The protesters quickly hung yellow crime scene tape on the black metal gates in the rear of the building. "By our yellow crime scene tape, we've identified this as a crime scene," said Patrick O'Neill, one of the protesters.*
>
> ~ Yonat Shimron, *The News & Observer*, April 1, 2010

Part 2

This sermon is titled, "Bodies Matter, part 2," because I preached "Bodies Matter, part 1" this morning in the town of Cary. Some of us held a footwashing service at a detention center operated by the Immigration and Customs Enforcement agency. I was there trying to wash the feet of the detainees, but they wouldn't let me. Pastors have been regularly refused access to prisoners at the detention centers throughout North Carolina.

But both of my sermons today are about the same thing: that God cares for our bodies, no matter who we are, no matter what we've done, and no matter where we're from. The act of footwashing is about how our bodies matter to God. This holy practice is how God's love flows over us and through us as the water washes over our feet. Listen to these words from the Gospel of John:

> Jesus, knowing that the Father had given all things into his hands, and that he had come from God and was going to God, got up from the table, took off his outer robe, and tied a towel around himself. Then he poured water into a basin and began to wash the disciples' feet and wipe them with the towel that was tied around him. (John 13:3–5)

Later in the evening, after Jesus washed their feet, Jesus tells the disciples to go and do likewise: "I give you a new commandment, that you love one another. Just as I have loved you, you also should love one another" (v. 34).

This is why in a few minutes you will walk up here and stand in line, waiting your turn to wash feet and have your feet washed. Through this practice, we are invited into discovering how our bodies matter to God; footwashing is how God's love flows through us and into one another—through our hands, and with the water. As we all know, each foot is ultimately attached to a face, the face of someone we love and someone who loves us—someone whom God loves. When we wash the feet of one another, we open our selves to learn what it means to love each other's lives.

This humble service is what love looks like, it's what love *feels* like—a foot in your hand, a hand on your foot. Love isn't simply a flighty emotion that comes and goes depending on your mood. Instead, love happens when you pour water on someone's foot and wash it and dry it and send that beloved person on her way to love and serve God. We can easily wash our own feet. Yet here we wash feet in order to give and receive God's love.

The mystery of God is the love that happens when you let someone take your dirty feet in her hands, and when you take her feet in your hands. That's what love feel like; that's what *God* feels like. We usually fail, writes Sebastian Moore, "to look forward to the point when the whole mystery of God will be known in the clasp of your brother's [or sister's] hand" (Moore, 141). God is a presence that passes through our lives—a presence who envelops our lives—with sustaining grace. And footwashing gives us a window to see what that grace looks like, to watch God's grace unfold before our eyes. Grace is the way someone takes our feet and washes them. This grace comes to us through people that want to serve us, to care for us, and to prepare us to show that same grace to whomever we may encounter as we go about our lives. Through footwashing we are invited to feel how bodies matter to our faith.

Bodies matter, even the bodies of our enemies. The scandal of the footwashing story in John's Gospel is that Jesus washes the feet of Judas as well, the betrayer, the one who hands over Jesus' body to be crucified.

Jesus washes the feet of his enemies. Jesus offers grace to the one he knows will betray him. The love and grace of Jesus know no boundaries. What would it mean for you to wash the feet of your enemy? What would it mean for his or her body to matter to you?

Desire

Heart's Desire

Psalm 20; 2 Corinthians 5:6–17; Mark 4:26–34

O God, our deliverer and our refuge, send out your light and your truth, that they may lead us, and bring us unto your holy hill and to your dwelling. Amen.

Time after time over the past week I've been shocked by a photograph on the evening news: it's a close-up of Abu Marsab al-Zarqawi's face after the blast of U.S. bombs killed him in his safe-house in Iraq on June 7. The picture itself is disturbing enough, and I'll spare you the details. Once upon a time the faces of the war-dead were not displayed for public consumption, but times have changed. Even more startling than the image of Mr. Zarqawi's face, however, was the context in which the photograph was aired. Initially, of course, we saw the picture of Mr. Zarqawi as proof that he had in fact been killed. But, by mid-week, the tenor of reports surrounding Zarqawi's death had changed. The photo is not just proof of his death, it is also proof that the War on Terror is progressing. CNN, FoxNews and MSNBC all ran stories this week in which the picture of Mr. Zarqawi's corpse was enlisted as proof that things are going well for President Bush. Mr. Zarqawi's death is proof that President Bush has and is executing a viable plan for the reconstruction of Iraq through political violence. By the end of the week, Mr. Bush's public approval rating had risen, even amidst his repeated insistence that U.S. troops will remain in Iraq indefinitely. His lightning-quick visit to Baghdad was enthusiastically endorsed and garnered a good deal of positive media attention. As President Bush stood on the platform speaking to an assembly of military personnel, his reference to the *justice* of Mr. Zarqawi's death was greeted by deafening cheers.

What do we say in a week like this when we read together the words of the twentieth Psalm?

> May [the Lord] grant you your heart's desire
> And fulfill all your plans.
> May we shout for joy over your victory
> And in the name of our God set up our banners.

At least one of the things I think we have to say is that today, in the wake of Mr. Zarqawi's death, the words of David's psalm seem like they were written for President Bush. The photograph of Mr. Zarqawi's corpse is proof that George Bush is having, in the words of VH1, "the best week ever."

I guess I shouldn't be surprised. This is, after all, our culture. Whether you agree with him or not, our culture valorizes people like President Bush, the ones who know what they want and won't falter on the relentless quest for self-fulfillment, the ones who overcome adversity and beat the odds to become who they want to be. We call it getting your heart's desire. Most of the time it's pretty innocent: earning a degree, landing a job, finding and marrying the love of your life. Other times getting your heart's desire is poignant: winning the battle against cancer, or walking again after a debilitating accident. Sometimes it's simply frivolous: getting a tattoo to display your countercultural edginess, or buying the right kind of car to display your pro-cultural conformity. In all of these instances, our culture teaches us that the psalmist's benediction is more or less spot on: the psalmist is talking about seeing your desires granted and your plans fulfilled.

If you are skeptical of this, think for a moment about all the people sitting in the congregations of mega-churches or the audiences of televangelists or those sitting at Purpose-Driven Life seminars. In one way or another they are being taught about their hearts' desire. They are being taught the prosperity gospel; they are being trained in the belief that God will give you what you want if you only want it earnestly enough. They aren't stupid people. More importantly, perhaps, they aren't any more morally incompetent than we are. They are being trained in a true message. The gospel really is all about getting what you want, having your heart's desire granted. But, it's a bit disconcerting, isn't it, when you stop and reflect that your heart's desire (that new job, or whatever) is cut from the same cultural cloth as President Bush's success in seeing Mr. Zarqawi dead?

When you think about it, it's hard to tell what distinguishes your heart's desire from that of President Bush. And this is because we're all machines of desire. We are what we want—or at least, we're defined by the pursuit of what we want. This isn't something you can escape. In fact, I'm not sure how our lives would remain recognizably human if we weren't defined by our desires. Our desires define us, *and God answers us in the language of desire; God responds to our desires in a language that our desires can understand.* The gospel really is all about getting what you want. The difficulty lies in knowing what your heart's desire is. So, here's the question we must ask ourselves: "What do we really want and why?"

The church is a school of desire. At its best, it teaches us to want the right things in the right way. We gather in church on Sundays because we think that there are right and wrong answers to the question, "What do you want and why?" We gather in church because we are convinced that our hearts' desires aren't self-validating—that the desires we know, plan for, and pursue might be misdirected. We gather because we believe that without a school of desire, without the church, we can't know what our hearts' desires truly are.

In his Second Letter to the Corinthians, the apostle Paul puts this point more succinctly. He writes, "We walk by faith, not by sight" (5:7). In twenty-first-century America, this verse is taken usually to support a kind of Christian cheerfulness in the grim face of reality. Because we walk by faith, we are able to disregard the more painful aspects of life—after all, our faith tells us that it will all come out in the wash. Because we walk by faith, we can act with a charming hopefulness that clear-eyed realists—those, by contrast, who insist on walking by *sight*—can't stomach. However, Paul's point in our text is altogether different. When he says, "we would rather be away from the body and at home with the Lord" (v. 8), it isn't because we wish to be spared the harsh realities of the world or the unpleasant truths about ourselves. Rather, it is because only then, when "we are at home with the Lord," will we "know as we are known," as Paul puts it elsewhere (1 Cor 13:12). Only then, when "we are at home with the Lord," will we "see face to face" (v. 12). Only then will we be able to recognize God's creation accurately. Only then will we be able to describe God's salvation realistically. Only then, on the day of judgment when each of us is called to give an account "so that each may receive recompense for what has been done in the body," will we know our hearts' desires and see the fulfillment of all our plans, "whether good or evil" (2 Cor 5:10).

For the time being, we are in a strikingly different position, one like that of the farmer in Mark's Gospel. Listen again to this parable of Jesus as Mark recounts it:

> The kingdom of God is as if someone would scatter seed on the ground, and would sleep and rise night and day, and the seed would sprout and grow, he does not know how. The earth produces of itself, first the stalk, then the head, then the full grain in the head. But when the grain is ripe, at once he goes in with his sickle, because the harvest has come. (4:26–29)

This is a hard word to hear for people who live in a culture of self-fulfillment. It is a word about patience, since the sower sleeps and rises night after night during the long period between sowing and maturity. And though we talk about patience a lot in church, we're generally pretty bad at it. Indeed, the very fact that we have to talk about patience so often is a good clue that we don't practice it. More importantly, though, this parable is also a word about the character of Christian faith. The farmer does not understand what is taking place in the mysterious process of growth. Nonetheless, he prepares for the harvest because he believes it will eventually appear. The kingdom of God will come when God's purpose is complete; we cannot hasten it. Our task is to learn to be the kind of people who, when God's kingdom does appear, find out that we fit in. And that happens by having our plans, wants, and desires retrained by attentiveness to God's Word, the life of Jesus, present in Scripture and in the church by the guarantee of the Holy Spirit.

Back in the late 1980s, Bill Cosby branched out from the phenomenal success of his sitcom, *The Cosby Show*, to give Lisa Bonet her own spin-off sitcom. It was called *A Different World*. The premise of the television show concerned Bonet's character, Denise Huxtable, who left home for college where she encountered new people, new ideas, new problems, and new resources for dealing with those problems. *A Different World* never matched the successful ratings of *The Cosby Show*, but it did air for six seasons, during which the show's characters had their wants, hopes, dreams, and plans reshaped so that they grew out of their unreflective youth into adulthood. Over the course of those six seasons, Denise, Whitley, and Duane Wayne found out that their lives were different from what they had grown to expect as children. They found out that they wanted things they never imagined on their first day of college. They also found out that life's most basic problem is not how to get what you want, but how to know what it is that you really want. Like the characters on *A Different World*, we too need to have our desires retrained, not simply because we've grown personally, but also because in the church it's a different world.

At least that's the content of the gospel according to Paul. He viewed the death and resurrection of Jesus as a world-remaking event. According to Paul, our heart's desire is only intelligible when we recognize—and try to fit into—God's reconciliation of the world. This is what we find if we turn again to our passage from 2 Corinthians:

> We are convinced that one has died for all; therefore all have died. And he died for all, so that those who live might live no longer for themselves, but for him who died and was raised for them. From now on, therefore, we regard no one according to the flesh . . . . So, if anyone is in Christ, there is a new creation: everything old has passed away; see, everything has become new! All this is from God, who reconciled us to himself through Christ, and has given us the ministry of reconciliation. (5:14b–18)

"If anyone is in Christ, there is a new creation." Please note that Paul's gospel isn't simply about personal change, though it certainly involves that. Paul's gospel is about the re-creation of the world. Professor Richard Hays notes that older versions of 2 Corinthians 5 obscured the cosmic dimension of Paul's proclamation by translating "the crucial phrase in verse 17 as '*he is* a new creation' (RSV) or—worse yet—'*he is* a new *creature*.'" Hays says that these translations mess up Paul's message because they make it sound as if Paul "is describing only the personal transformation of the individual through conversion experience. The sentence in Greek, however, lacks both subject and verb; a very literal translation might treat the words 'new creation' as an exclamatory interjection: 'If anyone is in Christ—new creation!' Paul is not merely talking about an individual's subjective experience of renewal through conversion; rather, for Paul . . . ['new creation'] refers to the whole created order" (Hays, 20).

For Paul the cross and resurrection of Christ create not just a new set of personal desires, but a new world. They do this especially when we remember that the first experiences of Christ's resurrection were absolutely disorienting: "the women fled from the tomb and said nothing to anyone, for they were afraid" (Mark 16:8). But closer to the heart of what we're about as Christians is the conviction that God, in Christ, has died and risen again to remake the world from within it. Everything is new, so of course we have to live by faith. Even our heart's desire is new, for Christ has died, Christ has risen, Christ will come again, and that means all the rules have changed. At the end of the day, this is all I have to say: remember that this school of desire we call the church is in a tight spot. We gather here on Sundays to be shaped into the kind of people who, when the Kingdom comes, find out that we fit in. But it's a different world, a whole new world that we try together to learn how to want. In this different world, our hearts' desires will surprise us because they come not through the violent plans of kings and presidents, and not through the relentless search for getting what you want from life. Instead, God's new creation comes as silently and mysteriously as when the harvest comes from the grain sown in the earth.

Faith and Love

Galatians 2:15–21; Luke 7:36 — 8:3

Tonight we have two texts that ask for an answer to this question: How do *you* know that your sins are forgiven? Think about the question for a moment. What is it asking? What are the criteria by which you could tell you had an answer to the question? How do you know your sins have been forgiven? If you're like me, the answer might be a lot like an Apple Jacks commercial: a goofy dad with his plaid shorts hiked up to mid-chest waddles into the kitchen, sees his kids eating Apple Jacks and says, "They don't look like apples; they don't taste like apples. Why do you kids like those things?" The kids grin, giggle, look at each other, shrug, and then laugh, "We just do!" Is that what our answer to this question, "How you know your sins have been forgiven?" is like? "We just do!" If so, no wonder the question lacks urgency for us.

The question didn't always lack urgency. In an earlier day, if I asked from the pulpit how you know your sins have been forgiven, you would have started to sweat. We would have a long conversation about the knowledge of election, or about the assurance of salvation. If I were good enough at my job, I could have ramped up this message, ending on a fevered pitch that brought you rushing forward to kneel at the rail and rededicate your lives to Jesus.

"How do you know your sins have been forgiven?" There used to be no better question to ask if you wanted to preach a sermon that stuck.

Yet, if you turn with me to our text from Galatians 2, you might at first blush have reason to feel confirmed in the "We just do!" approach to knowing your sins have been forgiven. There's no need for all that anxiety and fear and trembling. After all, we know it's a trick question, a question preachers ask when they need some extra money in the offering plate or when they need you to do something. But look, we say, here in Galatians Paul refuses to link justification with any work that we might do, whether the pastor scares you into doing it or not! Paul, it seems, is quite concerned to guard against turning righteousness into a contest to see who can pull off the best show, to do the most to win God's favor. Yes, if you are like me, that line from Isaiah, "Sacrifices and burnt offerings I do not desire," might be echoing somewhere in your heads right about now.

Galatians 2 is a hallmark of Protestantism; it preaches justification by faith. Everyone knows this. We know it so well that it has become second nature to us. Just think of this song: "What can wash away my sin? Nothing but the blood of Jesus. What can make me clean again? Nothing but the blood of Jesus." Or, more precisely, nothing but Jesus' blood *if I believe in him, if I have faith in him*. Justified by faith through grace: it's so close to us that we barely even think about it.

What is so striking about having our text from Galatians jammed together tonight with this text from Luke 7 about the woman with the alabaster jar is that none of the characters in Luke's Gospel seem to understand Paul's point in Galatians. Not even Jesus, at least not clearly. Of course, in verse 50 he says to the woman, "Your faith has saved you; go in peace"; but that line is hardly the focus of the story. Much more puzzling, and much closer to the center of Luke's theological vision, is verse 47: "I tell you, her sins, which were many, have been forgiven; hence she has shown great love. But the one to whom little is forgiven, loves little." *The one to whom little is forgiven, loves little.* If you're like me, your life is in large part a matter of tying up loose ends so that you have little to be forgiven. You want to love others extravagantly, generously, but you have little use for finding yourself in a position where you must swallow the bitter pill of someone else's generosity or forgiveness.

I think one of our deepest difficulties with coming to an awareness of what it might mean to know ourselves as forgiven has to do with our regular confusion of *sin* with *guilt*. We have this confusion ingrained in us from our earliest days: sin is a matter of doing something wrong that makes us guilty in the eyes of God. You commit a sin and become guilty, so you have to ask God for forgiveness. Then, when we're a little older, perhaps we hear about original sin—the idea that humans are bound to muck up their relationship with God, that sin is just part of the human condition. We're likely to think it's a little unfair that we are never told exactly what we've done to make us guilty.

The result of all this is that we wind up with a picture of God that's rather like my father's memories of boarding school in Rhodesia. When he was a boy in boarding school, my dad lived in mortal fear of mealtimes. Not because kids were going to steal his lunch money; not because he was afraid no one would let him sit with them (those were my anxieties). No, my dad was scared of lunch because the school disciplinarian was watching over their table manners like a hawk. If you slipped up—if you talked out of turn or failed to place your napkin properly on your lap—rap! right across the knuckles with the blunt edge of a heavy butter knife. The problem was that you could never live up to the expectations. Indeed, you rarely knew what the expectations were before you felt the back edge of that knife across your knuckles. Guilty!—and the arbiter of guilt and innocence really seemed a bit unreasonable.

I'll wager that's how many of us think about God when we think in terms of our own sinfulness. It is a relationship of guilt and punishment, and your task (since you can't figure out what it is that makes you guilty) is to figure out how to turn the punishment aside. Right? We catch ourselves engaged in this kind of project all the time. "O God, I didn't mean to cheat on my income tax return. How about I give an extra three percent of my income to charity this year? Is that good enough for you? Will that keep you from making the IRS bang down my door?" It's the "Just don't hit me again, God," approach to Christian faith.

Of course, if we're thinking with Paul in Galatians, "I'll be good, Jesus, just don't give me any more detention," isn't likely to cut it. Paul seems to see that approach to righteousness as writing a check neither our bodies nor our souls can cash. After all, even when we're at our most honest with ourselves, we aren't quite sure why God is so angry with us. Again, it rarely seems like we've done anything in particular that warrants God's anger—surely not eternal anger, for even human parents and human friends, when we've wronged them horribly, when we've broken their hearts, even they relent and welcome us back with open arms. Even they see us, embrace us, and say, "This son of mine was dead, and is alive again; he was lost and is found!" And they begin to celebrate.

But that isn't our picture of God. At least it isn't the picture that much of our Christianity has institutionalized. No, we have an image of God, the cosmic school disciplinarian, who we're desperately trying to please, before whom we acknowledge our guilt, and in the face of whom we realize there is nothing we can do to set the record straight. But we keep trying, don't we?

It's that obsession with our attempts to perform righteousness for God that Paul sees so clearly in Galatians. It's that fantasy of guilt and recompense that Paul says is delusional. Pay attention for a moment to the context of our passage. Paul is in the midst of recounting his apostolic biography to the Galatians; it's part of his attempt to convince them that they should trust the gospel he preached and not turn aside to "another gospel"—not that there is one, he says in 1:7, but that there are confusions of the true gospel.

Paul reminds the Galatians that even Peter was confused. Paul says that Peter ate with gentiles, until, that is, certain people approached James disapproving of Peter's life style. Then Peter stopped. He didn't want to be perceived as less than righteous. He wanted to walk the straight and narrow path, to make sure he wasn't doing anything that might make him appear to be guilty.

And Paul said to him something like this: "Look, Peter, by the logic you're using, all of us are already guilty. We know that no one fulfills the law. We know that even if someone were to do everything the law commanded, it would still be God and not the law that makes righteous. So stop performing. It isn't getting you anywhere. You see, Peter, the problem of sin is not the same thing as the problem of guilt. That's right: *the problem of sin is not the problem of guilt*. That's why only faith in Jesus Christ can make us righteous. Or perhaps better said, that's why only Jesus' faith, *the faith of Jesus*, can justify us."

It is at this point—when Paul reaches for the language of justification by faith—that a typical Protestant will talk about the alien righteousness of God. Let me explain. We've already seen that nothing we can do is good enough to get us out of our predicament of trying and failing to please God. God is infinitely better than all our attempts to be pleasing—there is nothing we have that we can give God that God needs, and so on. So, if we're trying to be made righteous before God, God will have to do it. God will have to impart to us God's own righteousness. Only God's righteousness will measure up to God's own standards.

The story we know about salvation starts here: God's alien righteousness—not anything we earned, but God's free gift of grace—is given to us by believing in Jesus, believing that he died to erase our guilt, believing that, if we trust in him, we "will not perish but have eternal life." Believing, with Paul, that through this act of belief we "have been crucified with Christ," and it is no longer we who live, but Christ who lives in us. Yet somehow I thought Christ living in me would feel a whole lot more inspiring than my life feels most of the time.

What I hope you see tonight is that if this story we've always heard about being saved is true, then we've only grappled with the problem of guilt; we haven't yet touched the problem of sin. We're still working with a picture of the angry God whom we've wronged, only now we've found the totem, if you will, that will finally make God happy. We've got belief in Jesus. If you believe in Jesus, God is happy and bing, bang, boom—we're on our way to heaven, glory hallelujah!

How do you know your sins have been forgiven? Guilt—that feeling of remorse we have when we realize we've committed an offense. Guilt—our sense of failure to live up to the possibilities life has laid out before us. In the picture of being made righteous that I've drawn out, God has given us a way to rid ourselves of that feeling of remorse, that sense of failure. God has gotten rid of guilt, given us an exit from the problem of guilt. So, how do you know your sins have been forgiven? Well, because I don't feel guilty anymore. But, I wonder: If you erase the symptom, has the pathology been cured?

Turn back with me to our passage from Luke's Gospel. There, too, we have a conjunction of our themes of sin, faith, and forgiveness. So, let's ask our question of this woman who appears with the alabaster jar, who kneels behind Jesus' feet, weeps over them, and dries them with her hair. How do we know her sins have been forgiven? The most obvious answer, of course, is that Jesus says so. Okay, that notwithstanding, let's test the Protestant reading of Galatians here . . . Oh, it appears to work out quite nicely: the woman realizes she's a sinner, she's convicted of her guilt, she believes in Jesus and performs this lovely act of devotion to him, and at the end Jesus sees the act of devotion and tells her that her sins are forgiven, that her faith has saved her.

But notice that the Protestant way of telling the story does not even have to mention the extravagance of the woman's response to Jesus. More importantly, it doesn't have to mention Jesus' own acknowledgment of her extravagance, which, in Luke, seems like the major point of the story:

> He said to Simon, "Do you see this woman? I entered your house; you gave me no water for my feet, but she has bathed my feet with her tears and dried them with her hair. You gave me no kiss, but from the time I came in she has not stopped kissing my feet. You did not anoint my head with oil, but she has anointed my feet with ointment. Therefore, I tell you, her sins, which were many, have been forgiven; hence she has shown great love. But the one to whom little is forgiven, loves little." (7:44–47)

If sin were merely a problem of guilt, like the Protestant reading of Galatians suggests, what would be the point of this emphasis on disparity in love? What would be the point of this last bit, "The one to whom little is forgiven loves little"? Are some people a little bit guilty and others really guilty? If you are honest with yourself, is that how you play the game of Christianity? "You know, I do get jealous every once in awhile of people who have more than I do. I would like my life to be a little easier, a little more like theirs. I know I've got issues. I know jealousy is a problem. But at least I'm not a thug, a drunk, or an adulterer. At least I'm not a homophobe. At least I'm not in the Army." We all have organizing fantasies about degrees of guilt, and that is part of the reason why the problem of sin cannot be reduced to a problem of guilt.

Something more fundamental than a fantasy of "I'm okay because I'm not as guilty as she is" is at stake in this story. The story isn't even posed in terms of guilt; it's posed in terms of sin and love. Something more fundamental than believing in Jesus is also at stake. If we were writing this Gospel today, we might pose this as a story about a person's sense of self-worth. Simon, the Pharisee, has a well-developed sense of his own worth. He is able to invite Jesus to dinner; he is able to talk shop with Jesus; he is even able to speculate about Jesus' status as a prophet. Simon is plugged into society. He is a player, a mover and a shaker. The woman, by contrast, is so unsure of herself, so withdrawn from the social fabric of the world, that she hides behind Jesus' feet while he is sitting at the table, almost like an animal, frightened to be seen, not wanting to be regarded by these men who know their own worth and therefore can measure her worthlessness.

We might say that it's this woman's feeling of worthlessness that shows us what sin is. We might say that sin is self-negation, withdrawal from our place in God's creation. Sin is the way we tell ourselves that we mean less than nothing, even though the God who created us only makes good things. The voice of sin in us doesn't first say, "Here's how you've mucked things up; here's why you need to be punished." That is the voice of guilt. That is the voice that will lead us to hold up Jesus before the angry God and say, "Look, God. I believe in your Son. Just don't hit me again." No. We don't worship an abusive God. The problem of guilt is not the problem of sin. So, look at this woman—cringing, behind the table, behind Jesus' feet—and hear the voice of sin in her. It says, "Yes, you are alone. In this entire universe, you are ultimately alone. You will crawl into a hole and die, alone. You are, after all, really no more than an animal" (Sebastian Moore, 69).

Or, that's what the voice of sin in her would have said, had she not come to know herself as forgiven. Jesus made it his mission to go to the dispossessed—those in whom the voice of sin echoed like thunder through the empty caverns of their lives—and he said, "Blessed are you who are poor, for yours is the kingdom of God. Blessed are you who are hungry now, for you will be filled. Blessed are you who weep now, for you will laugh." Those are words that bring love flooding into the world—extravagant love, beautiful love, love that overcomes our sense of worthlessness. If you want an answer to our question, "How do you know your sins have been forgiven?" look at this woman. "I tell you, her sins, which were many, have been forgiven. Hence she has shown great love." It is love like hers—love capable of overcoming our lonely withdrawal from God's good world—that proves the reality of forgiveness.

Closer

Isaiah 6:1–8; Psalm 29; Romans 8:12–17

*God created us without us;
but God did not will to save us without us.*
~ Augustine of Hippo

In April celebrities took over downtown Durham; Hollywood came to town. They were filming a movie called *Main Street*. Most of the young ladies were very interested in the star of this film, Orlando Bloom. But my wife was much more interested in the co-star, Colin Firth. In order for me to understand her admiration of this middle-aged British actor, Katie made us buy the BBC's six-part 1995 production of Jane Austen's *Pride and Prejudice*. Needless to say, we've been watching it for the past few weeks; and I'm glad, because now I understand the Trinity! Yes, I had to go back to 19th century England to understand the Trinity. The insight came to me as I watched Mr. Darcy learn how to love. But before we go to *Pride and Prejudice*, I should probably talk about the Bible first.

Our passages today offer plenty of interesting ways to get into the Trinity. Isaiah 6 has the Seraphs in heaven praising God saying, "Holy, Holy, Holy." Later Christian tradition has suggested that each "holy" is for each person of the Trinity—Father, Son, and Spirit. We could also focus on how the Word proceeds from the mouth of God in Psalm 29. The Psalm seems to assign a separate personality to God's voice. There is a constant repetition: the "Voice of the Lord" does this and the "Voice of the Lord" does that. The psalmist develops a rhythm that centers our attention on a Voice that seems to have a life of it's own. Is this the Word that John the evangelist says is Jesus in the prologue to his Gospel?

Even though the Trinity permeates the Scriptures for today, I think Romans 8 offers the most interesting way into our conversation about the triune God. Besides, it is one of my favorite passages; maybe it's the nihilist in me. I like all the stuff about groaning, the sighs too deep for words. It's there in verse 26: "for we do not know what we ought to pray for, but the Spirit intercedes with groans too deep for words."

Does it sound a little too unholy to start with the groaning in our gut? The Trinity doesn't belong there, right? Shouldn't we start up in heaven? Isn't it a bit self-centered to turn a sermon on the Trinity into a sermon about us? Isn't God supposed to be way over there, or way up there?...anywhere but here. As Isaiah says, "I saw the Lord sitting on a throne, high and lofty" (Isa 6:1a).

Now, to be fair to Isaiah's vision, God isn't completely distant: "The hem of God's robe filled the temple" (v. 1b). There is a point of connection between heaven and earth, and that is the Temple. But in Romans, Paul seems to think that God's presence is even more intimate than that: God is in us, in our groaning, in our sighs, in our prayers, God's Spirit is a companion with our spirit. Here's what Paul says: "When we cry, 'Abba! Father!' it is that very Spirit bearing witness with our spirit that we are children of God" (Rom 8:15b-16). Through the Spirit, God becomes intimate with us, interior to us, completely familiar, a companion. The Holy Spirit is present in our spirit, groaning with us, crying out with us. And with the groaning we begin to get a sense for the Trinity: we become the site of the work of all three persons—Father, Son, and Spirit. Our bodies become God's home. God rests with us, and in us, not as some outside power, not as some cosmic clockmaker, not as some bearded old king on a throne in heaven. God isn't an outsider to our lives. God isn't like a king or a president who might choose to save us by sending his troops. God doesn't send others to do the dirty work. God sends God. That's why we confess that Jesus is God. If Jesus is not God, then we worship a God who refuses to jump into our mess, then we serve a God who doesn't like to get dirty. If Jesus is not God, then we praise a God who doesn't want to get too close—a God who refuses intimacy, who refuses the risks that come along with becoming our friend, our companion.

This is why the language of God's *sovereignty* sometimes leads us astray. When we say that God is sovereign, we probably picture God as one of those kings who makes decrees from on high with an entourage of servants at his command. We picture God as a president who claims victory while never living in the trenches—a distant God, always once-removed from the action. And if that's what we mean when we call God sovereign, then we don't really believe in the God who is Trinity, which is simply another way of saying that we don't have a clue about what happens on the cross. Because on the cross that kind of sovereign God dies. Or, to put it more provocatively, the crucifixion kills our picture of a detached God. The crucifixion of Jesus kills our image of God as the sovereign victor who sends other people to do the dirty work, the risky stuff. The true God, the God revealed at the crucifixion, is intimate with humanity, familiar with our flesh. At the cross we see how God sends God to accomplish our salvation.

Now, the Holy Spirit is how God takes even one more step closer to us. The Spirit draws God even closer, maybe even uncomfortably close. Remember the beginning of the Gospel when the Holy Spirit descends upon Mary's womb and gives her a son, Jesus. Now that's close, very close—entering a womb is uncomfortably close. And we have Paul in Romans 8 using, interestingly enough, pregnancy language to talk about how the Spirit is doing things inside all of us—not just Mary. Each of us is groaning in labor pains, Paul says, undergoing the travail of the Holy Spirit, awaiting God's redemption in our midst, feeling the good news being born inside of us. At this point the Spirit reveals an important insight into the nature of God. That is, God doesn't overpower us. God isn't a super-sovereign, doing what he wants whenever he wants. God doesn't rescue us as if he were a SWAT team or a Navy Seal operation. God doesn't act like a foreign invader of our lives, forcing us to join the mission. None of those images describe God. Augustine of Hippo made this point when he said, "God did not will to save us without us." God doesn't save us without us. God doesn't use external force to get us to do the right thing.

Let me offer a few images to help us get a sense for what God is not. God is not like a surgeon who stands next to her patient and operates on the heart. God is not like a mechanic who looks under the hood and repairs the engine. God's life is much too intimate with ours for those images to be true. God saves us from the inside. God heals us as if healing her or his own body. It's hard to talk about this stuff. Our language seems to break down. That's why I'm using so many metaphors. The doctrine of the Trinity seems to push us into the limits of language and shows us that the best way to understand is to *feel* it, to be drawn into this relationship, to feel the Spirit working in your life, to listen for the groaning in your gut.

So let me offer one more picture of the way God works in our lives through the Holy Spirit. And this one involves that BBC production of *Pride and Prejudice*. The story centers on the relationship between Mr. Darcy and Elizabeth Bennet. Darcy is a gentlemen and one of the richest men around. Elizabeth comes from a humble family. Basically, Mr. Darcy falls in love with Elizabeth even though he shouldn't because of their class difference. It would be a scandal for a man like Darcy to marry someone from the inferior Bennet family line. Yet he can't help himself, and everything comes out one afternoon when he storms into Elizabeth's room and professes his love. But it's all wrong; he gets everything wrong. Darcy doesn't understand love. His kind of love is one that compels from the outside. Darcy knows his position of social power over someone as humble as Elizabeth. If he wants Elizabeth, he can take her and insult her in the process. Here's what he says in his profession of love: "My feelings for you have taken possession of me against my will, my reason, and almost against my character!" Darcy knows that a person of such high standing shouldn't love someone of such low status. So he admits that his love is *unnatural*, and insults Elizabeth's family. Not a very wise move. Darcy doesn't know that you can't come from on high and force someone to love you, that you can't make love happen on your own terms, that love is not coercive. When Darcy finally gets around to the proposal part, he goes on and on about how his kind shouldn't associate with her kind. He says, "I now hope that the strength of my love may have its reward in your acceptance of my hand." *The strength of my love*. Darcy thinks the strength of his love, the sheer power of his passion, should get him what he wants—a "reward," he says. Elizabeth's acceptance is a reward, something he earns through his confession. There is no need for him to think through whether or not he has made himself lovable. Darcy doesn't think twice about whether or not he deserves her love.

Mr. Darcy's love comes from one high, from the position of a gentlemanly sovereign, a benevolent aristocrat. That's not how God loves. Now, I should say a little more about how Darcy's character develops—Katie would not be happy with me if I left you with a bad impression of Mr. Darcy! Elizabeth rejects Darcy's declaration of love from on high, and so Darcy begins to learn that love must first become familiar, intimate. Love comes from companionship—so he spends the rest of the movie learning how to be a companion, and how to love Elizabeth's strange family. And it's this companionship that gets at what Paul is saying about the Holy Spirit. God is in our depths, groaning with us. God's love comes through intimate companionship—walking with us, praying with us, crying out with us. God doesn't overpower us. God's Spirit is a hidden presence—willing to go unnoticed, willing to be a humble companion. That is how the Trinity begins to unfold in our lives. It starts as a groan, something beyond words, a sigh. Perhaps a sigh from exhaustion with your life, or a disgruntled groan about the way the world works. You don't know what to say or how to change things or where to go. You're just plain stuck, without options. Yet the Spirit is there: your groaning companion, Paul says. The Holy Spirits turns that feeling in your gut into a simple prayer—or, as Paul says, "a cry" . . . a cry to the one who bore you, the creator, the mother of us all, "Abba! Father!"

The Trinity doesn't make much sense as a doctrine. But that's how it goes with the mystery of God. God is not a mystery for us to sit around and think about. The Trinity names an experience, an encounter, a relationship. The Trinity comes as a feeling in our gut, a prayer we don't know how to pray, a desire we can't quite get a handle on. This experience is how we know the Trinity is on the move. And if that's the case, then the best we can do sometimes, the best we can say when we don't know what to say, the best we can do when everything seems completely unsatisfying, is to go with our gut and groan. For our hope is that our deep sighs echo with the Holy Spirit who leads us into the intimate love of God, a God who is already our companion, a hidden presence among all his children. Paul is saying all of this in Romans; the Trinity comes with a cry:

> When we cry, 'Abba! Father!' it is that very Spirit [the Holy Spirit] bearing witness with our spirit that we are children of God, and if children, then heirs, heirs of God and joint heirs with Christ. (Rom 8:15b-17a)

If Our Hearts Condemn Us

Acts 4:5-12; Psalm 23; 1 John 3:16-24; John 10:11-18

In 1957 Cary Grant and Deborah Kerr starred in the classic film, *An Affair to Remember*. After a romance blossoms on a transatlantic voyage between Grant's character, Nickie Ferrante, and former night club singer Terry McKay, played by Kerr, the two agree to reunite at the top of the Empire State Building in six months. On her way to the meeting, McKay crosses a busy Manhattan street, oblivious of her surroundings because her gaze is fixed upwards on the spire of the Empire State Building where, she hopes, her lover waits for her. She is hit by an oncoming automobile and badly injured. Rushed to the hospital, McKay never makes it to the reunion.

Meanwhile, Nickie indeed waits for her. The minutes, then hours, tick by, and he becomes progressively more agitated as the elevator doors open repeatedly to reveal yet another crowd of passengers, but not her. Soon, Nickie is plagued by self-doubt: "I must have misunderstood her intentions." "She must have married her fiancé after all." "Did I do something to drive her away?" Self-doubt turns to self-loathing and, once he leaves the observation platform, Ferrante quickly loses himself in drink and despair. His emotional injury begins to heal only when he discovers, through a series of fantastic coincidences, that McKay fully intended to keep their appointment, but was crippled on her way to meet him.

While *An Affair to Remember* has a tidy comedic ending, it does ask serious questions about the place of love in our lives and the extent to which living a fully human life depends on love. Part of the film's attraction lies in its ability to turn romantic questions into existential ones, without trivializing the existential end of the spectrum in the name of romance. That most basic of human questions, "Who am I?" turns out to be the same as the questions, "Am I loved?" "Am I cared for by another?" "Am I attractive?" And Ferrante, alone at the top of the Empire State Building, having invested his entire being in this one love affair, can ask them to no one who will answer. They are questions he can speak only into the unanswering void of the city skyline.

Much current Christian spirituality has a pat answer for these questions, for the way we associate our existential anxiety with love. If Nickie Ferrante were a spiritual person, you could imagine him standing rejected in the rain on the 102nd floor of the Empire State Building reciting "Footprints." Or perhaps the 23rd Psalm: "Yea, though I walk through the valley of the shadow of death, I shall fear no evil, for thou art with me." The message of much Christian spirituality today is this: when I feel most alone, most dejected, most rejected, I simply have to remember that God is there too, shepherding me, caring for me, and consoling me. That is the story of God's love that we are asked to hear on a regular basis today. It is the medicine we prescribe not only for ourselves, but also for others in the throes of depression, disease, the nightmare of bad marriages, the grip of failed careers, and the death of those whom they cherished.

"Am I loved?" "Am I cared for?" "Am I attractive?" We're told that God answers "yes" to each of these questions even when no one else will. And I suppose that is consoling, at least for awhile, at least until fear begins to gnaw in the shadowy places of the mind, the fear that we made up the myth of God's love for just such an occasion as this, when we ask after our own significance and receive no answer.

I don't want that kind of consolation. If that's what God's love is, then count me out. I prefer human loves, with all their indiscretions, all their pettiness, all their disappointment. At least human answers to questions like "Am I loved?" are testable. At least I know where I stand with people. Fortunately, however, we don't have to be convinced by the picture of God's love that Christian spirituality has to offer.

Consider, for instance, the picture of God's love we find in 1 John. This letter is deeply defensive, drawing stark distinctions in strongly moralistic tones. We think this is due, at least in part, to the fact that the letter was written to a community that had just come through an internal conflict, one that left the community profoundly injured. So, the tone of 1 John is a function of a congregation that, as Robert Kysar writes in his commentary, is "threatened, fearful for its existence, uncertain of its identity, defensive and angry" (Kysar, 20). Yet, in the midst of some very pointed remarks about inside and outside, light and dark, good and evil, no other document in the New Testament speaks as often or as explicitly about love as 1 John. Even the thirteenth chapter of Paul's first letter to the Corinthians doesn't hold a candle to 1 John when it comes to discussing love.

Despite love's prominence as a theme in 1 John, there is little romanticism involved, for John's interest in love (much like Paul's interest in 1 Cor 13) derives from the earliest church's struggle for unity and integrity. 1 John is clearly directed toward a community torn apart by schism, which at least in part resulted from doctrinal disputes. In 2:19 the author made reference to the schism, saying, "They went out from us, but they did not belong to us; for if they had belonged to us, they would have remained with us. But by going out they made it plain that none of them belongs to us." And 4:2-3 gives some account of what had gone on to cause the split in the community: "Every spirit that confesses that Jesus Christ has come in the flesh is from God, and every spirit that does not confess Jesus is not from God." Evidently, some of the congregation thought that it wasn't essential to Christian faith to think that Jesus came in the flesh, that, in the words of John's Gospel, he was "made flesh and dwelt among us."

For the author of 1 John, however, it is only because Jesus came in the flesh that we know what love is. God's love is not primarily a disposition or a thought or emotion. It is instead an act like that of the model shepherd who is good because he lays down his life for the sheep. Love, according to 1 John, is an act which God has "willed and executed with all the energy of the crucifixion," as Karl Barth wrote (Barth, 786). That's the point of 1 John 3:16: we know what love is because Christ died for us.

Christ's death is the basis, the creative model, of true human love. Consequently, 1 John 3:16 continues to say that "we ought to lay down our lives for each other." We hear this often, but it startles us far too little. If the very human love of Christ's death is to show itself in our love for each other, then our loves are not chiefly internal dispositions but actions, the gift of our entire self. We're all familiar with this to one degree or another. We're told to love each other, so we put on pleasant faces and kid's gloves when we come to church, and we think that is loving. Yet, as the author of 1 John also says, "our hearts condemn us," for it is another question entirely to ask how much or little of our whole being is lacking when we love in our actions. However, when 1 John asks us to love "not in word or speech, but in truth and action," the author recognizes that no actual shortage in our love can be justified by reducing the love for which Christ's death liberated us to something merely inward, to feelings of warmth or general goodwill.

As I say, this startles us far too little. We are all-too-accustomed to hearing that authentic love is active, something more than warm fuzzies for the people whom we meet. And so our response is to externalize acts of love, to make sure that the love we say is in us is directed outward toward others. We do it when we gather our tithes and offerings, the vast majority of which goes to charity; we do it when we send people to Habitat for Humanity or Anathoth Community Garden; we do it when we pass the peace of Christ with hugs and warm words all around; we do it when we ask what this congregation needs to be doing in the community in order to validate our existence as a church; we do it when we forgive each other in public.

I'm not suggesting that we do away with any of these things. They are essential components of our life together. I'm simply asking us to recognize that everything we do is dangerous; that all of our activities, especially those we do at our most loving, are potential strategies for self-congratulation and self-protection. Externalize your love so that you can be sure you are loving—that's the recipe! Directing our loves outward is one of the ways we ask and answer Nickie Ferrante's questions about personal significance, about whether we too are loved.

This is the form sin takes in us: that we use our most faithful parts to satisfy our longing to know that we too are loved, that we too are significant. And, despite our best intentions, it places us in antagonistic and competitive relationships with our neighbors, our brothers and sisters. Love becomes a yardstick, a way to measure performance. We ask, most of the time subconsciously, what others are doing, how they're loving, how their love is active in the world. "Are those two really tithing?" "When was the last time he showed up to a church outreach activity?" "Whom do I need to greet with special openness this Sunday so that she knows I don't harbor grudges?" We encounter in the best bits of us the evil in which each of us unfortunately has a part. The person who loves, we think, doesn't compile a dossier about her neighbors, but that's precisely what we do. Or worse: we think the person who loves forgives with joy, and yet we forgive each other inauthentically. We come to possess a "refined satisfaction" by making a show of deep sympathy, of great readiness to forgive. Then we can set ourselves in contrast with our offending brother or sister and come out in a much better light, a light in which we now claim the moral superiority to posture, to teach, to model our own (better, less self-absorbed version of) love. It is terrifically easy to wait for others to do something wrong, to slip up, so that we may step in to play the part of the grand forgiver.

But God is "greater than our hearts," 1 John says, "and knows everything." We might be able to mask the inauthenticity of our loves from each other, we might even be able to deceive ourselves, but we can't hide from God. We can't trick God like we trick ourselves by externalizing our love, by putting it into action. We can't hide our relentless clamoring after personal significance from the one who created us. And so, rather than answering our questions about whether we are loved in kind, God gives us a savior, a shepherd, who lays down his life for us but refuses to be captured by the games we play with love. The shepherd, remember, is not part of the flock. The shepherd acts with an authority that doesn't belong to the flock; the shepherd's guidance is alien, it comes from elsewhere. So, the shepherd, unlike each of us, does not have to fear using his love for the flock in self-congratulatory ways. No, the image of the savior as shepherd is quite different from the image of the savior as one of us. We've heard a good deal in the last few weeks about the savior as one of us. We've heard how each of us is Christ to another and to the world, how we are the body that makes Christ available here and now. That image, I hope, can stay with us tonight, but I also hope that it can be tempered by the image of Christ as shepherd, by the image of Christ as God who answers our need to be loved by doing what we cannot: that is, laying down his life in order to take it up again.

You Shall Not Covet

Exodus 20:1-17; John 2:13-22

O Christ, who established the heavens by your wisdom and founded the earth upon the waters: Establish our hearts upon the rock of your commandments. Amen.

The philosopher and fiction writer, C. S. Lewis, often remarked on the fundamental problem of human life, the basic shortfall of the nature we all share in common. What is really, deeply wrong with us is simple, he said: we are "too easily pleased" (Lewis, 16).

Too easily pleased? That sounds preposterous. I could rattle off a list as long as my arm of the things I find unsatisfying and unfulfilling: my car, my job, my friendships, my marriage, family illnesses, the government, street violence, guilt, envy, resentment, the cold I had last week, the hole in my favorite shirt, loss of self-esteem, and Duke Basketball's prospects in the national championship, which are as good as anyone's, but still not good enough for me. I'm unsatisfied with all these things and more. I guess that each of you could populate a similar list, and if you can't, then I bet you simply aren't trying. What I am—my condition on any given day—is discontented. I'm not too easily pleased in the least; in fact, I'm never happy with anything. I want more, and I can't help myself. No, that isn't exactly true. The fact of the matter isn't that I can't help myself, it's that I don't want to.

The Bible's word for this disposition, for my way of being in the world, is "covetousness." Covetousness: unbridled desire. Covetousness: unslakable thirst. Covetousness: lust. The Ten Commandments end—

they are summed up—with a rebuke of covetousness: "You shall not covet your neighbor's house; you shall not covet your neighbor's wife, or male or female slave, or ox, or donkey, or anything that belongs to your neighbor" (Exod 20:17). Covetousness: it's condemned throughout the remainder of Torah; time and again the prophets rail against it; Jesus censures it in the Sermon on the Mount; and Paul frequently reprimands his congregations for it. But covetousness seems to be a normal condition that lies tremendously close to the heart of who we are, to our needs, drives, desires, and simple wants—the stuff that's part and parcel of what makes us *us*.

In *The Large Catechism*, Martin Luther wrote that the commandment not to covet places every one of us inescapably under the judgment of the Law. He says, "This last commandment . . . is addressed not to those whom the world considers wicked rogues, but precisely to the most upright—to people who wish to be commended as honest and virtuous because they have not offended against the preceding commandments" (Luther, 49). If, like the rich young man in Matthew's Gospel, we think that we can follow the rest of the commandments—if we can live our lives without committing adultery, without stealing, without worshiping false gods or dishonoring our parents, without lying or killing anyone, without profaning the Sabbath or the name of the Lord our God—if we can do all this, then the commandment, "Do not covet," will surely trip us up. After all, it isn't as if we have complete control over our desires. No, we want what we want when we want it; and if we can't get it, then we're dissatisfied. To say anything else would be less than fully honest.

So what, I wonder, could C. S. Lewis have meant by describing us as "too easily pleased"? Perhaps he didn't mean to question the fact that we're essentially dissatisfied so much as he meant to make us stop and take stock of the kinds of things we're perpetually happy to be dissatisfied with. Perhaps Lewis didn't consider our endless quest to gratify our desires to be the real problem. Perhaps his comment points to how paltry most of the things we covet are.

In *The Truth About God*, a book on the Ten Commandments in the Christian life, Stanley Hauerwas and Will Willimon tell a story about a friend of theirs who is a priest. Back in 1975, the priest went to see the movie *Jaws* when it came out. In the film a giant shark terrorizes a resort town in New England during the height of the summer vacation season. After Jaws swallows a small boy surfing on an inflatable raft, the town authorities send out a posse of fishermen to hunt sharks in the area. After awhile one of those boats comes back to port having caught and killed a 15-foot tiger shark—a huge fish, a vast eating-machine. It turns out to be the wrong shark because it didn't eat the little boy, which Richard Dreyfuss' character, a marine biologist, finds out by dissecting the shark in a laboratory. Anyway, out of the stomach of the tiger shark are pulled fish, an old tire, bones, a piece of a boat, and, in a nod to James M. Barrie of *Peter Pan* fame, an old clock, still ticking. The priest, watching everything the shark had eaten being divulged onscreen, exclaimed, "That's my congregation!" "We're so very desirous, so deeply empty and hungry, so omnivorous," that, like the shark, we constantly fill ourselves up with things that aren't food, with stuff that isn't good for us (Hauerwas and Willimon, 133).

But the commandment not to covet isn't just about us. It isn't there simply to remind us how measly our wants are, how prone we are to addictive behaviors. The commandment also shows us that we live in a world where gratifying our desires often means that others can't have what they need to survive, let alone flourish. Our world is very close to a zero-sum game, despite the enthusiasm we periodically show for renewable resources, charitable institutions, and pay-it-forward mentalities. I can hardly emphasize this enough: covetousness, envy, and lust aren't merely about what goes on in your head or heart. We aren't just talking about private feelings, since our covetousness has effects that belittle not only us, but also others and the world around us. The twentieth century Swiss theologian, Karl Barth, hit upon this point in an extremely poignant way when he retold what he called "the strange story of David and Bathsheba in 2 Sam. 11. 1-12, 25":

> [The army] of Israel . . . is encamped under Joab in the open fields. The king [David] has remained behind in Jerusalem, and has just awakened from a siesta . . . . He is there on the flat roof of his palace. It is not an evil situation, but it is not a very promising one. He gazes indolently at the courtyards of the lower neighboring houses. "Thou shalt not covet thy neighbor's wife." The gaping David covets the woman—Bathsheba, the wife of Uriah the Hittite, as he is told—whom he there sees washing herself. "Thou shalt not commit adultery." David wills to commit adultery with this woman. He has only to command her as the king, and he does so . . . . The woman becomes pregnant. Will he stand by what he has done, not only in her sight, but in that

of her husband, of all Jerusalem, perhaps of the child who is yet unborn? The king of Israel an adulterer? The consequences are incalculable. He is afraid of them, not unreasonably, but unjustly. Already, however, he is his own prisoner. It is only by further wrong that he can avert the consequences of the wrong which he has already done. First, he tries to practice a clumsy deception. Uriah is recalled. The ostensible reason is that he should report to David on the progress of the campaign. The real purpose is to restore him to his own house and therefore to Bathsheba. He will therefore think, and even at worst cannot prove a contrary opinion, that the expected child is his own. But this plan is defeated by an unexpected obstacle: "And Uriah said unto David, 'The ark, and Israel, and Judah, abide in tents; and my lord Joab, and the servants of my lord, are encamped in the open fields; shall I then go into mine house, to eat and to drink, and to lie with my wife? As thou livest, as my soul liveth, I will not do this thing." He will not do it even when he is pressed to do so, and invited to the royal table and made drunk, but sleeps two nights at the entrance to the palace with David's bodyguard. He "went not down to his own house" . . . . David has come up against a man—and it is almost a final appeal to himself—who knows what is right, and who keeps to it even in his cups. His only option therefore—if he is not to retreat, as he is obviously unable to do—is to cause this man to disappear, to die, in order that he may marry Bathsheba and conceal the adultery which he has committed. As king, he has the power to do this. "Thou shalt not kill" . . . . Well, he has the power to kill without having to admit it even to himself. And he does it by sending his famous directive to Joab, carried by the returning husband himself, to place him in the fiercest part of the battle against the besieged city of the Ammonites, and then to leave him in the lurch, so that he is killed by the enemies of Israel. His orders were obeyed, involving an unnecessary, imprudent and costly attack . . . The report sent by Joab concluded with the news which he had desired: "Thy servant, Uriah the Hittite, is dead also." This makes up for everything—even the death of the others who had lost their lives in this futile enterprise . . . . He can now enjoy the peace which he desires, and which is created by the death of Uriah that he has so skillfully arranged. Bathsheba mourns for her husband. "And when the mourning was past, David sent and fetched her to his house, and she became his wife, and bare him a son." . . . He could now be born without any scandal. It all belonged to the past. It had all been covered over.

"But the thing that David had done displeased the Lord." This was the message that the prophet Nathan had to give him. He had done what he should not and could not do as the elect of the Lord. He had contradicted at every point himself, his election and calling, and therefore the Lord. He had allowed himself to stray and fall into lust and adultery and [deceit] and murderous treachery—the one following the other by an iron law—and therefore into the sphere of the wrath and judgment of God. (Barth, 466-467)

David's sin shows us that covetousness leads, as Barth said, "by an iron law" to a betrayal of all the other commandments. But just because of how interconnected all the commandments are, there's a seed of gospel in our avarice and greed. The good thing about covetousness is that, "unlike some sin, it is not subtle. Its results are public, there for all to see" (Hauerwas and Willimon, 134), rather like the bazaar that Jesus found set up in the temple when he journeyed to Jerusalem for the Passover festival. "He told those who were selling the doves, 'Take these things out of here! Stop making my Father's house a marketplace!'" (John 2:17).

We hear a lot of conjecture about what Jesus was trying to accomplish by clearing out the temple in Jerusalem. Some New Testament scholars insist that, apart from getting himself killed, Jesus' riot in the temple was the one sure thing that he did in his ministry. A lot of others say that it's a symbolic action, by which they seem to mean that it made a statement even if it didn't accomplish anything material. A good bit of this is fairly embarrassing to Mennonites because Jesus' storming the temple with a whip of cords doesn't look altogether nonviolent, certainly not pacifistic. Fortunately, those conversations represent something of a red herring, because, if you consider Jesus' action in the context of the Ten Commandments, and in the context of what we've just been considering about how covetousness publicizes our sin, then his clearing of the temple makes sense as a strike at the heart of how even we, even God's elect, institutionalize ways of violating God's law. Jesus' temple action isn't merely symbolic, for the marketplace is one institution where greed is material.

Now, I'm not in any way suggesting that we could or should do away with marketplaces. But I am suggesting that, like those who were buying and selling in the temple, we live in a society that constantly bombards us with stimuli to unfaithfulness, and that these stimuli dig down deeply into our souls—so deeply, in fact, that we aren't going to be able to will ourselves out of covetous lifestyles by ourselves. "We need a community that enables us to rise above our natural covetousness and the rather relentless formation into greediness that characterizes [our lives today]" (Hauerwas and Willimon, 136).

The hope, I think, is that we could learn to call that community the church. But if we're to do so, then we need to do a better job at schooling each other out of greed. It isn't likely to happen elsewhere, and it certainly won't happen on our own. This is the one community we've got that hopes to flourish not on account of our covetousness, that hopes not to be too easily pleased by the wisdom of this world, but rather longs to be pulled into love by the grace of a jealous God, the Father of our Lord, Jesus Christ, who commands us to covet only communion in his Son's name.

Power

Illusions of Peace

Romans 6:1b–11; Matthew 10:24–39

Throughout the last century the summer vacation became a staple of American life, an identity marker for the leisured class, and a small but critical piece of the American dream. Where I grew up in South Central Pennsylvania it seemed as if everyone spent at least a week in July or August at the beach, or, more properly, "the Shore"—that stretch of coastal New Jersey from Atlantic City south to Cape May, where my own family still vacations every year. If you grew up in the United States or Canada, chances are that the word "vacation" conjures up images for you that are similar to mine: campfires, swimming in the ocean, digging for clams, and miniature golf—images having to do with rest and relaxation, with a break from the tension of everyday life, with a move into another world from which stress and strain are absent.

Of course, most actual vacations fail to measure up to the images we associate with them. Vacations can be plenty stressful, as you might know if you've ever taken one with your in-laws. Vacations can easily tire you out. How many times have you shown up at work on the Monday morning following your vacation thinking, "Okay, now I need a vacation so that I can recover from my vacation"? Vacations can be a tremendous amount of work, packing a year's worth of play into a week or two. They're odd things, these mixtures of rest and busyness we call vacations, perhaps most aptly captured by a T-shirt slogan I saw on the beach a few years back: it read, "Hurry up. Relax!"

And yet, the idea of a vacation remains extraordinarily appealing, and the ideal vacation is a powerful fantasy for many of us: couples save money for years while looking forward to those two weeks in Hawaii, and parents eagerly await next year when the children will finally be old enough to go to Disney World. In this sense, the ideal vacation is what Sigmund Freud, the father of modern psychoanalysis, called an illusion. An illusion is an idea or belief that works in our imaginations as a consolation, allowing us to cope successfully with how hectic or out of control things really are. In this vein, the Archbishop of Canterbury Rowan Williams once wrote that "We all . . . badly need images of achieved repose, of a state in which the process of 'becoming' is in effect over" (Williams, 45). And Freud himself, when he identified the "death drive," had in mind how we desire ways out of the pressures that come from balancing all the competing demands and joys our lives force upon us. The idea of a summer vacation, as well as many other escapes—church retreats, stints in the guest-houses of monasteries and abbeys, our blithe talk of "taking time for myself" or "a personal Sabbath"—all of these impress upon us our deep-seated desire to "take a step back" from the real workaday world of just one thing after another.

I often find myself wondering just how close my notion of peace lies to my illusion of the ideal vacation: peace as a release from pressure, peace as the absence of discord or disagreement, peace as play rather than work. I also often find myself wondering what it is that we imagine when we pray for peace. It feels like such a hard concept to envision, let alone actualize.

Another slogan, this time from a bumper sticker instead of a T-shirt: "If you want justice, work for peace." That's familiar fare for those of us influenced—even at a distance—by 1960s radicalism. The idea that lies behind the phrase is that justice is deeply complex. Justice is about giving to each her due, giving to each according to his need. And all of this involves us in intricate calculations, weighing what I deserve against what you deserve. No wonder we need so many courts: all that haggling over just deserts makes justice a recipe for disagreement and frustration. But peace—now that's something we can all get behind. Sane people don't want conflict; reasonable people don't want to involve themselves in the interminable dynamics of give and take. We don't want to have to hire accountants just to figure out the basics of distribution, like whose turn it is to make dinner or pay the bills, or which one of us should get up with the screaming kid at 3 AM. No, we want those negotiations to resolve themselves naturally, that is, peacefully. "If you want justice, work for peace." It seems logical enough until you get down to the tricky business of puzzling out what peace is all about.

The hard truth of the matter captured by each of these slogans—"Hurry up. Relax!" and "If you want justice, work for peace"—is that peace is often an illusion in our lives. I don't just mean that peace is illusory when George W. Bush claims that the military remains in Iraq to "keep the peace." I don't mean that peace is a fraud when stoners flip you the V-sign and say, "Peace, man," or when Eminem signs off his interview on MTV with, "Peace out!" I mean that for you and me—people who in this communion have committed ourselves fundamentally to the cause of peace—peace nevertheless often remains an illusion for us very much like the illusion of the ideal vacation.

Let me put some meat on that. In all strands of the Gospel tradition, Jesus is not a figure readily associated with peace in the sense of the serenity imagined in the ideal vacation. Visible harmony and human unity do not attach to him. Rather, Jesus provokes conflict and confrontation, and in our Gospel text for this evening, as he instructs the twelve disciples on how they are to go out into ministry, he says that he does not come bringing peace, but a sword (Matt 10:34). He continues by quoting to them the prophet Micah's denunciation of the social divisions of his day:

> The son treats his father with contempt,
> the daughter rises up against her mother,
> and the daughter-in-law against her mother-in-law;
> your enemies are members of your own household. (Micah 7:6)

Yet, there is a striking difference between Christ's word in the Gospel reading and Micah's prophecy, for Jesus laces what was originally a negative commentary on Micah's part with the authority of divine intent: "For I have come . . ." Christ says to his disciples that these divisions are the purpose of his advent on earth.

No matter how figuratively we read these verses—is it a spiritual sword that Christ brings, like the one imagined by the author of Hebrews, who wrote that "the word of God is living and active, sharper than any double-edged sword, piercing until it divides soul from spirit, joints from marrow . . . judging the thoughts and intentions of the heart"? (Heb 4:12)—no matter how much we tell ourselves that Jesus was really only challenging the overgrown and ossified kinship system of first century Palestinian Judaism, no matter what we do to soften the blow of these verses, this is not exactly a Jesus who resonates strongly with our images of peacefulness. He does not promise his followers repose or rest, release from the strain and stresses of the world. Instead, he suggests that because no disciple is above her or his teacher, we, if we plan to follow him, should not expect to be led along a different path than his, a path that inescapably culminates in the image of a man being tortured to death.

We face a powerful temptation as pacifist Christians to sanitize the gospel, to say that Jesus' work is simply the revelation that, after all is said and done, people really can get along. As has so often been said, it is very difficult to see why anyone offering such a bland message should have got himself crucified. If, however, Christ speaks truly when he says to the disciples that he comes to bring a sword, or, in Luke's casting of the same story, that he comes to bring "division" to the earth (Luke 12:51), then this should be a clue to us that the good news he proclaims will not be easily absorbed into our illusions of peace. If his identity as the Prince of Peace is to mean anything good and new to us, we need to see first why his peace is not obvious.

Christ's gospel is difficult to recognize as peace because the illusions of peace we long for involve visions of rest for the weary, withdrawal from the frenetic pace of our lives, and escape from conflict. Yet Paul speaks of a gospel that roots our lives in a conflict that brought the death of Christ. This gospel brings us "the newness of life," Paul says (Rom 6:4), as we are united with Christ in his death. This gospel has nothing to do with peace as escape or restful bliss. Instead, only if we have been united with him in a death like his, will we also be united with him in a resurrection like his (v. 5). Of course, the death Paul has in mind is the death of baptism, in which the body of sin is destroyed. We take a strange sort of comfort in that fact: baptism is, after all, only a ritual washing, a symbolic immersion into Christ's death. We tell ourselves that we do not really need to die in order to be united to Christ in his death, and so we breathe a sigh of relief. That sigh flows from two sources, intimately connected. One, it flows from the relief that we need not undergo bodily harm or injury in order to gain the rewards of resurrection—as Paul says, "the death he died he died to sin, once for all" (v. 10). Death can now be approached without fear. Two, the sigh flows from the supposition that by being united with Christ in his death we shall gain the peace we long for, the release from pressure that is synonymous with death. Death, or at least our images of it, especially after a long illness or if it comes in war, looks a lot like our illusion of the ideal vacation; it has the same texture as our illusions of peace: repose, rest, escape.

It should, however, be obvious that for Paul, Christ's death does not issue in this kind of peace. It issues in an active life, a life lived to God in Christ Jesus (v. 11). And this means that Paul takes the life inaugurated in our baptisms as seriously—no, more seriously—than he takes death. Death loses its dominion in Christ's resurrection; its hold on us is impermanent. Here's the lesson for us in death's instability: if we are to live into the newness of life of which Paul speaks, then we will have to give up on our illusions of peace, concord, and non-confrontation. We will have to reckon with the fact that the Prince of Peace brings a sword to the earth, a sword that issues a summons "to battle," as Karl Barth put it, "and not the telling of a dream which at the end necessarily leaves everything in the real world exactly as it was" (Barth, 679).

Battles and swords: these are not reposeful images. But they are images that speak of decision: the battle goes one way or the other, the sword divides as it cuts. Matthew and Paul, who are so often seen as opposites, are in fact deeply united in their visions of Christ's ministry insofar as for them Jesus represents the decisive climax of God's history, the messianic struggle of the king who arises to initiate God's rule. In response to him, men and women discover and decide the basic orientation of their thoughts and wants: we find ourselves judged, and only thus do we unearth in ourselves all kinds of hidden divisions and disunities. We can paper over those fractures with our illusions of peace, our faith in the ideal vacation, our hope in the repose of death. But Christ's peace is authentic only when our illusions of peace have been cut with a sword, when the rest and passivity we favor have been so upset that they bring to the surface all our resistance to the struggle of grace, which is Christ's new life flowing through ours.

Paul's Politics

Nehemiah 8:1–3, 5–6, 8–10; 1 Corinthians 12:12–31a;
Luke 4:14–21

There's so much talk about politics these days. If you pay attention to the news at all, you can't ignore the presidential fever in the air. Presidential hopefuls are putting their names in the hat for the race next year. And, of course, there's the recent power shift in Congress. Everyone is talking about bi-partisanship and what's going to happen on Capital Hill now that there are lots of Democrats in the House and Senate, while the president is a Republican. How will the politics play out? That's the question I keep hearing, and the pundits generously offer their predictions.

There was a book published a few years ago that has fed the political frenzy among Christians: *God's Politics* by Jim Wallis. Yes, *God's Politics*. Quite the title! I think it sounds a bit presumptuous, but that hasn't stopped anyone from buying it. When I was at Bluffton University to meet with students and preach at their chapel, I can't tell you how often people in university administration wanted to hear what I thought about *God's Politics*. Apparently Jim Wallis spoke on campus earlier in the year.

I'm not here to give you a book report. Nor am I going to attempt something so spectacular as outlining what I think God's politics really are. Instead, I want to try something a bit more modest. I want to talk about *Paul's politics*. Not God's politics, not even the politics of Jesus. Just the politics of Paul. And the reason why this is worth preaching about is because for Paul faith is political, Christian spirituality is political.

Last week we talked about the first part of 1 Corinthians 12 and heard how the Holy Spirit is present through each one of us as we gather to worship. As Paul says, "To each one the manifestation of the Spirit is given for the common good" (1 Cor 12:7). Worship is about the common good, Paul says. God gives us the Holy Spirit so we can offer it to one another and be joined together in God's love. God's Spirit is the grace that saves us from sin and binds us together. The Spirit shows us that we find life as we give it for the sake of each other. Thus, the local church is absolutely central for Paul. Through our gathering to worship God, we come to partake in God's abundant outpouring of grace. Mysteriously, our assembly overflows with God's Spirit, pouring out from each of us and binding us together in the love of Christ. That's why we need to look at what we do here with a mystical gaze, with patient eyes that learn to see God through our worshipful fellowship, because the Spirit comes through the material of our bodies.

Now this week, the lectionary moves us into the second half of chapter 12, where Paul further develops the spiritual reality of our worship. But this time around Paul takes up the language of politics. He calls the church in Corinth a *body*—and that's political language: "God has arranged the parts in the body, every one of them, just as he wanted them to be . . . As it is, there are many parts, but one body" (vv. 18–20). Paul insists that everyone is absolutely vital to the gathering. Just as the human body has many different parts, so it is with the church. As he says earlier, "The body is a unit, though it is made up of many parts; and though all its parts are many, they form one body. So it is with Christ" (v. 12). And since we all participate in the body of Christ together, "The eye cannot say to the hand, 'I don't need you!' And the head cannot say to the feet, 'I don't need you'" (v. 21). Everyone who is part of the church in Corinth is part of the same body. And every part of that body is absolutely indispensable, absolutely necessary.

This sounds great, right? It's nice to hear that we are all important, that we need each other in order to be Christian, to be part of the body of Christ. Paul's teaching in 1 Corinthians 12 makes sense of the quote I love so much from Herbert McCabe. I've repeated it too many times, but that won't stop me from saying it again: "Christ is present to us in so far as we are present to each other" (McCabe, xi). Or there's a famous line from Dietrich Bonhoeffer where he says the same sort of thing: "A person who is not in the church has no real living-community with

Christ" (Bonhoeffer, 161). Or how about Karl Barth? He also gets Paul right: "True Christianity cannot be a private Christianity, i.e., a rapacious Christianity .... Without one's fellow-person, God is an illusion, a myth. He may be the God of Holy Scripture, and we may call upon Him as the Yahweh of Israel and the Father of Jesus Christ, but He is an idol in whom we certainly cannot believe" (Barth, 442-443). This is exactly Paul's insight into what Jesus came into our world to create: we participate in the body of Christ, the church—the people who gathered together for worship in Corinth, and those of us who get together here in Chapel Hill. Our church is God's creation, and somehow, mysteriously, we are made into Christ's body where everyone is vital, where every body is part of the vitality of the corporate body of Christ. There are no expendable parts. We can't get along without each other. That's the point. And it's good news; it's the gospel, Paul says.

But there's more. This good news goes deeper. Scholars point out that Paul's letter to the church in Corinth bears striking similarities with other Greco-Roman speeches and letters. He used a style of writing and speaking called a "concord"—*homonoia* in Greek. Politicians would give speeches or write letters trying to convince the diverse people of the city—*polis* is "city" in Greek, and that's where we get the notion of "politics"—to unite in a common project, to share the same goals for society, to share a common politics just as they share the same life in the *polis*, in the city. This is where we can see that Paul used the same discourse, the same way of speaking or writing. In these "concord" addresses to the diverse population of the city, politicians called the society a body, just like Paul did in his letter to the divided church in Corinth. We are one body, politicians would say, so we need to act accordingly. We are one—united, bound together. Of course, politicians only made these speeches when they needed to: that is, when a dissatisfied section of society wanted to revolt (see Martin, 38–47).

With this context in mind, it almost sounds like Paul wasn't very original with this discussion about the body. He was simply repeating what other political leaders said. But once we compare what Paul was saying in his talk about the body with what the politicians were saying about the body of the *polis*, then we can see what's unique, then we can hear the good news. The politicians' concord speeches were part of the protective ideology of the establishment, part of a project to protect the empire—to keep the empire and the city hierarchically ordered. A good example from the Greek history books is a senator who needed to defuse the rebellious spirit of the lower classes—the poor, working classes—by saying that they were the necessary stomach of society: the poor do all the digestion work to provide nutrients for the head, which is the upper class of society who don't work because they have more important things to worry about (Martin, 45). The people assumed that the city was hierarchically ordered, and that the hierarchy could not be disturbed. Everything must stay the way it was for the sake of the common good. Some voices, by nature, were more politically relevant than others. So only a select few, the aristocracy, could provide the important leadership of the polis. The others, the masses, simply labored to provide for the movers and shakers of society.

Now here's where we can begin to hear the revolutionary politics of Paul. The good news according to Paul is that Jesus came and established a society, a community, a people that he called a body, but a very different political body than the Greco-Roman order. This new body of Christ is not hierarchically ordered; there is no protective ideology at work here; there isn't any concern to maintain the established order of things. Now listen to a passage from the middle of our reading from 1 Corinthians:

> those parts of the body that seem to be weaker are indispensable ... But God has combined the members of the body and has given greater honor to the parts that lacked it, so that there should be no division in the body, but that its parts should have equal concern for each other. If one part suffers, every part suffers with it; if one part is honored, every part rejoices with it. (1 Cor 12:22–26)

This is the shape of Paul's egalitarian politics, one where the weakest parts are actually the most important. With this logic, Paul turns our vision of politics upside-down. And what's more, each person bears the same suffering as every other. That's definitely not the way it works in the Greco-Roman polis. This new body has a new politics; the church is the body of Christ, a new political arrangement.

Here at our church there are no elected officials who are more politically important than any other. The only authority we have is this book, the Bible. As the late Baptist theologian James McClendon always put it, we are "people of the book"; this book determines our peoplehood—that is, our politics—by the way we gather around to interpret it with our lives (McClendon, 34-46). For this organizational strategy, we follow in the way of Israel. In our passage from Nehemiah we see all of Israel assemble for the reading of their Scriptures: "And all the people listened attentively" (Neh 8:3). They gather around the book. And as they assemble for the public reading of Scripture, they receive their political shape; their bodies become the body of Israel.

As the church, the body of the Messiah, we follow in the way of Israel. When we assemble as a worshiping body, we read the Bible, pray the Scriptures, sing God's Word in our hymns, someone preaches, everyone gets a chance to share insights, and finally we are commissioned to leave our gathering and continue to speak God's Word with our lives throughout the week. Church is the space where we learn how to submit our whole lives to the authority of the Word of God. But here's one difference between biblical Israel and us. For us—that is, the church—there are no priests. Or, I should say, there are no singular priests. The only priest we have, according to the Epistle to the Hebrews, is Jesus Christ. Instead of having a special class of priests, we believe in the priesthood of all believers—each of us is a priest, a vehicle of God's Spirit in the world. Our political shape—the shape of this body of Christ—is fundamentally egalitarian. We witness to the good news of Paul's politics by how we worship. That's why, for example, a few different people got up earlier in the service to read the Bible. No one person had that role. And they weren't the same people who did it last week, and different people will read next week. That's egalitarian politics. Then the preacher—that's me for today—gets up here and goes on and on about something from the Bible passages, but I will soon sit down and give up any authority I had over the Bible. Then someone else will come up here and ask all of us to share how we heard God speaking. That's politics. The power of God's Word flows from every corner of our worship space; there's no centralization of authority in this political body. Together, we listen for what the Holy Spirit may be saying to us from Scripture. I don't have any more authority about what God may be saying to us than you do. And everyone will have a chance to speak. It doesn't matter what class or race you come from, or what kind of power you may have in other venues. None of that counts here. As Christ's body our assembly performs the good news that everyone is a precious gift of the Holy Spirit. The good news Paul announces in 1 Corinthians is written again with the movements of our bodies at worship in the body of Christ.

Paul offers a completely different vision of politics than Jim Wallis' book. For Wallis, Christians are political when we vote according to the right morals, when we choose representatives based on so-called Christian values. Politics, for him, is primarily focused on the nation-state; some political theorists call this, "politics as statecraft" (Weber, 77). We are politically relevant, according to this logic, only when we use our convictions to make a difference for the nation-state. Although Jim Wallis thinks he's radical, he simply offers another side of the same political coin. In the end, he merely wants Evangelical Christians to be okay with voting for Democrats. But that's not radical; Wallis offers more of the same.

Paul's politics is radical: it digs down to the root (that's what the word *radical* means, getting to the origin or root) and plants something else. He plants the church as a different political body with a different politics. Through our worship, Paul says, we become a new political body, the body of Christ, in which we embody the resurrected life of Jesus. The power of Christ's redemptive life doesn't grow in the White House. God's radical politics is the fruit of the Spirit witnessed in our humble body. The relationships that form our church are the fertile soil where God plants his radical politics. This is what Augustine caught onto in the fourth-century when he called the church "the city of God," which is an *altera civitas*, an alternative city. In Christ's city our politics is determined, according to Paul, by how we treat the weakest among us. The basic political issue is whether or not we provide space for the weakest among us to speak. Does our communal body receive the giftedness of the weak? Your power is not determined by how much money you can raise to win a campaign. Airtime in our polis doesn't depend on your rhetorical abilities. The reputation of your friends won't win you more or less time in the pulpit. The movers and shakers in our church aren't necessarily the ones with a long list of successes and achievements. No, the power of Christ's body passes through everyone. We are a body that honors the weakest members of society.

I can see how this way of thinking about the church's political power can reinforce a certain sense of naval-gazing, an obsessive turn in our selves: if we are a political body, then what's the point of participating in the politics of that other body, the so-called secular body? Some people would be quick to accuse me of falling into the "sectarian temptation"—a withdrawal from worldly affairs. We do fall victim to that temptation when we forget that the very nature of the church is *witness*. The nature of our body is evangelistic, the church always reaches out. Our political arrangement is always open ended. We don't control the shape of our body because, ultimately, it belongs to God. We are determined by a politics that is always an open invitation. The borders of our polis are always open: we don't build walls to keep immigrants out. Instead, we actually want people to wander in and join our body politic. Anyone can walk through those doors, take a seat in our assembly, and have a chance to speak. We actually believe that they may have the gifts we need to help us discern what the Holy Spirit is saying.

I wonder if we should think about our evangelism in terms of an immigration policy: we are always interested in welcoming new citizens, which means our borders are never closed to anyone who wants to become a member of the people of God. This is called "conversion." Our immigration policy means that our doors are always open, and we mean that quite literally: at no point in our service do we lock the doors to keep people out. And we don't have immigration police guarding the doors—*la migra*, as my Hispanic relatives call them. Maybe a good way to envision this is to think about the church as a nation that unites the immigration agency with the department of tourism: like Jesus, we always seek out new people and invite them to join us. We aren't sectarians; the U.S. government proves itself a sectarian political organism through its closed-door immigration policy and its systematic deportation of undocumented residents.

As an extension of Jesus' life, the church continues in the way of Jesus. We re-present the good news of Jesus Christ. And to whom did Jesus say he was coming to share the good news? Not the powerful. Not the people with lots of resources. Not the power brokers. Not the movers and shakers in society. Apparently, Jesus didn't know what would be best for his political career; he didn't have a good campaign advisor. At the very beginning of his ministry Jesus laid out his agenda, his political platform. He offered a vision that shed light on the rest of his ministry. Jesus read a passage from the prophet Isaiah that shined through the rest of his life. The passage he read helps us see him for who he was and what he was all about. And, perhaps, it is also the way we can see who we are, to see how we can be identified with Paul's vision for the body politic of Christ. Here it is: He unrolled the scroll and found the place where it was written:

> "The Spirit of the Lord is upon me,
>   because he has anointed me
>   to bring good news to the poor.
> He has sent me to proclaim release to the captives
>   and the recovery of sight to the blind,
>   to let the oppressed go free,
>   to proclaim the year of the Lord's favor."
>
> And he rolled up the scroll, gave it back to the attendant, and sat down. (Luke 4:17–20)

That is our political spirituality.

Power in Weakness

2 Corinthians 12:2–10; Mark 6:1–13

They're about power, aren't they—these texts tonight? About power and what it looks like, its anatomy. It's a good thing, too, because power is a difficult concept to grasp. It's one of those words that we all use in vastly different contexts, often without paying much attention to what it means. Power. Who is powerful? Bill Gates? Ariel Sharon? Saddam Hussein? Brittney Spears? All those are powerful people, each in his or her own way. They have the social capital to get things done. And, in odd ways, we respect them for it. What about others? Your mother or father? Your wife or your husband? Your teacher? Your friends? They influence your lives, most of the time quite significantly. Those people are probably powerful too, at least to you.

But what happens when we turn to the gospel? Suddenly, power seems out of place. Power and the gospel seem strange bedfellows. Power, we say, tends to corrupt; the gospel improves and edifies. Power constrains and enforces; the gospel liberates—it promotes the freedom of those it attracts to its high ground. Those are our immediate impressions. But here tonight, in the New Testament, we have something more complex than this easy opposition between power and gospel. Jesus, God incarnate, finds himself in Mark's Gospel without power. Paul, in 2 Corinthians, is prompted to suggest that power is made perfect in weakness. God powerless? Power in weakness? We may have to think more closely and carefully about power, especially if it's the power of God in Jesus Christ that we're confronted with.

I love reading the Gospel of Mark. I think it's my favorite book in the Bible. If I had said that fifteen hundred or a thousand or five hundred years ago, people would have been shocked—Mark's just a pale imitation of Matthew, so don't waste your time. Even if I had said it a generation ago, I would've been greeted with raised eyebrows, especially among Mennonites. After all, Jesus doesn't do much teaching in this Gospel. There's no Sermon on the Mount to confirm us in our *Gelassenheit*. Maybe some of you are pretty sure I'm off my rocker, saying I like Mark best. Because, let's face it, by comparison with Mark any of us are fabulous storytellers. Mark's stories are more like the missionary biographies in this journal I receive called *Brethren in Christ History and Life*. The bios in it always follow a set pattern; there's no story except that time passes: So and so was born, then she did this, then she did that, then a little bit of this, a little bit of that, and then she died. And that's just what happens with Jesus in Mark's Gospel. Where's the story?

But every now and then Mark drops these soft hints and subtleties—like the one in our text tonight—that give us a glimpse of what's going on. Mark, in other words, if full of surprises. Consider this. From the beginning of the Gospel, we've been schlepping around Palestine with Jesus. The disciples, the crowds, the synagogue leaders—everyone is asking Jesus what's the point of it all. And by now, in the sixth chapter, we're all a little bit exasperated, because Jesus doesn't seem to care whether we have eyes to see and ears to hear—that, and frankly, we're all a little out of breath, because Jesus has been moving fast. First he's in the wilderness being baptized, then he's in Capernaum driving out demons, then back to the wilderness healing lepers, then back to Capernaum forgiving sins, then he's down by the lakeside eating with tax collectors, then he's in some cornfields. Finally, Jesus reaches his hometown, and we know home is where you go when you need to take a load off. So maybe now, as Jesus goes home, we'll get a chance to catch up and put it all together.

Apparently, however, Jesus has other ideas: immediately he's up to his old tricks, teaching in the synagogue. The people who hear him are "astounded." They were astounded back in chapter one, too. There, Jesus taught as one with authority and not as their scribes. But here they're astounded for an altogether different reason: Jesus, the carpenter from down the street, is showing off. You know people like that. They go away for a year of Mennonite Voluntary Service, or their freshman year of college, or they get a new position on the other side of the country, or they join the Merchant Marines, and when they come back they have to make sure everyone else knows how cultivated they are now that they've seen "the world," how much wiser and more mature they are than they were, and by implication, how much more entitled to their opinions they are than you will ever be. This happens all the time at high school and college reunions. It happens at professional conferences, too. People show off, and it "astounds" us; or rather, it makes us sick, because, of course, *we* never do any of this.

That's when the rumor mill starts grinding. "Well, you know what Ellen did to get that job in New York City, don't you?" "Yep, old Bill's made good; too bad what it did to his mama . . ." What we're doing when we make these comments is assuring everyone around, and perhaps especially ourselves, that we know better, that we still know how to place this person, that, appearances to the contrary, he or she is no one special. This is the kind of "knowing better" that the people in Jesus' hometown resort to in Mark 6 when they hear Jesus teach. So: "Isn't this the sawyer, Mary's bastard, the oldest of her brood of scoundrels? Haven't we made honest women out of all his sisters? And now he's showing up acting like he's the best thing since sliced bread? I don't think so: he can go pound sand."

In this context, Jesus' little quip about "the prophet without honor" is almost laughable. This isn't Socratic wisdom. It's not even sardonic ruefulness. It certainly isn't powerfully, immediately, and self-evidently true. It's chicken soup. It's pathetic. It's like when someone gives you a hard time, and all you can come up with is, "Nice hair." Prophets in their hometown. Right—"Good comeback, Jesus!" Still, something surprising is going on, because if Jesus' verbal response is rather lame, his activity is anything but. "And he was able to do no deed of power there, *except that he laid his hands on a few sick people and cured them*" (Mark 6:5). Oh really? Just that!

That's why I love Mark's Gospel. It's full of surprises. In fact, here there are two surprises. The first one: on the heels of the crowd's derision, Mark says that Jesus could not do any deed of power among them, yet he did heal a few sick people. *And* he was amazed at the people's unbelief. Mark seems to be linking unbelief with Jesus' wonderworking ability, or, in this case, lack thereof. Is that really what's going on? I think so, and it's extraordinary: to hitch up God's power with the posture of belief, with our readiness or unreadiness to be *transformed* by things we can't expect and never knew we should be looking for, to link that with what God does or is able to do—that's a surprising connection. Mark suggests that God's power has something to do with our willingness to see God's activity *as powerful*.

Now, let's be careful. We don't want to make it all about us. We don't want to say that everything hangs on perspective, as if one way of looking at the world is as good as any other. And that isn't what Mark is saying either. What he does say is that, while the crowds disbelieve and Jesus is unable to do anything powerful, he still does what he always does: in this case he teaches in the synagogue and heals the sick. But the crowds want something else.

I wonder—our text doesn't tell us—what the people Jesus healed thought. Did they think he was powerless, too? Or perhaps they, like the blind man in John's Gospel, said something like this: "I don't know whether he's a prophet or not; I don't even know if he's a sinner. What I do know is that though I once was blind, now I see. Though I once was sick, now I am well." We'll never know what they thought, because as far as the crowds are concerned, those people are the exception that proves the rule: Jesus can do no deeds of power here. There are a number of other explanations for why these people were healed, if you even want to call it healing. The point is that they don't count, just like last week the woman with the hemorrhage didn't count. The crowds can't see God's power in these people. So a few sick people get better when Jesus is around? Who cares? We want to see something impressive. Fireworks. Armies. Choreography. Something!

That fits, doesn't it? I bet that gets us all right in the gut. I don't have enough fingers to count the number of times in the last week I've wanted to see God's power powerfully displayed—all the times I've wanted God to give me something to go on. Even at my grandfather's funeral a few weeks ago, surrounded by hundreds of the holiest people I know, I experienced this all too human desire to find ways for God to come with power. We needed something powerful to validate this man's life to us—to assure us that God was active here. And the story of God's power took a predictable form of overcoming adversity. My grandpa was a missionary preacher, and he was a terrible stutterer. To the day he died he had problems spitting it out, at least in English. But, when he moved overseas to what was then southern Rhodesia and learned Ndbele, the language in which he would have to preach, he never stuttered once. He preached throughout Rhodesia with no translator. And we said: What a powerful testimony to this man's calling! That proves to us that God's power was in Lewis Sider.

The truth of the matter, and Mark's second surprise for us, is that God is not about to be kept out of our lives just because we want to see something impressive. No, Jesus heals even if you don't or can't or won't sit up and take notice. Instead, Mark's saying something like this: wanting to be impressed by Jesus is just another way of asking for security, the kind of security we always look for when we look up to powerful people. Yet Jesus won't give us that security; in Mark's story, Jesus says that wanting to be impressed by him is amazing unbelief.

Over in 2 Corinthians, Paul cranks this up a notch. After all, he's struggling with these issues of power as well. Paul's dealings with the Corinthians have from the get-go been ministries to people like us, people who desperately want to be impressed. At the very beginning of his first letter to them, the Corinthians are using their spiritual pedigrees to earn clout with others in the community: "I am of Cephas," "I am of Apollos," "I am of Paul." And Paul has to say, "No. Christ is undivided. I wasn't crucified for you, was I? You weren't baptized into my name" (1 Cor 1:12–13). Later on, the Corinthians have problems with money; they're letting the rich in their community have the loudest voice in their meetings. Then they have problems with spiritual gifts; they're undervaluing the less ostentatious, everyday gifts that keep churches running. Through all of this, the Corinthian Christians have a clear-cut picture of God's power: like any other power, God's power is social capital—it's the power to get things done. And Paul's task is to say over and over again: *No! The power of God is foolishness to the Greeks and a stumbling block to the Jews* (vv. 22–25).

By the time Paul writes his second letter to the Corinthians, they've evidently had just about enough of him telling them where they've gone wrong. So now he's faced with a new task: that of justifying his own power to the church. And it turns out to be a difficult juggling act, for here he's caught in a series of twisted, self-referential and agonizing contradictions: *I would not boast, yet I must boast. I don't want to boast, but you've made me do it. So I'll boast of the things that show my weakness* (see 2 Cor 11:16—12:10). Paul—trying to remind the Corinthians that God's power is always Christ's power, that God's might always looks like Jesus—confronts the fact of his own failure and folly, of his own inability to emulate his Lord. Paul has trouble being humble and meek and gentle. He knows that he can be a blowhard—bullying and manipulative. And so, he has to ask, one more time, and pointedly, *What is God's power like, and given what a roach I am, how can I convince you that it's manifest in me?*

The answer, in short, is that Paul *can't* convince the Corinthians that they ought to be impressed by him. *Paul* can't convince the Corinthians that they ought to be impressed by Jesus. Yet God's power is grace, gift, unexpectedness, and it's made perfect in weakness. Paul's own weakness, then, his own frailty, is paradoxically the only testament to God's glory and power that he *can* give. God's power doesn't defend itself or apologize for itself or build itself up. Paul's power, his weakness, does all those things. But God's power isn't bound up with being impressive. If it were, *our* vision of God would be all too clear. God could be whatever we think to be highest or strongest. God could be whatever is wisest or holiest *for us*, whatever we think most spiritually impressive. But here, Paul has nothing but the scandal of his own authority and experience, of his own crass need to be impressive, of his own botched attempts to witness to God in Christ. And yet God, he knows, will use that failure, that powerlessness, too. "Whenever I am weak, I am strong" (12:10). In a way, Paul's foolishness points us back to Jesus in Mark's Gospel: scorned by his kinsfolk, "powerless" before them, nevertheless doing what he always does—giving rest to the weary, blessing the dying, soothing the suffering, pitying the afflicted, shielding the joyous, healing the sick.

Preparing for Peace

Isaiah 2:1–5; Psalm 122; Romans 13:11–13; Matthew 24:36–44

Every year the Revised Common Lectionary appoints for the first Sunday of Advent texts having to do with preparation, awareness, and readiness. So we read in Isa 2:5 the prophet's plea, "O house of Jacob, come, let us walk in the light of the Lord," in Rom 13:11 we find Paul's proclamation, "now is the moment for you to wake from sleep," and in Matt 24:42 we have Jesus' own exhortation, "Keep awake . . . for you do not know on what day your Lord is coming." The theme, of course, has not to do with preparedness as such: it isn't telling Christians to be Boy Scouts. Rather, it has to do with cultivating in our lives the expectant and worshipful attentiveness appropriate to Christ's anticipated appearance among us. But even a cursory glance at the scriptures appointed for this year should make us wonder what all this talk about being prepared has to do with Advent. The passages for today that deal with Christ's appearance do not appear to deal with his first advent, but with his return, with his *parousia*.

Because Jesus lives, rules, and will judge as the particular person he is, the outcome of history will be different than we could otherwise expect; our thoughts are not the thoughts of Jesus, neither are our ways his ways. But Christianity is notorious for its vagueness about what exactly we can expect regarding the outcome of history given Christ's lordship. Put more directly, it's hard to know what the gospel promises. This makes our predicament doubly difficult. We have these Scriptures that tell us to be prepared, but they tell us to be prepared for the promise, which we're told we can't anticipate. Yet we notice another theme in these texts, especially in Psalm 122 and Isa 2:1–5—the theme of peace. "Pray for the peace of Jerusalem: 'May they prosper who love you.'" "Nation shall not lift up sword against nation, neither shall they learn war any more." And even in the texts from the New Testament the connection to peace is fairly transparent, although perhaps more so in Romans than in Matthew. So, Advent and *parousia*, peace and preparation—we're given this nexus of concerns to dwell in this morning.

Let's begin with Psalm 122: "A Song of Ascents. Of David." The first thing to notice about this Psalm—and it's the first thing to note about every Psalm even though we often forget it—is that it's a prayer. Israel uses it and includes it within the book of Psalms, what Dietrich Bonhoeffer described as "The Prayerbook of the Bible." Closer inspection shows that this Psalm is driven by a dynamic tension between, on the one hand, the Psalmist's presence in Jerusalem ("Our feet are standing within your gates," v. 2); and, on the other, the tone of the prayer, which conveys the sense that the peace Jerusalem represents is delayed. If the Psalmist must pray for Jerusalem's peace, then it is a peace that is not present, or at the very least is insecure. That sense of the fragility of Jerusalem's peace is strong—so strong, in fact, that it begins to erode our certainty of the Psalmist's self-location. Does he truly stand in Jerusalem's gates, or has going "to the house of the Lord" (v. 1)—being present in Jerusalem—become but a metaphorical expression of his deepest yearnings?

Scattered among the nations, with its best and brightest shipped off to Babylon, Israel begins to read the prayers of ascents in the Psalms as its eschatological calling. To be scattered, they begin to discover, is not a hiatus after which normalcy will resume. Rather, beginning with Israel's exile to Babylon, dispersion will be the positive calling of the Jewish community. Praying Psalm 122 in the context of dispersion makes both Israel's hope of a return to Jerusalem and the Psalmist's vision of standing within the gates of Jerusalem functional *as postponed*. The notion of going up to the house of the Lord has its meaning not as something Israel should bring about by its own strength, wait around to see happen, or plan for. Instead, it is functional as a metaphor for hopefulness in God renewing the life of faith anywhere. And that hopefulness requires the patience and faithful obedience of being willing not to be in charge, of being willing not to make sure history comes out right. This hope involves learning to live one's life as a prayer—the response to which is unanticipated, beyond anything we can ask or imagine. It is to live one's life as a prayer for the peace of Jerusalem.

The case is similar with Isa 2:1–5. The prophet Isaiah proclaimed his message to Judah and Jerusalem from 742 until 701 BCE, that critical period in which the Northern Kingdom was annexed to the Assyrian empire while Judah lived uneasily in its shadow as a tributary. During this period the prophet Isaiah undertakes a massive reorientation project, attempting to steer the gaze of Israel away from the period of monarchy, replete with its military and political disasters. Isaiah must put an end to Israel's paralyzing nostalgia for the security of its own political identity by pointing to a positive future for Judah and Jerusalem on the other side of judgment. For where there is no hope of newness, there is no hope for a living future. But that future is not one that either Judah or Jerusalem can bring about. Notice that the "house of the God of Jacob" follows the nations to the "mountain of the Lord's house" (v. 3). The vision of peace is sure only under the conditions of God's gracious activity. Only the Lord's work will give Israel the gift of its future. The hope that the peoples of many nations "shall beat their swords into plowshares, and their spears into pruning hooks" (v. 4), is one that Israel cannot secure on its own terms. It must learn to live in the uncertainty of accepting its fulfillment from beyond itself, and it must learn that life in that uncertainty is itself the material of obedience.

We have to come to the Gospel reading today with this sense uncertainty, the uncertainty that turns our life into a prayer for peace. Matthew 24:36–44 comes hard on the heels of Jesus' own apocalyptic oracle. Here, too, Jesus is talking about a future, the contours of which we cannot know. In this chapter of Matthew, sometimes referred to as "Matthew's Apocalypse," Jesus says that how the world will be made part of God's story—that is, how history is being worked out—is up to God. The task of Jesus' disciples is not to make history come out right, but to be alert and prepared, so that when history is worked out and the kingdom of God is established, they will find that they have become the kind of people who fit in.

Now, again, what does all this have to do with Advent? How do living our lives as a prayer for the peace of Jerusalem, reorienting our vision toward hope in an unanticipated newness, and being prepared so that when the kingdom comes we find out that we fit in turn us into good readers of the story of Jesus' birth? The answer, as I suggested earlier, lies in learning how to pay attention to the glimpses we catch in these Scriptures of Advent's connection to *parousia*.

The end of a story, scholars of literature tell us, always organizes the beginning and middle of the story. The end of a novel always imposes a kind of pattern on time and events within the rest of the novel. And herein lies the great art of storytellers: they always have to end a story in a way that gives it form and shape and yet does not neglect the haphazardness we know in "real life." Thus, on the one hand, stories have always preserved a tension between reflecting on accidental reality and, on the other, the form of a story, which demands harmony between past, present, and future.

In a sense, this tension between the harmony of a story organized by its ending and the contingency of reality is the same tension with which Paul is dealing in Romans. The passages we've been examining over the last weeks, and now again today, are central to Paul's reflections on the Christian state of life. For Paul, the Christian life supersedes the tension between storylike organization and haphazardness. Those aren't, however, Paul's terms. He configures the same tension in terms of the long conflict between law and lawlessness.

The beginning of Romans 13—"Let every person be subject to the governing authorities" (v. 1)—which we so often read as Paul's counsel that Christians should acquiesce to the demands of the state, is part of his comments on the tension between law and lawlessness. Often missed in Christian reflection on this passage is that Paul is discussing the possibility of a whole new world of relationships between Gentiles and Jews, which somehow is tied up in God's covenant with Israel. So, here's the question that fuels Paul's thoughts about the governing authorities: What does this new world in Christ mean for the lawless Gentiles and the people of God's Law, the Jews? Paul starts wrestling with this issue way back in 3:1, where he describes a community that has received promises and commitments from God on the one hand, and a sort of shapeless human conglomerate on the other—not really a "people" at all because they are not possessed by a firm corporate identity. There is Israel, which has a clear source of its sense of identity in the Law; and there is the non-community of Gentiles, who have no name of their own and no sense of a future that is distinctively theirs. But the problem that forms the subtext of Paul's argument is that the security of Israel has become ambiguous. Here is the ambiguity: the Law and the covenant are gifts to Israel, yet because they are expressed in terms of clear and identifiable demands like circumcision, it's possible to think that, as a recipient of this gift, you gain some kind of control over your identity and your part in God's story. If you are under the Law, you know who you are by doing what the Law requires of you—in performing a set of measurable duties that will define in unmistakable terms your identity and belonging. If you are not under the Law, then you are lawless, anonymous, and vulnerable to circumstance, incapable of placing yourself in God's story.

Paul, throughout Romans, claims that both these conditions—both Law and Lawlessness—are more than a matter of the ethnic or cultural prejudices that existed between Jews and Gentiles. Moreover, Christians are to put both conditions behind them because both conditions are locked in a demonic symbiosis of hostility. The life according to the Law (which can define itself through ordered practices), and Lawless life (which must locate itself outside of God's story)—*together* these forms of life create the pathology of the diseased and suffering world. They are the roots of violence and mutual rejection between people. And they are both challenged and transformed through the encounter with the new life begun in the advent of Jesus. Furthermore, the peace for which we hope and of which our lives are to be a prayer is a peace that stands against each of them alike.

Law and Law-lessness equally issue in an acceptance—tacit or admitted—of strife as humanly necessary. Both work with the assumption that the world is irreducibly a place of victory or defeat, in which it is unthinkable that very different people should be able to inhabit a common future. The two models of human practice have a hidden alliance; and to look at actual human societies is to see a fusion of these two impulses. The life of Law and the life of Lawlessness are both characterized by the refusal to sense that there might be a shared future, and they are both shaped by the myth that the story of the world is for humans to control. They therefore both exhibit a lack of resources to deal with the ways in which the future that has been promised in Christ is uncontrollable. They both display a profound impatience with time.

Violence is in large part a product of that impatience. We all know that violence and the sources of violence are too multiplicitous to reduce to any one cause. But it's nevertheless true to say that violence is at least the result of a lack of confidence in history as God's story, which is another way to say that we don't want to believe that we are not in control of how the story unfolds. Violence is enabled by the failure to understand our lives—that is, our future and the riskiness of that future's unexpectedness—as the gracious gift of being given ways to find out that when the kingdom comes we can be the kind of people who fit in. And because violence is always the failure to understand our lives as God's gracious gift, violence is also—like Law and Lawlessness—the attempt to create and maintain control over God's story. Our turn to violence betrays our secret distrust in God.

So, be lawful and subject to the governing authorities not because they're right or faithful, but because you aren't in control of God's story, and God uses them, too. Similarly, "live honorably as in the day, not in reveling and drunkenness, not in debauchery and licentiousness, not in quarreling and jealousy" (Rom 13:13), not because the Christian life is a life of law, but because those activities are ways of attempting to usurp control of God's story, the end of which is an unanticipatable promise.

This is why it is useful to think of the Christian life as a life of nonresistance, which, I'm sure, will make many of us uneasy. This word—nonresistance—caused quite a stir in the twentieth century, when during and after World War II, theologians and Christian ethicists began to use it to describe the ideal Christian life. Jesus, they argued with some justification from Scripture, was nonresistant in his life and death, and he called his followers to live their lives nonresistantly as well. This view was quickly disparaged, not least vocally by some Mennonite theologians. The arguments against nonresistance were various, and to review them all would take a yearlong course, not a sermon. But many of the arguments had a common refrain: Jesus and his immediate followers practiced nonresistance because they expected the kingdom to come soon. Their ethic, therefore, did not have to account for the maintenance of the social order. But Jesus and his early followers were wrong in their kingdom expectation, and two thousand years of history proves it. If Christians now continue to practice nonresistance, then they are irresponsibly abandoning the social order to non-Christians. Such irresponsibility is itself sinful, and therefore Christians cannot afford to be nonresistant.

That's the refrain. Now, apart from the fact that this argument assumes that Jesus' expectation of the kingdom was wrong, we need also to note that this argument against nonresistance reveals the same impatience with time that I have been suggesting our assigned lectionary scriptures school us out of. This argument against nonresistance—and let us be clear, it is an argument shared by many who allow the use of violent force in exceptional cases and many who practice nonviolent forms of resistance—is an argument for being in control of God's future. And if what we've seen in these texts today is even close to being true, then it is easy to see that the argument against nonresistance is neither quite biblical nor quite realistic, because Christian nonresistance does not abandon the social order to non-Christians, much less to evil and demonic powers, but rather to God's own ordering of God's own story.

At this point, the objection may be that the kind of nonresistance for which I am arguing turns Christians into passive pushovers. We've all heard this before: Jesus wasn't passive in his ministry, instead he stood up to the religious and political authorities of first-century Palestine and they killed him for it. All of that is true, but it is no argument against Christian nonresistance. Let us be clear: Christian theology from Paul on maintains that Jesus did not resist the powers that be. Instead, the powers resisted him. Nonresistance doesn't make you passive. It relieves you of the pretension to be in control. Not being in control is a scary thing, but the Psalmist, Isaiah, Paul, and Jesus all remind us that we were never in control anyway. The task for Christians isn't to make sure history comes out right. Rather, we are to prepare for the unanticipatedness of God's advent among us. Our task is, in a word, to live our lives as a prayer for the newness of God's peace.

Remembering Home

Genesis 41:41–57, and article 23 of the
Confession of Faith in a Mennonite Perspective

In a lot of ways the story of Joseph is a rags-to-riches tale. He's in a dungeon, but not for long. Soon he's discovered; Pharaoh hears about his gifts and takes Joseph to the very top of Egyptian power—from a filthy prison to the top of the world. The story reminds me of a friend in Los Angeles who works in restaurants while waiting for a casting director to discover his talents as an actor. There's a certain part of us that loves it when some no-name finally gets their break. And that no-name is Joseph.

Despite things going from bad to worse, the storyteller reassures us that Joseph will do just fine. We are told that "the Lord was with Joseph." We hear that sentence four times in Genesis 39 (vv. 2, 3, 22, 23). *The Lord was with Joseph*: there's still hope, his break will come, God won't abandon him in the pit of Egypt—that godforsaken land.

It finally happens. Pharaoh calls Joseph from the dungeon to interpret his dreams when no one else can. Joseph not only makes sense of the dreams, but also offers a plan for Egypt to prepare for the great famine. He says to Pharaoh, "They should collect the food of the good years and store up the grain under the authority of Pharaoh, to be kept in the cities" (41:35). Pharaoh likes his plan so much that he names Joseph as the man for the job. In a matter of minutes Joseph emerges from a dungeon, puts on royal clothing, and rides in Pharaoh's chariot with everyone bowing down before him. In Egypt, he is second only to Pharaoh. And he ends up saving countless people from starvation.

Is Joseph our model for how we relate to government and society? That's what we're focusing on today in our worship service. We're thinking through article 23 in our Mennonite Confession of Faith: "The Church's Relation to Government and Society." Should Joseph be our model? Like many of us, he resides in a country through no fault of his own. We didn't have a choice in being born into our nationalities. Citizenship just happened to us. So, since we're here, at the heart of the most powerful empire in the world, why don't we make the best of it and save some lives? That's what Joseph did, right?

Let me take a moment to anticipate a common misunderstanding about our involvement in society and government. Lots of people, when they think about society and government, focus our attention on presidents, senators, representatives and federal, state, and municipal governments. That's where government happens, they say. So, the question about our Christian relationship to government and society has to do with whether or not someone should get a job on Capital Hill or in Raleigh. But that way of thinking ignores all the ways that we are involved in everyday politics. There's no escape from being political. Aristotle called human beings "political animals." We are shot through with politics. We pledge allegiance when we swipe our credit cards or make a deposit in a bank account; we practice political responsibility when we save or spend our money. That economic stimulus check I received yesterday recognizes the political power of everyday spending. But our relationship to government and society is not only economic; it's also about the way we inhabit this land, land secured and sustained by powerful military forces and savvy leaders. The point is that all of us are involved in networks of political power everyday, for better or for worse. Even the Canadians in our congregation are involved in U.S. politics, even though they can't vote. Whether they like it or not, the Amish are also part of this system, although in different ways.

So, what do we do, or not do? The article in our Confession points us in helpful directions. "The church is the spiritual, social, and political body that gives its allegiance to God alone" (*Confession*, 85). And those of us who comprise this church are "citizens of God's kingdom," which is a statement that pulls the rug out from other claims of citizenship and belonging (ibid.). "Because we confess that Jesus Christ has been exalted as Lord of lords," it says, "we recognize no other authority's claims as ultimate" (86)—which means we can disobey the law if we have good reasons. The article also makes clear that despite the propaganda and wishful thinking, "at its best, a government cannot act completely according to the justice of God" (85). All governments trade in injustice. But that's no reason to think we can wash our hands of the matter: "We may participate in government or other institutions of society," just so long as we do so without compromising our Christian way of life, our fidelity to God and God's people (ibid). And that's what is so troubling about the story of Joseph: does Joseph sacrifice fidelity to God so he can accomplish good things in Egypt?

There's a lot in the story to make us wonder. Joseph takes on a new name, given by Pharaoh—so far in Genesis it's the Lord who changes names (Abram/Abraham, Sarai/Sarah, Jacob/Israel). Is Joseph acknowledging Pharaoh's power as a god, the one who changes names? Joseph takes as his wife a daughter of an Egyptian priest, whose name remembers the Egyptian goddess Neith—*Asenath*. The issue of forgetting God and God's people is summed up when Joseph names his children: Manasseh and Ephraim (Gen 41:51–52). Joseph names his second born, Ephraim, which he tells us means, "God has made me fruitful." Which God is Joseph remembering? He uses the generic name for 'God'—*elohim*. Is this the God of Israel, the God of his ancestors, the God of Abraham, Isaac and Jacob? Or, does this name remember the Egyptian gods of fertility, the ones who have made Joseph fruitful in this foreign land, the Egyptian god of his fruitful Egyptian wife? It's hard to know. It may be clearer when he names his firstborn son, Manasseh: "Because," Joseph says, "God has made me forget all my trouble and all my father's household." Joseph wants to forget. But the God of Israel, Isaac, and Jacob is not a god of forgetfulness. Is Joseph trying to forget the God of his ancestors so he can become Egyptian?

There's enough in the story for us to acknowledge that God's providential care for the children of Abraham involves the work of Joseph in Egypt. That's undeniable. In Egypt, God uses Joseph to provide for his people, perhaps even to save his people. But it's also important to notice how Joseph is the brainchild behind the emerging Egyptian empire. Joseph takes all the grain from the country, from the rural farmers, and stores them close to Pharaoh, in the cities. He consolidates Pharaoh's power. Later, in chapter 47, we hear that Joseph lets the people of Canaan and Egypt sell themselves into slavery for food. Joseph, sold into Egyptian slavery, ends up buying more slaves for Egypt! (47:18-25). Joseph single-handedly turns Egypt into the regional power that will enslave Israel. Ultimately, Joseph invites Jacob and his family into the very heart of the beast; Israel settles in Goshen, and they soon become Egyptian slaves. For a time, God may have used Egypt to keep Israel alive. But that doesn't make Egypt a chosen nation. In a few years, Egypt turns into the enemy of God, and God punishes Egypt with plagues.

We are Christians who live in dubious times and in an ambiguous land. There are Josephs in our recent past who brought us to North America—perhaps for religious freedom, or because of the good farm land, or to escape death at the hands of violent governments. But the story of Joseph also makes me wonder if I'm now working for the powers that will enslave the world. This is not to say that we shouldn't appreciate what we have and how God has sustained us. It's a wonderful thing to go where I need to go without waiting at military checkpoints. I am grateful that I can meet with you in public places and pray and study our Bibles. It's an incredible blessing that we don't go hungry; in our community even the homeless can find food. But we must also remember that Israel enjoyed much prosperity in the beautiful land of Goshen. It was only a matter of time before slavery. And even before Egypt formally made the residents of Goshen slaves, Joseph was already at work amassing slaves for Egypt.

Are we a bunch of Josephs? Are we in Goshen, enjoying the comforts of Egypt, tending to Pharaoh's cattle, while slaves are amassed? It's hard to know for sure. It's hard to predict the future, or even see what's happening in front of our eyes. But maybe that's the problem—*prediction*. Joseph wants to predict the future and make sure his team comes out on top. He does what he thinks is best and ends up enslaving his people in the process. Perhaps the problem is that Joseph forgets—or at least he tries to forget—so he can get on with his magnificent future in Egypt. He forgets his home and he forgets his God so he can move on.

So, what should we remember? On this Fourth of July weekend, we remember that this place is Goshen at best. We remember that our people, the people of God, extend beyond the borders of this country. When there's famine in distant places, we remember what Joseph forgets: that there are people over there who are part of our family. When our Egypt declares war, we remember that our family members live among those foreign countries. When our candidates talk about universal healthcare, we remember that they are merely provincial thinkers who don't really use the word "universal" like we do when we say that we believe in the church universal—that is, the catholicity of the church, which means our body of faith reaches across the globe, transgressing national boundaries. Finally, we remember that our God remembers us even while we are away from home, dwelling in Goshen, sojourning in Egypt. God remembers us. God goes into Egypt with Israel, and God will set Israel free. Even though we may not feel like slaves now, the time may soon come when this empire will also enslave us. When it does, we must remember that God sent Moses, and we must remember that God sent Jesus, who never leaves us nor forsakes us.

Money

Caesar's Coin

Exodus 20:1–6; Hebrews 1:1–5, 10–14; Mark 12:13–17

How many of you have ever visited a psychologist, counselor, or therapist? If you have, you might have noticed the following: therapists like to ask questions. "How would you describe your relationship with your mother?" "Do you do anything that you consider to be a bad habit?" "How do you relax in your spare time?" "Just how long have you been afraid of purple corduroy?" The quiz seems endless. Not only do they ask a lot of questions, but therapists are also able to answer any question you ask with another question. "I thought I saw you in Barnes & Noble the other night. Was it you?" "Why is it important to you to know whether I was in Barnes & Noble?" I don't know about you, but I find this trait a bit frustrating. I asked you a question, please just give me a straight answer.

After reading our text from the Gospel of Mark for this morning, I have to say that I feel some of the same frustration with Jesus. "Is it lawful to pay taxes . . . or not? Should we pay them or should we not?" (Mark 12:14–15). A yes or no answer, including a bit of explanation, would do the trick, wouldn't it? "Yes, pay your taxes because . . ." or "No, don't pay taxes, and here's why . . ." But here, as we see elsewhere in Mark's Gospel, Jesus gives very little straightforward advice. Instead, Mark's Jesus seems to prefer elusive riddles about his identity, his authority, and his purpose; he seems to prefer the Socratic method to setting clear guidelines for his disciples' conduct. In this passage, Jesus acts like a psychiatrist: ask him a question and he answers you with another question.

Of course, therapists have excellent reasons for redirecting their patients' questions with other questions. My frustration with the tactic notwithstanding, I have to admit that when someone answers a question I've asked with another question, I often learn something about myself; my motives, anxieties, desires, and so on, come into clearer focus. The fact that I find people who answer questions with questions frustrating tells me something about myself, and so I'm led to wonder if my frustration with Jesus this morning shouldn't be similarly instructive.

I'm struck, for instance, by how much I'd like Jesus to answer the question the Pharisees and Herodians ask him in the terms that they ask it: black and white. "Taxes: should we pay them or shouldn't we?" Yes or no—clear-cut binaries with no wiggle room in between. I, too, crave the clarity that they ask for. It reminds me of being a child and having to ask permission to do things like have a snack or go outside and play. My mom always had a clear answer for me with a reason attached. As an adult who doesn't have to ask permission for things anymore, I find that I quickly tire of deciding, deliberating, making judgments, and having to accept responsibility for my own actions. Black pants or brown, shoes or sandals, cold cereal or oatmeal? I'm easily consumed by those choices, trivial though they may be. It is not surprising that I want a black and white answer to the question of taxes because when I get right down to it, what I realize about myself is that I'd like Jesus (or maybe Scripture) to be my authority figure and to do my deciding for me. Unfortunately, this isn't the way it works. I'm always frustrated. I can't get what I want. And if we can't get what we want from this passage, we should spend some time wondering what exactly we are looking for. What do we expect from this piece of Scripture?

I'm not sure whether it was an accident that you asked me to preach from this text the day before Independence Day or not, but it is interesting that Mark 12:13–17 is a regularly prescribed lectionary reading for national holidays. Memorial Day, the Fourth of July, Labor Day, these are days on which the task of balancing one's discipleship to Jesus with the demands of citizenship loom especially large, and churches with a pacifist heritage feel this burden more acutely than most. At the very least, we all recognize how difficult a balancing act it can be—being good citizens and good disciples. We think that it's altogether appropriate to look to Scripture for guidance on how to live in such a confusing situation. However, we have probably also noticed that passages like ours for this morning can be extraordinarily divisive—so divisive that they threaten our unity as the body of Christ. Some of us are war-tax resisters, meaning that we refuse to pay the portion of our income taxes that is earmarked for military support, while others of us think that the state is rightfully due the loyalty and support of its citizens in all that belongs to it. I am sure there are middle-ground positions. However, I'd bet that most of us honestly believe that our position on this issue is the right one. Given the opportunity, most of us would welcome the chance to convince others of our stance.

I'm not about to stand up here and tell you that paying taxes is an unimportant issue, but I would like to sound two notes of caution. First, because this is such a divisive issue, it demands conversation, not only so that we can reach some kind of consensus as a community, but also (and, more importantly) to ensure that reconciliation can take place between people whose practice offends each other. Second, because entering into potentially divisive and painful conversation with the intent to reconcile demands openness to each other, all who enter the dialogue must expect to have his or her point of view changed. That's very easy to say, but it's a much harder thing to do. The biggest risk in assessing a passage like this one isn't that we'll get the answer wrong, but rather that whatever answer we come up with will divide the church.

Regardless of how or why we come to Jesus and this question about taxes, it's unlikely that we'll approach him in the same way that the Pharisees and Herodians did. We're told that they asked the question because they wanted to trap Jesus in what he said: the question is itself a trap that sets the tone for the entire conversation that ensues. Not only does this trap color everything that comes after it, the very fact that it is a trap also ought to clue us into what we should (and shouldn't) expect in Jesus' response to his opponents. If we look to this passage for good advice on whether or not to pay our taxes, then no matter what answer we come up with, we will probably be out of sync with the logic of the story.

Here's an analogy to help illustrate what I'm talking about. We all know the story of Goldilocks and the Three Bears. Goldilocks happens upon the three bears' house in the woods, and although she doesn't know who lives there she enters, sits in their chairs, eats their porridge, and then goes upstairs to bed. "This bed's too hard; this one's too soft; oh, this one's just right." Any sensible person could imagine all kinds of questions they'd like to ask Goldilocks at this point. "Goldilocks, do you think it's okay to wander into a stranger's house and help yourself to their possessions?" "Goldilocks, I know you like your porridge medium-warm, but otherwise, which is better, hot porridge or cold porridge?" "Goldilocks, didn't you see the bear fur on the bed pillow when you laid down for your nap?" All of these are reasonable questions, given what we know about Goldilocks and her situation, but they're abstract in the following way: they don't make much sense if we're paying attention to the story. They show that we're out of step with the plot and don't understand what's going on. These questions show that we're interested in things other than what the bears are going to do when they get home and find this silly little girl sleeping in Junior's bed.

Something like this happens when we ask Mark's Gospel for advice on paying taxes. I propose that rather than coming to the text with an abstract question in mind, we spend the rest of our time paying attention to the way the story unfolds. The story itself doesn't give much indication that there is a right answer to the question. In fact, if there were a clear answer, then the issue of paying taxes to Caesar wouldn't be a good way for the Pharisees and Herodians to trap Jesus in his words.

The episode opens when the Sanhedrin—who have been hounding Jesus since the end of chapter two in Mark—realize that he's gained a lot of popular support that prevents them from arresting or attacking him openly. They search for a new tactic and find it in an unlikely alliance with the Pharisees and Herodians (the religious moralists of the day coupled with those who have royalist and, hence, imperial sympathies). They send these two groups to pepper Jesus with questions so that they can catch him in his teaching. The trap will be sprung when they ask about taxes because it will put Jesus in a proverbial "catch-22." If, on the one hand, he answers that they should refuse to pay the tax, he will be guilty of sedition against the state, and the Roman procurator will have a real claim against him. If, on the other hand, he says that they should pay the tax, then he's likely to upset the crowds who form his popular support and upon whose shoulders fall squarely the main burden of Roman taxation. Clearly, the point of the trap is that however Jesus answers the question, he will be unable to say the right thing.

Before the Pharisees and Herodians spring the trap, they must first lay the bait, which they do in verse 14 by way of flattery: "Teacher," they say, "we know that you are sincere [or "forthright"—the Greek word is usually translated "truthful"], and show deference to no one; for you do not regard people with partiality, but teach the way of God in accordance with truth." They make two appeals to his truthfulness or fairness and remind him that he isn't usually swayed by public opinion. They dare Jesus to commit himself to an answer, and they seem to know their target: given who Jesus is, it's unlikely that he'll stoop to equivocation or compromise.

Consequently, when Jesus responds, he does so, Mark says, "knowing their hypocrisy" (v. 15). On the face of things, hypocrisy seems like a strange word for Mark to use. What, after all, is a hypocrite but someone who expresses as her own a feeling or belief that she doesn't, in fact, hold? Mark doesn't call the Pharisees and Herodians hypocrites just because they've asked Jesus a question that was designed to function as a trap. He doesn't call them hypocrites simply because they're acting from insincere motives. No, he calls them hypocrites because they've baited Jesus into committing himself on a politically volatile issue when they won't commit themselves! They've given Jesus enough rope with which to hang himself, and now they're ready to stand back and watch the fun.

The tables start to turn on them, however, when Jesus tells them, "Bring me a denarius and let me see it" (v. 15). Apparently, Jesus doesn't have a coin. Indeed, if you take his follow-up questions seriously—"Whose head is this, and whose inscription?"—Jesus isn't even very familiar with the coin. Mark might simply be telling us that Jesus was one of the working poor who constituted the majority of his following. In other words, he's poor enough that he can't pull the right currency out of his pocket. Be that as it may, the story doesn't focus on Jesus' standard of living. Instead, it focuses on the coin itself and two things in particular: the image on it and the title it bears. First, let's deal with the image. A denarius, the common currency of Rome, bore on its face the bust of the current emperor. Such an image or icon should have settled the matter for observant Jews since many of them refused to use Roman currency on the grounds that the coins violated the first and second commandments: "I am the Lord your God, who brought you out of the land of Egypt, out of the house of slavery; you shall have no other gods before me. You shall not make for yourself an image, whether in the form of anything that is in heaven above, or on the earth beneath, or in the water under the earth" (Exod 20:2–4). That Jesus asks about the image on the coin shows that the basic issue at stake for Mark, in the question about paying taxes to Caesar, is idolatry. The fact that the Pharisees and

Herodians can produce a denarius with an image—or, more to the point, an *idol*—of the emperor on it shows that they've already ceased to be observant Jews and, moreover, that this question about the "lawfulness" of paying taxes is a smokescreen for something else: namely, a way to trick Jesus into getting himself arrested.

Second, the inscription. As Mark's audience would have been well aware, any denarius was minted with a title on its back that read something like "Caesar Tiberius: August and Divine Son." Obviously, that presents a problem, like when we look at the back of a dollar bill and wonder which "God" it is in whom we are supposedly to trust. Mark, however, had something else in mind, which he highlighted by using the word "title" or "inscription." That word only occurs one other time in his Gospel, in Mark 15:26, when Jesus was crucified: "the inscription of the charge against him read, 'The king of the Jews.'" On the one hand, Mark presents us with the emperor's inscription, but on the other hand, our imaginations are likely to be drawn to that other inscription posted above Jesus' head as he hung on the cross. It sounds to me as if we're being asked to sort out our loyalties *once and for all*, as if this question about paying taxes to Caesar is really just an extended way of reminding us that we cannot serve two masters.

If the basic issue at stake in the text is idolatry, if Jesus was in fact speaking to Jews who knew the Law—who knew they were to have no familiarity with fabricated images, who knew as well that any rival claimant to God's kingdom was not to be tolerated let alone trusted—then there is really no question about whether or not Jesus was telling his opponents to pay Caesar's tax. This is not a text about how to *manage* your loyalties in a complex world, and no Jew in the first century who was aware of the Law and of the Lord's command from Moses to the people, "Hear, O Israel, the Lord your God, the Lord alone" could have thought it was. In the context of the story, "Give to Caesar what is Caesar's, and give to God what is God's," could only be heard as a reminder that everything lives and moves and has its being in God, and that everything already "belongs" to God in a far more radical way than it could ever belong to Caesar. In the terms of the parable that immediately precedes our passage this morning, all rulers and all authorities are merely tenants in God's vineyard. These are things of which any observant Jew of the period would have been aware.

Of course, Mark's first readers weren't Jews, and we aren't Jews either: we're Gentile Christians. When we talk about idolatry, we begin by remembering what the writer of the letter to the Hebrews says about the Son: that he is "the reflection of God's glory and the exact imprint of God's very being, sustaining all things by his powerful word" (Heb 1:3). Our claim is that the imageless God of Israel has been perfectly "imaged" in the person of Jesus, and that this image is of a humanity reborn in and as God's creative newness, a humanity no longer captured by the need to *sort out* divided loyalties, an expansive community that witnesses to a humanity without borders other than Christ. This is not, let me hasten to add, a community of new creation in which all our relationships and affiliations are cancelled out. The church is not an escape hatch from the history of our families, our friendships, *or* our political systems. Rather, the church is a place where we are asked to stop and take stock of whether, and if so how, all of our existing patterns of belonging can collaborate with the patterns of the new creation. It is a company where we are given the opportunity to ask how, if at all, the goals and priorities of our lives can be brought together with the constructive work of God's Kingdom. For us, for you and for me, those are questions that cannot be posed in the abstract. These questions can only be asked and addressed in conversation with those in our congregations and with our neighbors who may or may not claim our allegiance to Christ.

I think that the question about taxes, much like the more general question about how we navigate in the life of this nation, fits into that category of question that cannot be answered in the abstract. It is rather a question that has to be answered in terms of the type of humanity it fosters. What degree of flourishing does it enable? What level of mutual care? What capacity for vision that is more than local? Those are contexts that you and I are well positioned to address, but we must be aware that they won't address themselves. They will take conversation, dialogue, patience, and abiding in a spirit of openness and especially in the spirit of God's good news, in a spirit of expectation that *we* may be questioned, surprised, and enriched by a message that grips each of us again and again as both good and as new.

Dirty Money

Luke 16:1–13

We knew that Michael wasn't like the rest of us at our church in Tucson, Arizona. He had lots of money and we didn't, but he wasn't obvious or audacious about it. He dressed like the rest of us and had a house in the same part of town as most people at church.

I started to get a sense for the money he had when my dad and I went with a bunch of other men to the Promise Keepers convention in San Diego, California. Mike rented the van we drove in from Tucson to San Diego and paid for all of the gas. He covered the cost of our hotel rooms, our registration, our dinners, and he even rented a boat one afternoon so we could cruise around the harbor.

One Saturday afternoon some time later my dad got back from lunch with Mike and told me that Mike was in trouble. Something bad was going to happen soon. My dad didn't exactly know what it was, but Mike told him that he was involved in activities that he now regretted and couldn't get out of. He said that things might get bad really quickly. Sure enough, the following week, Mike showed up on the front page of our local newspaper. Apparently, he was part of an extensive drug ring, and was responsible for making sure that drugs got through Nogales, on the Mexico-Arizona border and got to the regional suppliers. Now he would spend much of the rest of his life in prison.

Our small church was part of how he was working through the guilt and regret he felt about the way of life he had chosen. Now, as a middle-aged man, he realized that he was in so deep that he couldn't get out without getting killed or putting his family at risk. Our small church in Tucson benefited from his dirty money.

Luke tells us a story about dirty money. The manager has a terrible job. He's the representative of the richest guy in town to the money-hungry merchants and traders. The manager must combine the slippery skills of a politician with the money-smarts of an investor who trades in commodity futures. If he pours too much of his master's money in olive oil, and it's a bad year, then he'll be out of a job. Back then there wasn't anything like picking yourself up by the bootstraps. If you messed up, you were done and spent the rest of your life among the expendable class—the beggars and day laborers. There wasn't another firm or investment group to work for in town. In the story, the manager finds himself in deep trouble when the town's traders send nasty rumors to the manager's boss. They either want the manager canned or, perhaps, the merchants just want to show their strong arm to the manager in order to let him know who's really in charge.

I think we misunderstand this story if we think of the manager as a dishonest thief who steals from his boss. That's not what this story is about. This story is about a guy who is stuck right smack in the middle of an unjust, dog-eat-dog system. The translators lead us astray when they call the manager "dishonest" (Luke 16:8), which is not the case at all. The word in Greek is *adikia*, and it means unjust or unrighteous. He is not an unjust or unrighteous manager; instead, he is the "manager of unrighteousness." But, what does it mean to be a manager of unrighteousness? It means that he's caught in the middle of an unjust economic world, a world that operates in unrighteousness, a system that charges interest and creates debtors in violation of Torah, of God's law. What is a faithful Jewish manager supposed to do in this kind of system? How is he supposed to handle all the unrighteousness?

This is our question as well. We go about our business in a sinful economic system. That's right, I said "sinful." It's too easy, and perhaps a bit delusional, for us to preach against war and stand up against violence and somehow think that we are innocent in a world at war, and can wash our hands of the spilled blood in Iraq and elsewhere. Here's our problem: the currency we use means nothing without U.S. military power. Our economic system needs wars, it needs violence, it needs oil, it needs to maintain our borders, it needs to maintain our expanding global markets. Without this land and without the armed forces that protect it, our cash means next to nothing. Our money, the way it circulates, the way it means anything in the global market, would come to nothing if we didn't have sophisticated weapons and well-trained soldiers. Our dollars wouldn't have any value if those seventeenth-century European entrepreneurs hadn't set up shop here in the so-called "New World," and later annexed some large chunks of land through genocide to be maintained with bloodshed. The economy is sinful: it feeds on a history of bloodshed. The harsh truth is that we participate in those violences. We benefit from those violences when we earn money and spend it and invest it and use it. Our hands our dirty—they become filthy from our money. We should be honest about this. We don't live at peace with the world, and we can't because people shed blood to protect our livelihood, our money. As one New Testament scholar put it, "All money gets dirty at some stage in its history" (Manson, 269).

I told you about Mike, about how he got himself stuck in the middle of a drug ring and went to prison because he couldn't escape from it. His money was dirty, which is pretty easy for us to see. He managed drug money. I went to Promise Keepers on drug money! Of course our money isn't as obviously and directly dirty as my friend Mike's. We don't sell or traffic drugs—or if you do, I haven't heard about it . . . yet! But just because we didn't choose the economic system in which we participate, just because we didn't make Mike's bad decisions, doesn't mean we are innocent of its unrighteousness. We are participants in injustice by birth, by happenstance, by chance, by the roll of the dice.

So now what do we do? There's no way to escape the system, and so we have to go straight through the thick of it. Wise as serpents, innocent as doves. We learn how to handle our dirty money from our friend the shrewd manager in Luke's story. He is the manager of unrighteousness, someone in our position who the Lord recommends to us. And what does he do? What does he do as the manager of injustice? He forgives debts, or at least reduces them substantially. In forgiving debts, he helps us to imagine the possibility of that prayer we prayed with Jen Graber earlier in our service: the Lord's Prayer, in which we are called *to forgive debts*. The wise manager helps us begin to imagine what it means for Leviticus 25 to come true: the year of jubilee, the Sabbath year, the year of our Lord—when debts are forgiven, slaves are set free, and property is scattered among the people. The faithful manager helps us to imagine what it means for the pentecostal church of Acts to treat possessions as if they belonged to everyone: "All who believed were together and had all things in common; they would sell their possessions and goods and distribute the proceeds to all, as any had need" (Acts 2:44–45). This is the vision that captured the imagination of the early Anabaptists, our ancestors of the faith: *Omnia sunt communia* was their rallying cry, "All things in common."

Now, if you're like me, then all of this sounds a bit too crazy for our modern sensibilities about money. Yet, even if we don't want to be like the church in Acts, it is important to notice the ways in which we do share and how that sharing is the embodiment of what it means to live faithfully with our dirty money, while hoping that God redeems it, sanctifies it, and makes it holy through our sharing. As Jesus says in our passage, "I tell you, make friends for yourself by means of unrighteous *mammon*"—that is, your unjust wealth, your dirty money (Luke 16:9). We become good managers of unrighteous mammon when we use it to sustain our friendships. That's why it makes sense for you wonderful people who came from Pennsylvania, Virginia, Chicago, and Ohio to spend your dirty money on traveling for our church reunion so that we can share meals, enjoy fellowship, and worship together. This gathering is about using our dirty money to sustain friendships and to be present with one another because this reunion is all about the friendships that make up the body of Christ. Our worship is about the friendships that redeem our lives, the friendships that set us free from the bondage of money and free from mammon. And that's why most of us get together every other week and share a fellowship meal. Sure, we do it because it's fun, but it's also the way we share things in common, even if only for an evening. The time, effort, money we use to make food for one another is nothing other than the redemption of our dirty money, the sanctification of our unrighteous wealth. It's how we make and sustain friendships. It's how we weave our lives together. Our gathering creates the space to share our ordinary and messy lives. Sharing what we have is how we come to depend on one another, and in that dependence, as we are wrapped up with each other, we come to see our lives bound together in the Holy Spirit and woven together in the body of Christ. We are welcomed into the eternal home Jesus mentions in our passage as we share what we have and provide time and space for our lives to flow into the person seated next to us, and behind us, and in front, and the ones we will sit with when we eat in a few minutes.

This is where we come to find those friendships that beckon us into eternity, friendships that lead us along the narrow path, friendships that last forever. Sitting at these tables, and eating and talking, is the appetizer before the eternal banquet, the wedding feast, where we will abide forever in the loving embrace of our God.

With all of this talk about feasts and food, you are probably wondering when I'm going to stop talking so we can get to the real business of the kingdom—sharing and eating. But before I stop, I must leave us with a line that sums up what I'm trying to say. Many of the regulars at Chapel Hill Mennonite will find this quote all too familiar, but I thought I could say it again because I haven't said it in a while, and because there are people here who haven't heard it before. It comes from a Dominican priest, Herbert McCabe. He says, "Christ is present to us insofar as we are present to each other" (McCabe, xi). That's a concise summary of the gospel. McCabe names the presence of Christ that happens in our worship. Yes, we gather to celebrate Christ's presence, but, for McCabe, Christ's presence is also a calling: we are called to be truly present to each other because that's how we get caught up in the flow of God's love poured out for the world. So, our money, even if it's part of this passing system of injustice, makes sense as long as we remember that it's supposed to be used for being present—for sustaining our friendships and inviting others to join us in the friendships that make up the kingdom of God. Use it to make friends for the kingdom.

When you enjoy Communion together, remember that the way you make yourself available for friendship this afternoon is the very presence of Christ. And what Christ weaves together, what God joins together, nothing can separate because it is the permeating embrace of God's love that holds us through our friendships, for eternity.

Irresponsible Stewards

1 Corinthians 15:1–11; Luke 5:1–11

❝ [Jesus] got into one of the boats, the one belonging to Simon, and asked him to put out a little from shore. Then he sat down and taught the people from the boat" (Luke 5:3). After Jesus finished we can almost see a smile flash across his face as he sat in Simon's boat. It's the sort of smile that you get at Christmastime when you know you've bought the perfect gift for someone. You know they are going to love it. They pick it up from under the tree and you can't help but smile. That's what I see on Jesus' face as I read this story. Jesus wanted to bless this fisherman beyond his wildest dreams, if only he would listen and obey. However, obeying Jesus probably wasn't an easy thing for Simon to do at this point in his day. He was exhausted after a long day's work. The text says that Simon and the others were already finished with their strenuous work and were cleaning their nets. They were ready to call it quits for the day and head home for some rest so they could do it all over again tomorrow in hopes that they would have more success. It was a bad day at work. But Jesus comes up with a whimsical idea: miraculous fish, a multitude of fish. He tells Simon to go out further into the deep waters and try for another catch. Simon had already done this traveling preacher-man a favor. He had taken him out into the sea in his boat so Jesus could preach to the crowds. And after all of that, after his generosity, this guy wants to go on a fishing trip! "Simon answered, 'Master, we've worked hard all night and haven't caught anything. But because you say so, I will let down the nets'" (v. 5). You can hear the fatigue in Simon's voice. Yet, despite himself, he calls Jesus his *master* and goes where Jesus desires.

Simon is not among the seekers. He isn't among the interested crowds who gather around Jesus in order to listen from a distance to the word of God. Simon doesn't stand with them. Instead, he's around the corner minding his own business. He's a laborer, doing what he always does: cleaning his nets after a tough day at work. Simon doesn't seek Jesus; it's Jesus who seeks Simon. And that's what we call *grace*. Grace means that God acts first. It means that God offers us something we weren't even looking for. Grace is the way Jesus comes after us and offers us a chance to participate in the wonderful work of the kingdom, something we couldn't ever dream up on our own, something beyond our imaginations. And when God's grace has moved in our lives, all we can offer are our willing hands—hands that are ready to do his work and receive his miraculous gifts. Grace is the way Jesus comes up to Simon even though there were probably others who wanted intimacy with Jesus more than he did. Grace is how God comes into our lives when there are probably others who deserve it more than we do.

When grace moves, we can't help but go with Simon as he follows wherever the call may lead. Jesus sees us in the distance, comes to us, and draws us into the kingdom of God . . . *if* we are willing to call Jesus "master," like Simon does. That's the question Jesus asks us: Will we call him our master? And a follow-up question: What does it mean to call Jesus our master? Would our lives look any different?

The best way to get at these questions is to see how Simon's life changes. All of a sudden he's got tons of fish, more fish than he knows what to do with. Simon let down the nets as Jesus commanded, and now I'll pick up the story in verse 6: "When they had done so, they caught such a large number of fish that their nets began to break. So they signaled their partners in the other boat to come and help them, and they came and filled both boats so full that they began to sink." What an image of Jesus' extravagant grace, right? This is extreme grace. Jesus gives an over-abundance of fish, more than enough, too much even. The boats start to sink from the weight of the fish. Simon calls Jesus his master, and look what happens to him: he gets more than he could ever imagine!

I wish I could leave us with that message—leave us there on the shore with Simon and Jesus and that multitude of fish. I wish I could leave us with a gospel message that says that being a Christian means

God will make us rich. But that's not what grace means, and that's not how this story ends. Let me give you a window into my life as a way to frame the ending of this story about the fish.

I'm actually only employed half time as pastor of Chapel Hill Mennonite. With the other half of my time I work on Steve Jolley's construction crew. We remodel, build additions and decks—those sorts of projects. The livelihood of the small crew depends on the work we have. We are only able to do the work because we have tools. Steve has a trailer he pulls around with a multitude of tools for every task we may encounter. If you've ever been to Home Depot or Lowe's, you've noticed that tools aren't cheap. I'm sure Steve is still paying off some of those specialty tools, but we need them in order to do our job and make a living. Now, what would happen to our crew if one day, after a very productive day on the jobsite, Steve decided to leave all the tools there on the street corner and move out of town? We would be out of a job. No way to pay the bills. It would be completely irresponsible of Steve. No concern for us, or for himself.

Yet, that's how our story from Luke ends! This is exactly the sort of irresponsibility we are left with. Yes, this is an amazing story of a miraculously productive fishing trip, but it is also a story of a miraculously irresponsible surrender of all blessings, all profits, all economic gains, and all earned income for the sake of a journey into the unknown. The punch line of the story comes at the end. *After* Luke tells us about this amazing miracle and the wonderful blessing that Jesus gives Simon and his friends, something crazy happens. Jesus invites Simon and his business partners to join him in his work, and this is what the last line of the passage says: "So they pulled their boats up on the shore, left everything and followed him" (v. 11). *They left everything!* Think about it. They had just caught the most fish they'd ever seen. They could take that catch to the market and make some real money. Perhaps this was the break they had been waiting for. Now they could finally expand their business, make greater profits, buy another boat, and hire more workers. I'm sure they could have provided a handful of needed jobs for the unemployed in their village. That would have been a responsible decision, a choice that would help them while helping others. That's probably what it would have meant to be good stewards of the gifts God had given them, but that's not what they do. Instead, they throw it all away. They don't even give it to the poor. That would have been a better option. That's exactly what Jesus tells the rich young ruler to do later in Luke's Gospel: "Sell everything you have and give to the poor, and you will have treasure in heaven. Then come, follow me" (18:22). But that's not what happens in this story. This is not about charity. This is not about being good, about being pious, about storing treasures in heaven. What happens in our story for today is much more irresponsible. The fishermen leave their miraculous catch to rot on the shore. They embody bad economics and poor stewardship. And what's worse, they leave their nets and their boats too! They leave their jobs, their investments, and their livelihood behind . . . and for what? They really don't know. So they can follow this man they hardly know into what will turn out to be a bleak end to their earthly life—the cross? Jesus and Simon both get killed on crosses.

This isn't an easy passage. Sure, there are ways to make this story easier to swallow. I could spiritualize it and turn the story into something psychological, something that happens in our heads. I could say: "This is about how we need to be *willing* to give up all we have for the sake of the gospel; it's about our *attitude* toward wealth. We can keep it as long as we don't let it control us." To be honest, I like that message better because that's the way I actually live. I have lots of things, like the nice car my wife and I drove this morning. But our Scripture today won't let us live comfortably with our wealth, even if we try to be responsible with it.

This story shows us what it means to believe in the sheer grace of God—a mysterious grace, a dark grace. A bloodstained cross is the best image we have of God's grace. Jesus beckons us into the darkness of the cross. This kind of grace calls us and empowers us to leave behind all of our securities to follow this mysterious man from Galilee into a hazy future, into a land we can only faintly see on the horizon. This same gracious call led Abraham to leave his country, his people, and his property, and trust that God would bring him into unimaginable promises. The call of God's grace led the people of Israel out of Egyptian slavery and across the Red Sea, only to wander for forty years in the wilderness where they lived by the daily grace of manna and quail. In Luke's Gospel this morning, we hear the gracious call of God, down by the lake, which leads Simon and his friends to leave behind all of their securities, all of their assets, all that they have, and follow this unpredictable savior.

Yes, God pours out loving grace in order to save us, but the way God's grace saves may not be what we thought we needed. Grace saves us by helping us let go of everything—to let go of our lives, to lose control of our selves, and to step into a new life and a new path. And we go forward into the unfamiliar, the unknown, because we've heard a strange story. We've heard that this man was buried, and "that he was raised on the third day according to Scriptures" (1 Cor 15:4). God's grace leads to our death—the end of how we sustain our selves—and leads us into a new life that depends completely on the same Holy Spirit that raised Jesus from the dead. The grace Jesus offers is the same grace he offered Simon: a flow of grace that moves Simon to leave everything behind and follow Jesus to the cross. Like his master, Simon's earthly life ends on a Roman cross, which is the birthplace of resurrection.

"So they pulled their boats up on the shore, and left everything and followed him" (Luke 5:11).

Human Enough

Matthew 18:21–35

When Will Willimon and Stanley Hauerwas discuss forgiveness in their book on the Lord's Prayer, *Lord, Teach Us*, they begin by recounting the story of Reginald Denny, a truck driver who was pulled from his rig and beaten severely in the aftermath of the first Rodney King verdict. "After his painful recovery," the authors say, Mr. Denny "met face to face with his attackers, shook hands with them, and forgave them. A reporter, commenting on the scene, wrote, 'It is said that Mr. Denny is suffering from brain damage'" (Hauerwas and Willimon, 78).

No matter how you account for the reporter's comment, the implication is clear: only a crazy person would forgive people who had so deeply wounded him. I think we'd do well to dwell on that reporter's insight for a moment because despite how comical it seems, the response to Mr. Denny's act of forgiveness seems somehow natural.

In the wake of the Amish school shooting in Nickel Mines, the country watched as the Amish community forgave the attacker and made gestures of reconciliation toward his family. The general public was stunned. We live in a culture that makes school shootings altogether too common. Consequently, we have a normal range of responses, from tighter security in schools, tougher gun laws, and mandatory sentencing for juvenile offenders, to school-side shrines and martyr cults for the victims. However, in the case of Nickel Mines, watching an entire community respond to such a tragedy with forgiveness—as if that was a normal response—put the watching public out of its depth. The media attention lavished on the Nickel Mines community after the shooting didn't accuse the Amish of being crazy like it accused Mr. Denny, but it did look at them in an uncomprehending manner, and it quickly trotted out religious "experts" to normalize and make sense of the community's response for the nightly news consumer.

These two stories confirm that we don't live in a society based on forgiveness. Forgiveness is an anomaly when it occurs in a public context, the exception that proves the rule, so to speak. Whenever I talk about forgiveness in our Introduction to Biblical Worldview class at Bluffton University, students are surprised by the claim that we don't live in a society based on forgiveness—until, that is, I ask how many of them expect their lenders to forgive their student loans. No one has ever raised her or his hand, and most of them laugh. It's preposterous to think that lenders might be in the business of debt forgiveness, and when the students think about it, they realize that they are only able to come to school because loan corporations don't routinely forgive debt. For better or worse, we find that much of what we think is important in our society happens because we don't forgive debt.

If these three examples tell us anything, it's that Willimon and Hauerwas are right. Forgiveness is an outrageous human activity. I'm tempted to say that it's so outrageous that it's possible only with God's help, but that's a silly thing to say, since nothing we do is possible apart from God. So, here's the thrust of what I'm going to say instead: if Christians are going to understand and practice forgiveness as part of the good news they are to proclaim, then forgiveness needs to be understood first and foremost as a human activity. Christians often make a mistake of assuming that our first experience of forgiveness comes from being forgiven by God. That may be true, but if it is, it's really unfathomable. Let me suggest that each of us learns what forgiveness is by being forgiven by other people. A little boy lies to his mother about having tormented the family cat. He feels guilty and tells her that he lied to her, perhaps he apologizes, and she forgives him. One friend gossips about another friend and hurts her in the process. Once she realizes she's hurt her friend, she tells her so and is deeply sorry for the gossip, and her friend forgives her. It's in contexts like these where we first learn about forgiveness. They are human, interpersonal, and completely mundane. From there we move to talking about God.

I think today's text from Matthew's Gospel bears this out. Notice that no one even mentions God until the very last verse of the story (Matt

18:35). I'd like to leave it that way for us. When we talk about forgiveness, let's agree that God doesn't come up until the end; otherwise it's too easy for us to use God to make forgiveness safe, comfortable, and above all impersonal. What happens in the story before God comes up is what I'd like us to focus on. First, Peter asks Jesus a question about forgiving his sister or brother in the church. The initial impetus for this teaching on forgiveness is interpersonal. Second, Jesus' response to Peter's question isn't just a saying, but also a story about money. Thirdly, the unmerciful servant in the parable has the opportunity to forgive the debt he's owed, and in refusing to do so, he diminishes not only his own but also his debtor's humanity.

First, the entire teaching about forgiveness is interpersonal. We are altogether prone to forget this, and, indeed, that seems to be just the mistake that Peter makes. He doesn't see that forgiveness isn't primarily about him. He's an egotist who can't see that forgiveness is how God draws him out of himself and into another's life. So, he comes to Jesus and says, "Lord, if *my* brother or sister sins against *me*, how often should *I* forgive? As many as seven times?" (v. 21). The message I've heard preached on this passage is basically this: Peter wants to turn forgiveness into a math problem, and Jesus won't let him. So, Jesus' response to Peter reminds us that we shouldn't set limits on forgiveness; instead, we should be extravagantly forgiving. That is an important lesson, and it might be especially pointed for us if we take the context of these few verses to heart. Peter's question to Jesus follows hard on the heels of Jesus' own teaching about church discipline. Mennonites, more than any other church, have been tempted to read those verses as a formula or a how-to manual—as though we only need to worry about getting the steps in the process straight, and the healing and reconciling work of church discipline will take care of itself.

To us, it looks like Peter has missed the point of forgiveness almost entirely. It looks like this is going to be another of those "poor Peter, bless his heart" moments in the Gospel. *Silly Peter*, we say, *stop keeping count. It isn't seven times or seventy-seven times or four hundred ninety times. Jesus is saying that you're to learn to be perfectly forgiving.* However, this might be just what Peter means. He says, "Should I forgive seven times?" If we know anything about biblical numerology, we know that seven is a perfect number. So Peter has already, in essence, said to Jesus, "Lord, do you mean to say that I need to be perfectly forgiving?" It isn't so much that Peter gets the answer to his question wrong, but that Peter's question demands Jesus' response because he has failed to think of forgiveness in a non-egocentric way: again, if *my* brother or sister sins against *me*, how much should *I* forgive?

Peter's got me down to the tee. Does he speak for you, too? We'd like to think of forgiveness as part of a self-improvement program, wouldn't we? We know that forgiveness isn't always easy for a variety of reasons: maybe you just don't like the person you're supposed to forgive, maybe you like her altogether too much, maybe the injury you've sustained has been staggering, maybe you're just tired, or perhaps it's all these things rolled into a ball. And, if forgiveness isn't always easy, we think, at least it had better be good for us. We're told then, or we tell ourselves, that if we learn to be forgiving we will be less resentful, more resilient, happier, and better-adjusted as we make our way through the day.

I'm sure all of this is true, but this is the gospel as self-help for dummies, and, what's more, if we stop with the psychological benefits of cultivating a pay-it-forward mentality in life, we'll have missed what's most startling about Jesus' parable. The story he tells is not about me or you and the happiness we get from being forgiving. It's a story about the kingdom, and it is above all a story about money. My students at Bluffton are usually surprised that we are talking about money in theology class. The topic was supposed to be forgiveness, and here I am talking about the Student Loan Corporation. I think it's telling that the New Testament changes topics like this as well. In the Lord's Prayer, Jesus teaches his disciples to pray for forgiveness in a way that immediately calls money to mind ("forgive us our debts"); and in our Gospel text for this Sunday, Jesus answers a question about forgiveness with a parable about money.

It is certainly the case that when we talk about forgiving debts, one of the most natural things to speak about is money. I bet that most of us have the sense, however, that forgiveness needs to involve more than simply cancelling debts. Indeed, the list of arenas in which forgiveness is called for is comprehensive. You won't find an area of human life in which somebody, at some point, doesn't need to be forgiven. So, we'd be silly to assume that we could reduce the practice of forgiveness to one aspect of life, say, the financial one. And yet, it is more than a coincidence that when Jesus speaks of forgiveness his illustrations are economic.

Money is one of the main ways in which people attach value to things. From a half gallon of milk to a vacation house on the beach, we know what things are worth by how much money they cost. Money is tricky as a medium for assigning value, however. Anyone who has ever tried to replace an old automobile with a new one knows that your old car was far more valuable to you than it is to any car dealership. Money is also an arbitrary and impersonal mechanism for determining worth. A book costs pretty much the same in a bookstore whether it was written by Toni Morrison, Dostoevsky, or Danielle Steele, but an education at Duke is a lot more valuable than an education at UNC, at least if the price tags on tuition and room and board are to be trusted. Obviously, this isn't all there is to be said about value; it's a much more complex system than simply how much money something costs. For better or worse, however, we use money to assign value to things.

We do this with people as well. In our culture, one could assume that medical doctors are more valuable than teachers by looking at their respective salaries. Both are more valuable than the housekeeping staff that keep both schools and hospitals clean and safe environments in which to work. If you have a lot of money, you are worth more than people who lack money, and not simply in terms of how much money you actually have. People with money are also happier, more trustworthy, and more fun to be around than people without money—or so the collective wisdom of our culture, as represented by Visa and MasterCard, maintains. Money allows you to pursue what is good in human life, or so we're told, and the implication is that if you lack money you won't be able to live well as a person. Wretched poverty or crushing debt are dehumanizing forces, not only because of the risks to long-term health that come with personal economic instability, but also because people who are economically dependent on others tend to be overlooked in society; they tend to go uncared for, and they fall out of public perception, except when it comes to collecting on the debts they owe. Those, too, are ways that money assigns value, not just to things, but also to people.

If we think about money and value in this way, then our connection to Christ's teaching on forgiveness might become clearer. Peter's mistake, as I've said, is not that he's not willing to be forgiving, it's that he fails to see the humanity of the other person with whom he's engaged. For Peter, forgiveness is about him, and consequently, it's a way of dehumanizing the other. Jesus' parable addresses Peter by asking him to recall the humanity of others, by asking him to recognize that forgiveness is about the reintroduction of estranged people into truly human and life-giving relationships.

The story is about a king and his slaves. The king seems to be rather average: he is not especially vindictive, but then again he's no bleeding heart liberal either. A slave who owes him a massive sum, more than ten thousand times what he was likely to earn in a year, is brought before him. The slave cannot pay the debt. Indeed, the debt is so great that it is past the point by which it might be worked off. So the king orders the slave—including everything he has and everything that is dear to him—to be sold to pay off the debt. It won't be enough, mind you. Even if the slave lived to be 100 years old, there would still need to be 100 of him to pay off his master's debt. In the king's eyes the slave is no longer human—if he ever was. He has been dehumanized, simply a medium of exchange, money in the master's pocket.

His cry for mercy is startling precisely in that it makes the king aware of the humanity of the subject that stands before him. The slave's plea, "Be patient with me, and I will pay you everything" (v. 26), isn't realistic; instead, it's a last ditch attempt on the slave's part to be seen as a person. And somehow it works. The king takes pity on him and forgives the debt, which reinstates this worthless slave into the realm of truly human relationships. That is what forgiveness does: it takes a person who is in a paralyzed and inhuman relation to the world and gives her or him back their humanity. Just like having a massive financial debt lifted off your shoulders can make you feel respectable and worthwhile, so also forgiveness is about the cultivation of the humanity that we hold in common as a bond of trust and faith between us.

That is why the slave's refusal to forgive the debt of his fellow slave is so tragic. By not forgiving the debt of the other slave, the forgiven slave diminishes the humanity of his peer. If we only become fully human in relationship with each other (and I think it's important to remember here that God's first words to humanity were, "It is not good for Adam to be alone" [Gen 2:18]), then our refusal to treat others as worthy of relationship ostracizes them, cuts them off from the network of social relationship, and makes them less human. This is precisely what the forgiven slave does with his fellow slave. In place of the money he's owed, he takes his peer's humanity away. In the process, of course, he himself becomes inhuman; for the refusal of relationship is not only taking something from someone else, it is also your own self-diminishment. That, by the way, is all I'd ever want to say about sin. Sin is the diminishment of our humanity. It is often, though perhaps not always, self-diminishment, but sin is always our failure to be human enough.

The king's response makes sense only in this context. It is not that the king has changed from being merciful to vindictive; it is rather that where he responded earlier to the forgiven slave's humanity, that same slave is now in the business of stealing the humanity of others, and so has ruined his own. And that, I think, is the point at which we need to begin to talk about God. This is, after all, a parable of the kingdom of heaven, but I think we do well to not identify God with the king in the story. I think we should identify God rather with the overwhelming concern for the humanity of others that characterizes the moment of forgiveness. God is far more concerned with the effect that our failure to be human enough has on others and us than God is concerned about the things that we do. God is concerned with what happens when we close ourselves and others off from joy and life. For God is in Godself the full measure of our humanity (that's what it means for Christians to talk about Jesus), the gift of new life and new hope that calls us in our relationships with others out of our self-diminishment and into effusive, abundant, and joyful human life.

Salvation

Companions without Paychecks

Genesis 22:1–14

People need a paycheck to survive. We work—sometimes we enjoy it and sometimes we don't—so we can get a paycheck. Everyone has bills to pay. As far as I can tell, my dad has never enjoyed his work, but he works hard for the family and I respect him for it. He works for a paycheck. Sure, he's made some friends along the way, and learned some mechanical skills, but at the end of the day—at the end of the week, at the end of the month—his labor finds meaning in a paycheck. When it's time to retire, he will not return to the factory and put in a few hours on one of the machines for the heck of it.

Isn't that how we think about salvation sometimes? Think about it. All this following Jesus stuff, all this Christianity, don't we do it for a reason? Isn't there a payoff? Don't we participate in church life for a paycheck? Isn't heaven or salvation our paycheck? We make our investments now—call it "discipleship"—so we can get paid at the end of time. To use some words (probably out of context) from the Sermon on the Mount, we give to the needy so that our heavenly father will reward us someday. We don't spend time padding our bank accounts and investment portfolios now, because we have a more important fund to look forward to: it's called heaven. "Do not store up for yourselves treasures on earth, where moth and rust destroy.... But store up for yourselves treasures in heaven" (Matt 6:19–20). We do all of it for a payoff at the end—something that will make it all worthwhile. Isn't this what we believe?

This is why the story of the binding of Isaac is so difficult to figure out. Abraham does everything in his life for one promise: that God will make of him a great nation—"Leave your country, your people and your father's household and go to the land I will show you. I will make you into a great nation and I will bless you." That's what God says to Abraham in Gen 12:1–2. God gets Abraham to leave everything behind for a promise: that he will give birth to a great nation. Abraham makes a cost-benefit analysis. He has a decent life in Haran. But if he invests his life in God's project, then Abraham will have an unbelievable life. He'll be the father of a great nation. So he goes. The investment is worth it. All along the way, God reaffirms this promise, and each time God is a little more specific. After the painful separation with Lot, God says to Abraham: "I will make your offspring like the dust of the earth, so that if anyone could count the dust, then your offspring could be counted" (Gen 13:14f.). In chapter 15, God says the same sort of thing, but this time uses stars instead of dust to talk about the promise of descendents: "Look up at the heavens and count the stars—if indeed you can count them. So shall your offspring be" (15:5). In chapter 17, God again affirms his promise: God changes Abram's name to Abraham and says, "You will be the father of many nations. No longer will you be called Abram; your name will be Abraham, for I have made you a father of many nations. I will make you very fruitful; I will make nations of you, and kings will come from you" (17:4).

One reason why God reminds Abraham of this promise is that it seems impossible given the circumstances. Abraham and Sarah are too old for children. Yet God does the impossible and Sarah bears a child, the child of the promise, the one who will make Abraham a great nation, as numerous as the dust on the ground and the stars in the sky. Abraham took God at God's word, the word of promise, and with Isaac it finally looks like Abraham's sacrifice will pay off. Abraham will begin to see the beginning of his rewards. Isaac is the first payment on Abraham's investment—and this first dividend is an important one, because it makes all the future payments possible. The great nation will come through Isaac.

Now we can begin to feel the significance of what happens on Mount Moriah. Abraham faces the possibility that it's all for nothing. With Isaac on the altar, this is a sacrifice of the promise, of his investment, of his hope, of his reason for being. We all know the story well enough. Abraham and Isaac walk together. Isaac carries the wood, Abraham carries the knife and fire. Abraham puts Isaac on the altar, atop the wood.

He raises his knife. "Abraham, Abraham," says the angel of the Lord (22:11). Abraham lays down his knife and says, "Here I am." *Here I am.* That statement is what God wants to know, what God needs to know. "Now I know," the angel of the Lord says in verse 12. What does God now know? God knows that Abraham follows God, that Abraham walks with God, for no other reason than love—and Abraham's love does not depend on future rewards, on paychecks. That's why this event is called a "test" at the beginning of the story. God needs to know if Abraham is in it for the investment, for the payoff; or, is Abraham in the relationship for sheer love, for the companionship.

Here I am. This story is about Abraham's ability to say, "Here I am"—to be wholeheartedly available, to be present to the one who beckons, to be completely present. Abraham says "Here I am" at the beginning and the end of our story: "After these things God tested Abraham. God said to him, 'Abraham!' And he said, 'Here I am'" (v. 1); then at the end of the story the same thing happens, "The angel of the Lord called to Abraham from heaven and said, 'Abraham, Abraham!' And he said, 'Here I am'" (v. 11). God needs to know if Abraham is in it for the promises of glory, if he is in it to be the father of a great nation; or, if Abraham is in it because he is completely devoted to God. God needs to know if Abraham will run away when he gets what he wants from the relationship. God wants to know if Abraham will walk with him, if Abraham will be God's companion, an intimate ally, a friend. Will Abraham walk with God when he calls? Or will he abandon God?

Will Abraham hide like Adam and Eve hid in the Garden of Eden? Remember that story from Genesis 3. Adam and Eve "heard the sound of the Lord God walking in the garden during the evening breeze, and the man and woman hid themselves among the trees from the presence of God" (3:8). In the story God comes to take a walk with Adam and Eve, but they hear God and hide; they run away from the presence of God. They refuse to be God's companions; they refuse the intimacy of walking with God. Now will Abraham do the same? God needs to know.

God wants a companion, someone with whom to walk, someone who is completely available, someone who will say, "Here I am" instead of hiding in the trees. This desire for companionship is at the foundation of God's covenant. In Genesis 17, in the account of the great covenant of circumcision that will mark God's people forever, God starts by telling Abraham to walk with him, to be a companion: "Walk before me, and be wholehearted" (17:1). *Walk before me*—literally, *walk to my face*. God is saying: Walk so that I can look at you; so my face can shine upon you; so I can see you; in my presence, always by my side, with me, my companion. *Be wholehearted*—literally, *be undivided, simple, complete*. Be with me completely, God says. Be there for me without hidden motives, without deceptions, without running. Be undivided, faithful, singular in your desire for me: "Be wholly there for me," as Professor Ellen Davis puts it (Davis, 283). God needs to know if Abraham will be a true companion. And after the test God says, "Now I know."

To understand this story of the binding of Isaac, we have to believe in a God who desires a companion—a God who wants us, who wants to walk with you face to face. It's hard to believe that anyone would want our presence all the time, that someone would want us to be with her forever—constantly, always in front of her face, always at the center of her vision. Yet, that is what God wants from Abraham.

Another detail of the story, often overlooked, adds more color to the biblical portrait of God. Our trusted translators frequently ignore the fact that God says "please." The binding of Isaac is a story about a God who says "please," not a God who remains distant, a God who stays outside the give-and-take of friendship. No, the God of Genesis 22 is a *beggar* God, a God who looks more like the hungry person on the side of the road than the president of the United States who wouldn't think of coming over for a meal at my house. Like someone desperate for company, the God of Genesis begs. God needs to know if Abraham will be a companion. This "please" is there in verse 2: the Hebrew has *na*, which means "please." God says, "Please take your son."

What kind of God says please? This isn't a harsh command from a remote sovereign. Instead, it is a heartfelt request; God is begging. Some Rabbis pick up on this word for "please" and offer this translation: God said, "Abraham, take—please take; take, I beg of you—take your son."

What does God want from Abraham? God needs to know if Abraham will work for free. Will Abraham walk with God even if the promise of a great future doesn't happen, even if there are no descendents, even if he won't be the father of a great nation? Will Abraham be God's companion without expectations? Will Abraham walk wholeheartedly with God without the hope that has sustained him so far? Is intimacy with God enough to make it all worthwhile? God has to know, God needs to know, God is dying to know, if Abraham is in it for a paycheck.

This story takes us into the very heart of our faith. Would we work without a paycheck? Would we walk with God even if heaven was not a possibility? Do we live for the promises, or do we live for the companionship? God is wholeheartedly devoted to us, to you, without expectations. And God is wondering—no, God is *begging*, God is hoping—that you want nothing else but intimacy, nothing else but companionship. Is it worth it? Do you need the promise of a paycheck to follow? Do you need to think about your glorious future in heaven in order to keep on going, to keep on walking with God?

Life on the Vine

Acts 8:26–40; John 15:1–8

Let's begin by pausing over this remarkable story in the book of Acts. Philip receives an angelic command that takes him away from the site of a successful mission in Samaria and drops him in the middle of a wilderness, on a desert road at high noon. In other words, Philip finds himself in a place wholly barren of opportunities for Christian work. He's gone, to turn the metaphor on its head, from riches to rags, from the embarrassing wealth of a situation in which the work of the Lord is evident everywhere to a place where one is bound to wonder what work there is to be done at all. Rather like being "promoted" from a middle management position in Raleigh to the head of the Butner branch office, Philip's circumstances don't appear terribly promising. Yet oddly enough, he meets another traveler on the wilderness.

The traveler Philip meets fits the circumstances perfectly. That is to say, he's as weird as the situation is. In almost every possible way this Ethiopian is an outsider, at least from Philip's perspective. He's a Gentile from the far south, worshiping Israel's God in Jerusalem. But that isn't all. On the one hand, he's almost unimaginably wealthy: he rides in a chariot, he reads Greek—moreover, he apparently has the cash to purchase scrolls, because he's reading the Scriptures right then and there—and finally he's in charge of the entire treasury of the Queen of the Ethiopians. On the other hand (and this is a big problem), he's a eunuch, and, according to Deut 23:1, eunuchs are forbidden entry into the temple of God. If I'm Philip, right about now I'm thinking, "God, what in the world am I supposed to do with *this*?"

Philip doesn't get that far, because he receives, for the second time in our story, a divine command: "Go over to this chariot and join it" (Acts 8:29). So, in the midst of all the social anxiety that's built up—a strange place, a strange traveler of a higher social station than Philip's in a chariot on a wilderness road fraught with dangers (think of the story of the Good Samaritan)—Philip runs after the chariot to catch the Ethiopian. As he's running, he hears the eunuch reading the prophet Isaiah, and so he proceeds to ask whether the eunuch understands what he's reading. And *we* know (don't we?) how situations like *this* work out: the eunuch will stop the chariot—after all, this clown in the dust poses no threat—and will look down his nose at Philip and sneer, "*Really*, you filthy peasant? You're asking *me* if *I* need help understanding what *I'm* reading?"

But that isn't quite the response Philip gets. Unexpectedly, the Ethiopian confesses, "How can I understand this, if I have no one to guide me?" (v. 31). And then he invites Philip to join him. Unheard of! Maybe Philip's clothes, or his accent, gave him away as a Jew, as someone who could help interpret Jewish Scripture. But that isn't at all clear, certainly not from this story. Remember that, just a few weeks ago, when we were looking at John's Gospel, we saw Greeks approaching Philip precisely because Philip was from Bethsaida in Galilee, that is, *because* he looked and acted Greek.

In any event Philip's on a roll, because his luck (is that the right word?) doesn't give and he is invited to join the Ethiopian in his chariot. The passage the Ethiopian reads from Isaiah provides a golden opportunity as a launch pad for Christian witness: "Like a sheep he was led to the slaughter, / and like a lamb silent before its shearer, / so he does not open his mouth. / In his humiliation justice was denied him. / Who can describe his generation? / For his life is taken away from the earth" (Isa 53:7ff). The passage forms part of the so-called Servant Songs, which tell of the humiliation and suffering of God's anointed, who bears the consequences of others' sin, making some kind of atonement for that sin, and is *therefore* exalted by God. It isn't exactly the clearest point in the Old Testament. Indeed, in the early Judaism of Philip's day, there are a lot of options for making sense out of a passage like this. So, the question the eunuch asks, "Of whom is the prophet speaking, himself or another?" (Acts 8:34), isn't a bad one at all. Jeremiah, for instance, had used the form of prophetic poetry to describe his own suffering; thus, the prophet Isaiah could plausibly be speaking of himself in this passage.

On the other hand, the Scriptures are also replete with instances of God referring to the *people* Israel as his servant. The servant could therefore easily be the nation as a whole. Both of these views were current in first century Palestine. What isn't clear is whether any self-respecting Jew in the first century would have equated the servant in Isaiah with the Messiah of Israel, and therefore, possibly, with Jesus.

But that's what Philip does, and, as the story's pace picks up, they approach some water where the eunuch asks to be baptized. Philip agrees, they go down into the water, Philip baptizes him, and then the Spirit of the Lord snatches Philip away, setting him down twenty-five miles along the Mediterranean coast in the town of Azotus, where Philip starts over, "proclaiming the good news to all the towns until he came to Caesarea" (v. 40).

There are numerous moments in this passage that, when juxtaposed with our passage from John's Gospel for this evening, tell us something important about the church that I am prone to forget. The lesson involves the radical mobility of God's saving activity. God's movements often defy our expectations, and so demand a readjustment of our settled routines of faithfulness.

That sounds trite, doesn't it? After all, each of us is aware at one level or another that God surprises, that God will not be managed or confined to the boxes we find so convenient for our purposes—so useful, so familiar, and so comforting. Each of us understands in one way or another that the God we call "King of the Universe" might just show up not only when we gather to worship, but anytime and anywhere. Even if that's a fairly scary thought, we have nevertheless made our peace with the possibility. Because here we sit, don't we? How many of you are bored to the verge of tears right now? Flannery O'Connor, the southern fiction writer, evidently felt this too, and it provoked in her a sense of outrage. She once remarked that if Christians really believed what we read in our Bibles and proclaim from our pulpits, we'd all wear hard hats to church and buckle ourselves into our seats. *Our God might just show up!* God's power, as we see with Philip and the Ethiopian eunuch, is radically mobile. God's power isn't bound by law-like regularities, nor is it governed by the assumptions, which we make every day, that the way things are is the way they have to be.

The Quaker movement in seventeenth-century England, and later, the Pentecostal movement in late nineteenth-century America, were based on just that kind of scary, disturbing thought. Quakerism was based on the felt realization that God "hath yet more light to break forth from the Almighty Word." Pentecostalism was based, at least in its early stages, on a fundamental remembering that the God who is the same yesterday, today and tomorrow, is also ever new. If many of us, as Mennonites, or perhaps for other reasons, have issues with the Quaker and Pentecostal movements, might it not have something to do with the threat that they represent to our settled lives?

Consider for instance the premium we place in this fellowship on the word "community." It means mutual support and moral accountability, friendships and fellowship. Some of us are even convinced that this word "community" has to do with Christ's body and the very life of God. None of this is wrong. None of it deserves to be bulldozed or downplayed, yet "community" can also have less positive connotations, ones having to do with parochialism and routinization, with an immobile localism, with comfort zones and a resistance to leaving or stretching them. In these registers an otherwise laudable emphasis on community can hinder and inhibit our openness to God's work.

The story of Philip's encounter with the Ethiopian eunuch asks us to test the limits of our grasp of community. It asks us to reconsider how and by whom the work of the church is accomplished. The story makes us imagine a wildness and a wideness to God's grace that calls us out of the places we thought we were supposed to be and into places, like Philip's wilderness road, where our vision of God's goodness might require a new focus, where our version of what community entails might be reshaped.

If we speak of a wildness and a capaciousness to God's grace that works on us and stretches us—that compels us in our life together to be pliable to God's will, as Philip was pliable to God's will—then we might be able to enter more easily into the imagery in the fifteenth chapter of John's Gospel, where Jesus says, "I am the true vine, and my Father is the keeper.... I am the vine, and you are the branches; live in me" (John 15:1ff). The metaphor obviously regards the church, the community of disciples gathered around Jesus. How many times have you considered, hearing these verses, what vines are really like? I remember the flannel graph lesson for this passage. The Sunday school teacher stretches out this thin, slightly curved piece of brown flannel with two green flannel leaves sticking out of the top. Then you take your thin brown piece of flannel with green flannel leaves, write your name on it in smelly markers, and stick it to the side of the first brown piece of flannel. The lesson isn't a bad one: "Oh. I'm a branch. I depend on Jesus." However, what you end up with when the whole Sunday school class has stuck their flannel branches to the first piece of flannel never looks much like a vine, does it? It looks more like a tree or a small bush. But Jesus didn't say, "I am the true shrub." Instead, he said, "I am the true vine." So I find myself wondering what it might mean for the church to be shaped by that metaphor, to grow and to live like a vine.

I wonder about this because I fear we may be altogether more shrub-like than we are vine-ish. The differences between the two types of life, I think, cycle us back to this notion of God's mobility and the possible resistances we erect between ourselves and God's call for movement. Shrubs, trees, and bushes are all instances of ongoing growth, the patterns of which we can pretty clearly anticipate. That's why the acorn was Plato's favorite example of organic potential. The acorn, Plato insisted as he held it in his palm, contains within it the idea of—the form of, the potential for being—an oak tree. Once Plato says "oak" we all know what he's talking about. If we were each asked to draw a picture of an oak tree and had a way of adjusting for our differing levels of artistic ability, the trees we drew would look strikingly similar. There's nothing wrong with that. Shrubs, trees, and bushes are appropriate metaphors for some kinds of life and growth. But, I think it's instructive that those aren't the metaphors Jesus uses to describe the shape of the church's life. Because shrubs, trees, and bushes are all metaphors for forms of life that we can control, manage, and imagine clearly—if *this* oak tree is to look right, it needs another branch just *here*, growing like *this*. Symmetry, appropriateness, and fittingness: these are the registers of association for shrub-like lives. Yet they aren't particularly apt metaphors for lush lives that surprise us, for lives that we can only receive as prodigious gifts of God.

Consider by contrast the life of vines. Vines grow in twisted shapes and patterns, sometimes following a pre-given pathway, as when they race along an arbor, sometimes tumbling out of the pattern we had hoped for or imagined. They loop around and loop back on themselves, here and there shooting off new branches as well as new roots that sink deep into the ground, nourishing it at points we could not have envisioned when the vine was planted. There is mobility and almost an improvisational quality to life on the vine. This kind of growth fits life in the church, especially as Philip's encounter with the Ethiopian eunuch portrays it to us. The image of a vine reminds us that any moving forward will involve unpredictable loopings back and around—to Scripture, to the history and traditions of Christianity, to our experiences together. If our life together is like the life of a vine, then we can't assume we've gotten it right and can just move on, as if we're branching off from a trunk whose pattern of growth is so obvious that it never needs retracing. If our life together is life on the vine, there will be a constant and unanticipated potential for the reformation of our lives, perhaps even a readiness for that reformation to be radical. The wholesome life of a church, as Jesus' metaphor of vine-ishness suggests to us, is a movement of the constant interruption of organic growth and the chances for roots to dig into the ground anywhere. Like Philip, you may find yourself in Azotus, having been only moments before waist deep in a wadi somewhere between Hebron and Gaza, baptizing a man you had met an hour before.

Deliverance from Egypt

Exodus 12:1–14; Romans 13:8–14; Matthew 18:15–20

Last week we read a story from Exodus 3, where God comes to Moses at the burning bush and says, "the cry of the Israelites has reached me, and I have seen the way the Egyptians are oppressing them. So now, go. I am sending you to Pharaoh to bring my people out of Egypt" (Exod 3:9–10). Now in our passage for today Israel is on the verge of escape. God will deliver the people. So they eat with anticipation: "you shall eat your meal hurriedly," God says in verse 11. The Exodus is imminent. They are on the edge of new life.

This is an explosive narrative. African slaves heard this account of escape from Egyptian oppression as good news for their time and place, which happened to be right here in North Carolina not so long ago. From hearing the story, they knew that God would set them free. Early Anabaptists also heard this narrative and believed in Israel's God. The peasants who later became Mennonites retold the story of Israel's redemption as their own story. Itinerant preachers proclaimed the hope of Passover and Exodus across the countryside, saying: "The people shall go free; and God alone will be lord over them" (Müntzer, 94). Passover was how Israel celebrated that good news in anticipation of their salvation from Egypt. The good news inspired hope among the enslaved Africans, it spread the Radical Reformation across Europe, and it is good news for us, too. What would it mean for us to be set free from Egypt? Think about that for a moment. What are the powers of Egypt that enslave us?

On Friday morning, as I made my way back to the kitchen for more coffee, I noticed a CNN video Katie was watching on the computer. I was stunned as I saw a protestor in the streets of St. Paul, Minnesota, trying to get to her feet but being rammed back to the ground by police officers on bicycles. I couldn't shake that picture from my head. In the afternoon I searched the web for more footage. Although I couldn't find the same video, I did find incredible scenes of mass protest over the past few days.

I get mad at the world sometimes. There are times when I hear news on the radio when driving, and I yell at whoever dropped more bombs and "accidently" killed some kids. I make sure, of course, that I'm alone and the windows are rolled up. Nobody likes an angry pastor. Or I get angry when I hear about friends who do the best they can, but it's never enough. They are up against the world and there's no way out. There's not a clear villain, just an assembly of forces that seem to set everyone against you. There's no escape, it seems. All you can do is protest—make some noise, burn some tires, and get in the way. Then, usually, everyone goes home or to jail and it's business as usual soon enough. The same powers that enslaved Israel in Egypt are still at work in the world today and they always seem to win.

Don't get me wrong. I have nothing against protests. In fact, I admire the people who participate in them. I don't have the courage to face down riot police. Instead, when I get angry I put on my Rage Against the Machine album and sing along to "Killing in the Name of." When I realize that listening to a few songs does absolutely nothing to change the world, I grow melancholy and put on Radiohead, preferably *OK Computer*. I have my personalized protest in the comfort of my home, without the possibility of police brutality. But my personal protest also means that I don't experience the thrill of crowds of friends at my side. Sure, a protest doesn't last very long, but it seems like the protestors experience the power of solidarity, even if for a fleeting moment.

What if I said that church is a kind of protest? Sure, it's a stretch. It doesn't take much courage for us to get together for worship. We don't have to worry about police batons or tear gas. Yet there's a way in which church is a protest, however mundane, against Egypt, against the powers of this world—at least that's what the apostle Paul argues. We usually take Paul's Epistle to the Romans to be a dense theological treatise— chapter after chapter of tedious argumentation. But I think Paul is more like a rogue organizer than a meticulous theologian, disseminating news of an illegitimate new movement. The logic of Romans works more like a contagious virus than a brilliant thesis. Paul, of course, has his theological training, but that's not his passion. His passion is the protest. He lives for the gathering crowds of protest. Everything else is a preamble that clears the way for the assembly to happen. He wants people to get together, meet together, and organize. But there are some people who don't want these meetings to happen. These enemies want to preempt Paul's explosive message by raiding the communities before he can get there and spread his viral movement. The enemies don't want Gentiles and Jews eating together, worshipping together, and talking with one another. It's not that Paul simply wants to stir up trouble and make some enemies because there's nothing better to do. Instead, Paul is at the mercy of the power of love and nothing can separate him from that divine love. As he says earlier in Romans, "I am convinced that [nothing] will be able to separate us from the love of God that is in Christ Jesus our Lord" (Rom 8:39). In order to join in God's movement of love, Paul will go to the ends of the earth. Through the power of the Holy Spirit, Jesus Christ is at work creating a dwelling place for God's love, a people who will be God's home. How does Paul think we should go about creating a people who welcome God's presence?

"Owe no one anything," Paul says, "except to love one another" (13:1). To love one another is the organizational principle for God's assembled people. The whole purpose of the law is to tell the people what to do in order to love one another: *don't commit adultery, don't murder, don't steal, don't covet,* and so on. These are not random rules. They give us the basics so we can be together, so we can truly and deeply love one another, so we can assemble. That's the point of the law, Paul says.

This command to love is familiar; we've heard it before from Jesus. Someone comes up to Jesus and asks him, "Which is the greatest commandment in the law?" And Jesus replies, "You shall love the Lord your God with all your heart, and with all your soul, and with all your mind" (Matt 22:37)—Jesus quotes Deut 6:5, what is called the *shema*. But Jesus goes on to add a second commandment: "You shall love your neighbor as yourself" (Matt 22:39)—Jesus quotes Lev 19:18. For Jesus, the first commandment is to love God, then comes the second, to love your neighbor. Isn't it strange, then, that Paul leaves out what Jesus says is the first and most important commandment, to love God with all your heart? —"the commandments . . . are summed up in this word, 'Love your neighbor as yourself'" (Rom 13:9). But what about God? How can Paul leave out the commandment to love God? What kind of theologian forgets about God?

Or, perhaps Paul helps us discover the radical nature of Jesus' statement in today's passage from Matthew 18. In verse 20 Jesus says, "For where two or three are gathered in my name, I am there among them." God is present in and with the people. Thus, because God is present among the gathered, to love God is to love one another. To love God with our heart, soul, and mind is to love one another. To love your neighbor as yourself sums up all of the other commandments, including the command to love God. Our love for one another is a demonstration of God's love for us and our love of God.

That's what Paul wants, and he can't wait to join in God's love that is happening among the Christians in Rome. At the beginning and the end of his letter, he talks explicitly about this longing. In chapter 1 Paul comes right out and says it: "I long to see you" (Rom 1:11). Then again, at the end, in chapter 15: "I have been longing for many years to see you" (15:23). And a few verses later: "Pray . . . that I may come to you with joy and together with you be refreshed" (v. 32). This desire is the pulse of Paul's letter. Paul has heard about the presence of God in this Roman community and he can't wait to be with them, to taste God's love at work in their midst. *Keep up the faith*, he tells them, *never stop loving one another no matter what anyone says.*

Paul's longing for God's love invites us into Israel's anticipation of deliverance from Egypt. To put it clearly: our love for one another is how we actively await our exodus. Like Israel at Passover, with sandals on our feet and a staff in our hand, we are on the verge of God's salvation. Paul tells us to get ready: "Now is the moment for you to wake from sleep. For salvation is nearer to us now than when we first believed" (13:11). *It's here. God is here. Now is the moment of our exodus!*

What does it mean to be set free from Egypt? The powers of the world infect our lives in all sorts of ways. That's why Jesus' teaching in Matthew 18 is so important to how we love one another. We let each other know when Egypt—that is, the powers of this world, the infection called sin—has a hold on us. We are "a people who," as Stanley Hauerwas puts it, "love one another so intensely that [we] refuse to let anyone go astray—or for us to go astray through unspoken resentment" (Hauerwas,

165). We expose the hidden grip of the powers of this age as we make our sins known to one another, which is how we make public our protest against Egyptian slavery. Sin is not only an action we do, sin is also the way we are under the dominion of evil powers that squelch the life out of us. Sin is slavery. Sin is like the powers of Egypt: they keep us barely alive so they can use us as cheap labor for their projects of destruction. That's why we are a protest movement, as Karl Barth puts it in his commentary on today's passage from Romans 13: "Love of one another ought to be undertaken as the protest against the course of this world" (Barth, 492).

Church is like a protest, even if it's an underwhelming protest. We gather in the face of a world of sin and destruction. Every Sunday we assemble, we get in formation, say some words about God, enjoy our solidarity, read litanies, and do some strategic planning. Then it's all over and we go home and wonder if our gathering made a difference. The world, it seems, hasn't changed. Yet there may be more going on even when it looks like not much is happening. We must remember what Joe Wiebe said last week in his sermon: God's presence is weak, so we don't know when it comes or where it goes. We can be certain that God is here and something is happening to us, even though we don't quite know where we are being led and why. That's why we continue to gather in expectation, as Israel did and the Jews continue to do on Passover. We are like protestors who hit the streets knowing the problems, but not quite sure what the solution may be or where we'll end up when we have to face down the police. We continue to assemble as a church, anticipating God's redemption and protesting against sin. We are disciples who await God's presence, even if we don't know what it looks like. We are like Matt Thiessen, who mentioned last week during our time of discernment how he continues to work at our community garden even though nothing important ever happens. God's redemption doesn't usually overwhelm us with obvious effects or rewards. Yet we gather nonetheless, and we love wholeheartedly because our salvation is nearer now than ever before, as Paul says. It may have happened while we were busy looking for undeniable results. Our fixation on a strong kingdom and a powerful God may have blinded us from the One who is among us in weakness.

Salvation Is Created

Isaiah 61:10—62:3; Psalm 148; Galatians 4:4–7;
Luke 2:22–40

"Salvation is created. Salvation here on earth. God. Alleluia." Pavel Tchesnokov's Christmas hymn celebrates the central mystery of our faith: that, in Christ, the God who created us without us did not redeem us without us, as Augustine wrote. God's salvation is not apart from us, not different from you and me, for salvation is a human being. That is the Christmas gospel. Salvation is created here on earth. Therefore, as the Psalmist says, let all creation praise the Lord, from the heavens, angels, sun, moon and shining stars to "ye sea monsters and all deeps" (Ps 148:7). The "torch of salvation," the "vindication of Jerusalem" for which Isaiah yearned has been found to be none other than God in a stable, and "the new name that the mouth of the Lord will give" (Isa 62:1-2) is none other than that foretold by the angel and given to Christ at his circumcision: *Jesus*. Salvation is created, salvation here on earth: God in an earthy way, as we are reminded this evening when we read of Jesus' presentation in the temple.

Imagine that you or your spouse just had a child. The two of you bring your child to church, maybe for the first time, for a baby dedication like the one we had a few weeks ago for Tristan Plummer. The pastor, or whoever is conducting the service, says the right words, prays over the baby, asks God to protect her, or to bring him up in the paths of righteousness, and so on. The dedication concludes and you take your child back to your seats. What are you feeling at that moment? Perhaps a little pride in your beautiful child presented before the congregation, happiness and hopefulness that this child will be brought up in a nurturing body of believers, maybe relief at having done your duty.

How would your feelings change if, at the end of the baby dedication, an older man whom you respected, even one whom everyone recognized as above reproach, entered the church, took your newly dedicated baby in his arms, looked down at him or her, and said, "Now, I'm ready to die because I've just seen salvation"? I bet that would suck the pride, hopefulness, and relief right out of you. You would be anxious to get your child back in your protective arms. "Hey, old man," you would think to yourself, "You look at my kid and you see salvation? We look at him and we see a promising young doctor. At any rate, he's not even six weeks old! At least give him a chance to discover his own destiny."

This is why it seems right to me that Luke's Gospel doesn't tell us that Mary and Joseph were overjoyed to hear Simeon praise God concerning Jesus (Luke 2:28–33). No, they were amazed and disoriented, like an audience at a magic show. You know how at a magic show each new trick astounds you? Even though you've just seen fifteen other tricks that were amazing in their own right, you're never quite prepared enough not to be surprised by the magician's next trick. I imagine that's how Mary and Joseph feel as one surprising event leads to another. It just doesn't stop with this kid! First, there was the visit from the angel and the unaccountable pregnancy. Then she had to traipse all the way to Bethlehem for that wretched census, and Joseph couldn't even find them a hotel room. Without a proper place to stay, Mary's contractions started while they were huddled in a barn and the only place to deliver her baby was a feed trough. Then a bunch of shepherds show up for a baby shower that very night when all she wanted to do was get some sleep. Now, after the whirlwind of events surrounding the birth of Jesus settle down—after a normal circumcision, a normal purification rite, a normal sacrifice in the temple—Simeon shows up and talks about seeing salvation in the face of baby Jesus, the "glory of . . . Israel," "a light to enlighten the nations," and life becomes bewildering and magical again.

The pageantry of Christmas celebrates the magic of the season. Christmas trees, presents, nativity scenes, carols in the night—all of this commemorates the surprising events recounted blow by blow in Luke and Matthew's Gospels and reminds us just how strange and unusual Jesus' birth was. We love to celebrate the magical pageantry of Christmas, and this isn't a bad thing. Psychologically, I think, it's healthy for us to take breaks from the humdrum, featureless, ordinary terrain of our lives. But, we also need to be honest with ourselves and recognize that we are very good at valuing pageantry at the expense of the everyday. We look forward to the spectacular in a way that often makes us less than fully attentive to the goodness of the ordinary, as if we live our lives by getting from one peak experience to the next.

Perhaps our propensity to value the stand-out and unusual times of our lives at the expense of the mundane is part of the reason why Paul, in the letter to the Galatians, insists that when God "in the fullness of time" sent the Son, he was "born of a woman" (Gal 4:4). When Christians say the Apostles' Creed, we too insist upon this critical point: Jesus was born of a woman, "born of the virgin Mary." Yet, often, when we reflect on this phrase, we fixate on the word "virgin" because the concept of a virgin birth offends our sense of biological propriety. So, we think to ourselves, *Here's another miracle, another bit of the magic of Christmas that we can celebrate.* But that's barely half the story. The apostle Paul's accent in Galatians is simply that God's Son was *born* at all.

I suppose that it's clear to us that God did not have to redeem the world through a Son born in human flesh, not if the problem of redemption concerns how to erase the debt and stain of sin. God could have achieved our redemption in an infinite number of ways. We could let our imaginations run wild. A student one year wrote an essay on this very point and insisted to me that God could have saved us by shooting lasers out of his eyes. While I'm not sure how useful it is to spend time thinking about what God could and couldn't do, I did understand the student's point. Whatever the case, God could have put a little more magic into the vehicle of our salvation, like lasers.

Instead, "Salvation is created. Salvation here on earth." Jesus Christ was "born of a woman, under the law." In other words, his was a birth like every other birth. The birth of the Messiah was an ordinary way to come into the world. For all the strange and magical events that surrounded his birth, "Jesus Christ [was] the real son of a real mother, both of them as real as all the other sons of other mothers" (Barth, 185). We see evidence of this mundane reality in Luke's Gospel when, after Christ's circumcision, Mary goes to Jerusalem for the rite of purification (Luke 2:22). Torah (specifically, Leviticus 12) stipulated that after the birth of a son, a woman is unclean for seven days and should be kept away from all holy things for a further thirty-three days. Then, she should offer a lamb as a burnt offering and a dove or pigeon as a sin offering. If she was too poor to offer a lamb, then a second dove or pigeon would suffice as a burnt offering instead.

Notice two things about our text tonight. First, Mary needed to be purified in accordance with the Law for giving birth to the savior of the world. This is more than a respectful nod by Luke to Jewish custom, and more than an effort to show that Jesus' parents were observant Jews. Here we find that the mother of the God of the Law is made unclean according to the Law when she becomes God's mother. Secondly, Mary offers two turtledoves, which is the sacrifice of the poor. It doesn't get much more humble, much more mundane than this.

The Lord of time took the time to bind himself to one human story, to enter so fully into humanity that we, by coming into contact with Jesus, might be drawn into God's very life. For all the magic, all the expectation, and all the prophecy that attended Jesus' birth and life, he was a human being—"one of the many, not infinitely but limitedly many, possibilities of historical humanity" (Karl Barth, I.2, 138). He stands inside human (specifically Jewish) history. After all, his parents took him to *Jerusalem*. "In the history of the Jews," writes Rowan Williams, "God's Spirit [had] been for centuries pressing this people toward a complete openness, receptivity, and vulnerability that will 'clear a space' for renewing grace to flow freely" (Williams, 18). Mary is the figure who displays this vulnerable receptivity within the Jewish people. She is the climax of the Spirit's movement of grace through the story of Israel. Mary's fiat, her "let it be to me according to your word" (Luke 1:38), is how room is made for God's salvation through Jesus Christ. With these words, she received God's gift: "a daughter of Israel finally realized Israel's destiny by putting herself utterly at God's disposal," Williams continues, "so that the new human life [begun] in her body is a life in which God's Word is indeed set free, given space to work in the world and make it new" (Williams, 19).

We tend to think of salvation as a process of being made holy, of being affected or shaped by the work of Christ's Spirit. Because we are a part of this process, we tend to think of salvation as depending on us— not in the sense of our initiating the activity of God's grace in our lives, but that we are called to cooperate with grace, not to fight against it. Simeon, in Luke's Gospel, models much of this picture of salvation. He is righteous and devout, one on whom the Holy Spirit rests, one whose life has shown itself to be so open and receptive to the leading of God that the Holy Spirit can guide him to the temple at exactly the right time to see Jesus. What more could Simeon need? We long for his kind of life, a life in which God's will is concretely and affirmatively knowable, a life marked by intimacy with the Holy Spirit. Yet, as he holds Jesus in his arms, he says that *now*, for the first time, he sees salvation (Luke 2:30). Salvation is a baby. With Simeon, we discover that salvation is fundamentally a created human life, God's own life created as a human gift of love. We see it here: an old man holds in his frail arms the even frailer Maker of All, a child born of a woman, born under the Law. As this child, God bewilders us, disorients us, amazes us, bursts open the frontiers of all possible and imaginable experience and comes among us. "Salvation is created. Salvation here on earth. God. Alleluia."

Strangers

Do You See This Woman?

Psalm 5:1–8; Galatians 2:15–21; Luke 7:36—8:3

An unknown woman—uninvited, unexpected, and suspicious—enters where she doesn't belong. Unnoticed, she stands in the shadows, behind Jesus, outside the circle of fellowship. She doesn't even have the dignity of a name, of being named in the story; she's completely anonymous.

However, the dinner host recognizes her. Simon the Pharisee says to himself, "If this man [Jesus] were a prophet, he would know who is touching him and what kind of woman she is—that she is a sinner" (Luke 7:39). Simon doesn't need to know her name. He already knows all he needs to know: this woman is a *sinner*. Nothing else matters, and she has been among these people long enough to know that she doesn't matter to them or to anyone else. That's why she is cowering in the shadows where she thinks she belongs. She is the product of a society that has convinced her that she is unworthy, that she is dispensable, that she doesn't belong at the party. She, of course, has a place in the world, but it's not with these people. I'm sure she is needed for something . . . but not for anything going on here at Simon's house. She can enter the room where the Pharisees dine, but she must stay outside the inner circle, along the wall, invisible. For some reason—and the text is silent on this point—but for some reason the woman without a name emerges from the shadows. She makes her way to the table without a hint of confidence: she is bowed low, nearly crawling, with her face in the dust because she doesn't dare look anyone in the eyes, which would be something that equals would do. Not her, because she is a *sinner*.

I wonder what first announces her presence to Simon and the rest. I bet it is the tears and sobs—as Luke says, she stands "behind [Jesus] at his feet, weeping, and [begins] to bathe his feet with her tears and to dry them with her hair" (v. 38). She speaks with tears, so many tears that she drenches Jesus' feet and needs to wipe them with her hair. Apparently Simon doesn't hear the love the woman speaks through her weeping. She communicates her love to Jesus in a language that Simon does not understand. He would never go to such extreme measures to reach out and make a connection with someone else. Simon doesn't need to because people come to him; he is an esteemed leader in the community.

This woman speaks not with words but with a bowed body, and Simon does not have ears to hear and eyes to see her humble act as the language of love. While he can't help but focus his gaze on the woman at Jesus' feet, Simon's eyes see what he has always seen when he passes her on the city streets: she is *that* sinner.

Have you ever felt the unease of people staring at you?—all of those eyes piercing into your back, burning holes through the back of your head. I remember watching a woman walk out of a bathroom with a strip of toilet paper tucked into the back of her skirt. After a few moments she felt the pressure of all of our stares and realized why people were looking at her. She quickly returned to the restroom to attend to the issue.

I imagine the unnamed woman in our story feels something like that, although the stares that pierce into her back are probably more merciless. That's why the woman is crouched down, bent over, with her face in the dust. The judgmental stares of the dinner guests beat down on her, forcing her to become more like an animal than a human. She crawls to Jesus because she can barely manage the weight of their moralistic gazes.

We don't know why Simon calls her a "sinner." The text is silent about what she has done to warrant such name-calling. Although many interpreters suggest that the woman is a prostitute due to her flowing hair, the Jewish *Mishnah* indicates that only married women were to put up their hair. So, from her hair we should only assume that she is unmarried, not that she is a loose woman as one commentator suggests: "Letting her hair down in this setting would have been on par with appearing topless in public" (Green, 310). Nevertheless, Simon's response indicates that the woman occupies an ambiguous place in his society, a social position that renders her questionable. He sees her and places her in a category called "sinner." Whatever the reason Simon has for putting her in that social class, the woman shows us the nature of sin as it works its way into a human being.

As she crawls like a dog, we can overhear the voice of sin reverberating throughout the room and echoing into her mind. Sin is that voice of deception that tells her that she is worthless, that she deserves to grovel in the dirt. Sin is the demonic voice that insinuates its way into her head through the people around her and convinces her that she is something other than God's beloved creation. Sin is the power of dehumanization—the force of privation—that begins to suck the life out of her, like a parasite. Sin eats away at the truth that she is part of God's good creation to the point where there is nothing left of that truth. Gradually, she finds herself conspiring with the voice of sin and disfiguring her own God-given beauty.

In a sermon Alex Sider preached on this passage from Luke a few years ago, he helped us get a sense for what sin sounds like when it speaks to us: the voice says, "Yes, you are alone. In all this universe you are ultimately alone. You will crawl into a hole and die, alone. You are no more than an animal after all." Sadly, this insidious voice is so convincing that *we* speak it—it speaks through us and becomes our voice—in ways that we fail to recognize. We express the voice of sin by the way we live; for example, by the way we are content to let some people work to make our lives possible without ever eating at the same table. We allow those who make our lives possible to remain anonymous, to subsist in our world without a name, like the woman in our story. These people live on unmarked streets and work in the shadows of factories, crouched over machines—or in fields bent over rows of vegetables, crawling to make a living. In our world there are so many unnamed people who make our lives possible, and we will never see where they live or meet their children. With the way capitalism organizes the world, the fact is that we do not need to care about them, or waste a moment of valuable time to wonder about their lives. We need not seek out their names. This is one way we speak the voice of sin with our lives: we are satisfied with division, with broken communion, with anonymous economic relations.

There is, however, still hope for us because there is still hope for Simon the Pharisee. In our story Jesus doesn't dismiss Simon as another lost cause, another person who fails to catch the vision of the kingdom of God. Instead, Jesus offers an invitation to look again at the woman and let her love break apart the divisions of Simon's hardened categories:

"Then Jesus turned toward the woman and said to Simon, 'Do you see this woman?'" (v. 44). This is an amazing image. Like everyone else in the room, Jesus also turns his eyes to the woman at his feet. But he does not look with the same eyes that weigh down the woman with guilt as she walks around town. Instead, Jesus' eyes pierce her with the light of God's love, eyes that awaken the forgotten loveliness that suffuses her being. The loving gaze of Jesus sees and understands the woman's tears and her gentle act of washing of his feet. Jesus doesn't merely glance at her, give her a moment of his attention, then turn to Simon and ask him a question. No, Jesus doesn't move on from the woman at his feet to more significant people and more important matters. At this moment in the story there is nothing more significant and no one more important than this woman. He takes time to receive the profound gift that she offers. Jesus waits with this woman without a name, whose cringing and lowly body shows the severe effects of a lifetime under the weight of sin.

"Jesus turned toward the woman and said to Simon." Jesus' eyes are fixed on her—steadfast and unswerving—and he invites Simon to see this woman the way he sees her. This invitation from Jesus leaves open the possibility for Simon to look again and see the woman as a beloved member of God's kingdom, a sister not a sinner. Despite his name-calling, Simon is not yet a lost cause because we are not given Simon's response to Jesus' question. "Do you see this woman?" The story doesn't let us hear Simon's answer. We don't hear him say something like, "Yeah, I see her, she's the scum of the earth. We have a place for her, but it's not here." Nor does Simon say, "Gosh Jesus, I guess I've never seen her the way you do. Thanks." We don't have anything like that in the text. Instead, Simon is left on the threshold of a decision. Luke cuts away from the scene before we get an answer. Since the question is left open, it easily jumps off the page and into our lives. We can't help but wonder how Simon might respond, which leads us to consider how *we* might respond. In wrestling with the open-ended question, we read ourselves into the story and wonder how we are like Simon. Jesus also asks you and I, "Do you see this woman?" If we are ever surprised with the opportunity to glimpse her cowering in the corner, with what kind of eyes will we look at her? Will we offer her a passing glance and remain undisturbed. Or will we take time with her and try to see her with the eyes of Jesus?

"Do you see this woman?" becomes a question that challenges how we process the world and how we engage with others as we go about our days. However, there is a subtle danger that sneaks up on us with the challenge. The problem comes in thinking that we have everything to give and nothing to receive. It's the danger in thinking that people are out there waiting for our benevolence and our attention—waiting for us to discover them. All of this is very narcissistic: "We've got God's salvation, God's kingdom, and we need to go hand it out." According to this logic, all of the needy people we discover are dependant on us for God's love. Yet, that is not the logic of Luke's story as Jesus asks Simon if he sees the woman. Jesus invites Simon to see this woman and to understand what she is saying with her tears, because the woman has the power to see what Simon cannot: that Jesus is Lord, that Jesus brings God's promised kingdom, that the love of Jesus belongs to the people Simon calls "sinners." In Luke's Gospel the kingdom of God's love is a reality that the excluded and lowly are more able to see. The people at the bottom have a better line of sight into the kingdom of God. As the unnamed woman crawls so low to the ground, the love and forgiveness of Jesus washes over her in ways that Simon and his dinner guests cannot know due to their position in the community. This dynamic is the scandal of Luke's story, and it is a reality at work throughout his Gospel. God comes for the oppressed.

In Jesus' first public address, he opens up the scroll of the prophet Isaiah in the synagogue and reads this passage:

> The Spirit of the Lord is on me, because he has anointed me to preach good news to the poor. He has sent me to proclaim freedom for the prisoners and recovery of sight for the blind, to release the oppressed, to proclaim the year of the Lord's favor. (4:18–19)

And later, just a couple chapters before the story of Simon and the unnamed woman, Jesus says,

> Blessed are you who are poor, for yours is the kingdom of God. Blessed are you who hunger now, for you will be satisfied. Blessed are you who weep now, for you will laugh. (5:20–21)

Jesus doesn't stop with good news for those who weep like the woman in our story. To the blessings for some, Jesus adds bad news for others:

> But woe to you who are rich, for you have already received your comfort. Woe to you who are well fed now, for you will go hungry. Woe to you who laugh now, for you will mourn and weep. (vv. 24–25)

In other words, it's no mistake that the scorned woman is drawn to Jesus in ways that Simon is not. This woman is part of the blessed people who can see and receive God's kingdom: *"Blessed are you who weep now."* The story in chapter 7 of the woman crying as she washes Jesus' feet fulfils these words of Jesus in chapter 5.

We suffer from hazy vision; our eyes are clouded by our comforts. Like Simon, we are well-established benefactors of the world. Yet, it is the lowly who receive the kingdom. The ones who know their need are in a position to see the wonderful reality that Jesus offers. The question Jesus asks us, "Do you see this woman?" soon leads to another, "Do you see what this woman sees?" And there's no way of knowing what she sees until you ask and receive what only she can give: a vision of the kingdom of God.

I think the story of the so-called sinful woman can turn on us one more time, because there is a sense in which you and I are that woman as well. By no means are we made to feel as unwanted and worthless as she, I'm sure, feels. Yet, we too live in a world of sin where powers manipulate us into something less than God's good creation, and we too internalize the voice of sin and speak sin upon others with our lives. Depending on what we do for work, the color of our skin, our sex and gender, or social class, others evaluate our worth. On the basis of these and other categories, we are *evaluated*: that is, we are assigned a "value" in society according to our function. And sin is the way those valuations insinuate themselves into our being and corrupt our acceptance of God's unconditional love, which defies all of our calculations of value or earnings. If the voice of sin infects our ears in such a way that we have a hard time hearing the voice of God, we slowly begin to take that lying voice as reality and go about messing up our lives trying to be something we are not, trying to live up to some foreign value structure, and trying to satisfy ourselves with whatever those lying voices tell us will make our lives meaningful.

Christianity doesn't inoculate us from this temptation. We can easily start to think that doing good, religious activities will convince God that we belong to him, that he should love us. But God doesn't need convincing. This is the grace-filled message of the apostle Paul in our passage from Galatians. Jesus Christ is a living testimony of God's abundant love for us—the Christ who, as Paul says, "loved me and gave himself for me" (Gal 2:20). Grace means that we are held in God's eternal embrace of love through the faithfulness of Jesus Christ, without equivocation. We are already forgiven, we are already invited into fellowship, and we are already infinitely loved. It doesn't matter what we think about ourselves or about God. God already loves us and nothing can separate us from the love of God, not even the claims of those voices all around us and inside of us. That's what we see when Jesus does not refuse the humble act of love from the sinful woman, no matter how the voice of sin determines her value at Simon's table, and no matter what she may have come to believe about herself. Jesus receives her love, and in turn speaks God's restorative blessing into her life: "go in peace" (Luke 7:50).

The good news of this Gospel story fills out a verse from our Psalm for today (the gospel of God's grace is not just a message found in the New Testament): "But I, through your steadfast love, will enter your house" (Ps 5:7). God's love is steadfast, unswerving, constantly knocking down the walls of loneliness and worthlessness that all of us erect. God's steadfast love emerges in the lonely woman in Luke's story. She should have stayed in the shadows, but she doesn't because she has heard rumors in the village of the good news: that Jesus offers a kind of love that dissolves the boundaries created by sin with divine forgiveness. So, the nameless woman emerges from the dark places where the voices of sin have told her to stay, and she makes her way to the feet of Jesus, weeping—not proud, but moved by love, and sent out in peace.

Strangers

Genesis 45:1–15; Romans 11:1–2a, 28–32;
Matthew 15:21–28

In a memorable scene from the Broadway musical *Annie*, Oliver Warbucks' personal assistant escorts the eleven-year-old orphan Annie from Ms. Hannigan's squalid orphanage to the Warbucks mansion. As Grace, Mr. Warbucks' personal assistant, flings open the double doors, Annie nearly trips over her own two feet in her excitement, drinking in the wonder of a place she'd never imagined could exist. She eagerly flits about the foyer in wide-eyed disbelief and amazement, until she sees a tall, bald, stern-looking man in a business suit standing at the top of the staircase. She stops dead in her tracks, scurries back to Grace, and nervously peeks out at the man from behind Grace's dress.

The scene is one of my favorites from the musical because it sums up wordlessly what it's like to meet a stranger. Daddy Warbucks and orphan Annie don't know each other at all when she sees him standing at the head of the stairs, and all of the mystery and promise of the future hang in the first gaze they share. While mystery and promise infuses their first encounter, the scene is also marked by less comfortable feelings, like uncertainty and awkwardness, and even outright fear.

Strangers present us with some of the richest hopes in our lives; for we remember that every person whom you hold dear was once a perfect stranger. Yet, strangers also present us with potent fears of the unknown, of danger, and of the loss of control. It isn't accidental that many early elementary school social studies curricula begin by reinforcing the same lesson: "Don't talk to strangers." Where strangers are concerned, we easily identify with Orphan Annie, clinging to any shred of security as we peer out at this new and different person with both fear and excitement, with curiosity and uneasiness.

Our Scripture passages for today have to do with meetings among strangers, meetings that evoke all of the ambivalent feelings we harbor toward others, especially other people who are very different from us. I wonder if Joseph's brothers in Genesis 45 felt like Little Orphan Annie when they met Joseph in Egypt. A lot had happened during those long years since his brothers sold him into slavery. Joseph distinguished himself as a capable steward in the household of Potiphar, Pharaoh's captain of the guard. He got tossed in prison because he refused the advances of Potiphar's wife. Even while languishing in the dungeon, he was put in charge of the other inmates. Two years later, when Pharaoh had a dream that none of his seers could decipher, Joseph was hauled out of prison to tell Pharaoh the meaning of his dream. Pleased with his interpretation, Pharaoh rewarded Joseph's wisdom by making him second-in-command. Joseph oversaw Egypt through seven years of plentiful harvests, during which he told the people to store up grain for the approaching years of famine that he had foreseen. Due to Joseph's keen predictions, Egypt alone was prepared for the severe drought. When he was sold into Egyptian slavery, Joseph was only seventeen years old. By the time of the famine when his brothers sought him out to buy food from the Egypt storehouses, Joseph was thirty-nine.

It is no wonder that Joseph's brothers failed to recognize him, for in the twenty-two years since they had last laid eyes on him, Joseph had undergone a remarkable transformation. Then, he was merely the youngest son of a minor wilderness goat-herder; now, he had two sons of his own and could describe himself as a "father to Pharaoh." Then, he was nothing but a foolishly ambitious and arrogant boy; now, in his wisdom he commanded the entire nation of Egypt. Then, he was cast into the bottom of a pit; now, he sat high on Pharaoh's throne. So complete was Joseph's transition that it's safe to say that even if his brothers recognized his face, the Joseph whom they met in Egypt would have remained a complete stranger to them.

Yet, Joseph's strangeness to his brothers proved to be the way God exercised providential care over Joseph's family: "God sent me before you to prepare for you a remnant on earth, and to keep alive for you many survivors. So it was not you who sent me here, but God" (Gen 45:7–8a). Had Joseph not been torn away from the land of his birth, had his brothers not given Joseph's father (Jacob) his coat of many colors soaked in goat's blood so that Jacob would believe him dead and not go searching for him, had Joseph not been adopted into a foreign culture (we see this especially in the text when we read that Pharaoh gave him an Egyptian name and even an Egyptian wife), had Joseph not become so thoroughly assimilated to that culture that he could rise to the utmost heights of governmental authority—in short, had Joseph not become an utter stranger to his own family, the promises God made to Abraham, Isaac, and Jacob would have been proven false.

A second encounter with a stranger occurs in our passage from Matthew's Gospel for today. While Joseph—the stranger in Genesis—was in the position to offer aid to the people of Israel, the situation in Matthew is reversed. In Matthew, it is a foreign woman—the stranger, the one outside the promises of God—who stands in need of help, and the one who can offer help is none other than Jesus. Although, when the woman hails him as "Lord, Son of David," and asks him to have "mercy" on her and her daughter who is "tormented by a demon," Jesus does not treat her as we might expect (Matt 15:22). He certainly doesn't respond to her with the generosity and charity that the people of God were from ancient times expected to extend to foreigners and strangers. Instead, Jesus first reacts in a way that feels very familiar to me. He ignores her, just as we probably would do to someone who approaches us on a street corner in the city, and says, "Hey, buddy, can you spare some change?" If you are like me, your internal dialogue might sound something like this: *Look straight ahead; whatever you do, don't make eye contact; be sure your car key is in your hand; keep walking.* Jesus ends up acting similarly when this Canaanite woman comes up to him and makes a request, which seems like an inappropriate way for someone to act who claims to "bring good news to the poor." Matters only continue to worsen when she persists in hounding him, because then Jesus gets downright offensive, likening both her and her people to dogs: "He answered, 'It is not fair to take the children's food and throw it to the dogs'" (v. 26). Why does he treat this stranger so callously?

If we take the story at face value, there's no easy answer to such a question, and I won't try to make one up so as to reassure us that Jesus is really a nice guy after all. The Scripture does not tell us that Jesus was testing the woman's faith, though her faith did prove great enough that her daughter was healed. The text also doesn't tell us that Jesus knew the woman's heart or that he could foresee that everything would turn out all right in the end. Instead, the only explanation we have from the Scripture is that the "lost sheep of the house of Israel" (v. 24) have the privileged place of children at the banquet table of God's salvation, while the Gentiles (which includes all of the non-Jews among us, too) are fit only for the leftovers—not that leftovers are so bad. We might notice, for instance, that just a few verses later Jesus feeds over four thousand people with only seven loaves and seven fish, and his disciples clean up seven basketfuls of leftovers. As we can see, God provides abundantly for human needs. The encounter between Jesus and the Canaanite woman might be another story about how God always acts with overabundance: God's saving grace passes beyond the doors of Israel's house, beyond the boundaries of the promise to the Jews. The lesson of the story might be that the Spirit of God is sufficient enough to flow outside the family of the covenant; God's power can overflow the chosen routes of grace and election.

The contours of God's grace and the boundaries of the chosen people are at the center of Paul's reflections on Israel in Romans 11. What has happened to God's covenant with Israel? As we watch Paul wrestle with this question, we often misunderstand his argument when he claims that the Jews are "enemies of God for your sake" (Rom 11:28). It would be a mistake to think, as many Christians have done for two millennia, that Christianity replaces Israel in God's plan of salvation. Instead of the church superseding the Jews, Paul asks us to envision a flood of grace and mercy that overflows the boundaries of God's promise to Abraham, Isaac, and Jacob, without washing away the borders of the chosen people of God. In deep sympathy with the prophets, Paul claims that Israel has estranged itself from God. Yet, despite Israel's rejection of God, they have not ceased to be God's chosen people, "for the gifts and the calling of God are irrevocable" (v. 29).

There is an important line of continuity between our passage from Genesis and this part of Paul's Epistle to the Romans. In Genesis, if Joseph had not become a stranger to his family, God could not have used him for their salvation. In Romans, Paul claims that because the Jews have become strangers and enemies of God, God's saving grace and mercy are now available for all.

So far I have been talking about strangers, which, as I noted earlier, is a subject that makes many of us very nervous. But my sermon has been a fairly comfortable talk, because the strangers I've mentioned have turned out to look a lot like us; they've turned out to look a lot like I suspect we picture ourselves. We're altogether more likely to identify with Joseph than we are with his brothers because we also have stories of moving away from home. We're altogether more inclined to see ourselves fighting for scraps under the master's table than we are to imagine being seated at the table with the dogs scuffling around our feet because it hurts when we remember that our privileged lives keep other people under the table. And, of course, the majority of us identify more strongly with the Gentiles to whom Paul writes than we do with the Jews.

Yet, the ease with which we can identify ourselves with the strangers in each of these texts tonight ought to make us uneasy. If you're like me, you'd much rather be orphan Annie cowering behind Grace's skirt than the imposing Daddy Warbucks standing at the top of the stairs. In other words, if you're like me, you find it much easier to think of yourself as the outsider, as the morally innocent party, as *the stranger*. I know that my eagerness to be Little Orphan Annie blinds me to other strangers, as I was reminded when a friend told me a story of an orphan named Tom who went to his church.

Tom was four years old when his parents found out that he was autistic. The doctor told his mother, "You're going to have to raise him like he was a dog." By this the doctor meant that Tom would need to have extraordinarily clear boundaries and routines in his life if he was to have a chance at developing his capacity for relationship and self-sufficiency. But, Tom's mother and father heard the word "dog" and it infected their perceptions of Tom and his place in their lives. Soon, Tom's father left home. Tom's mother continued to raise Tom on her own, but she found that she lacked a support network as her family pulled back farther and farther away from any involvement with them. Her family treated Tom like a complete stranger. Even Tom's own brothers, when they moved out, quickly grew more and more distant. After some time, Tom's mother started taking him to church, and it was there that they discovered Tom's passion for music. He learned to play the piano, and he sang, developing into a powerful bass. Tom appreciated the richness of music so fully that he would become ecstatic upon hearing a Mozart concerto.

Then Tom's mother died, and many of us would say that he was left alone. But God's world is full of astounding reversals, where the last are first, the hungry filled, and the lost found—where strangers become wellsprings of grace. Tom worked for the rest of his life as a gardener in a local care home, and died suddenly one day at the age of 46. At his funeral the first four rows of seats usually occupied by family members were mostly empty, but behind those pews the sanctuary overflowed with people. As the service proceeded, one story after another was told that explained why the church was so full. One woman recalled that when she first began attending the church, she felt like a stranger, like she didn't fit in. But, she kept coming back because of Tom, whom she simply watched every week as he sang in the choir, his face enraptured—and she wanted to be like him.

Who Are You?

Isaiah 61:1–4, 8–11; Psalm 126; John 1:6–9, 19–28

It wouldn't be too much of an exaggeration to say that many of the texts in the New Testament were written as a result of a disagreement. Much of the time, people write in order to correct someone else's misunderstanding. In our attempts to understand a position or an argument, we frequently get it wrong and have to engage in disagreement and discussion. Actually, misunderstanding isn't necessarily a bad thing. The early sections of John's Gospel are good examples of how "getting it wrong" can be positive. In those opening passages we find instances where talking with others is often fueled by misunderstanding; misconceptions and differences provide an opportunity for further conversation.

"'I am not the Christ.' 'Well then,' they asked, 'are you Elijah?' 'I am not,' he said. 'Are you the Prophet?' He answered, 'No'" (John 1:20–21). This is simple and direct communication between the Jerusalem priests and John, yet the encounter is perplexing despite the seemingly straightforward dialogue. As the passage continues, the priests' frustration mounts. Their irritation seems to increase as they try yet fail to hear what John is saying. "*Who are you*? Let us have *an* answer for those who sent us. What *do* you say about yourself?" (v. 22; italics added)— *Please, John, give us something we can hang onto; we're trying desperately to understand you.*

"I am the voice of one crying out in the wilderness, 'Make straight the way of the Lord'" (v. 23). This is a mystifying answer on John's part because it is a direct response that, in a sense, refuses to respond. Instead of speaking for himself, John quotes from Isa 40:3, which would have been a familiar text for his conversation partners. He doesn't say, "*I am one crying in the wilderness.*" John says, "I am *the voice.*" John's response creates more questions than it answers. Is "the voice" someone other than the one who cries out in the wilderness? John seems intent on making sure that the priests can't get a handle on him. When he responds, it almost sounds like he is saying, "If you still think I'm the point of what I'm up to, you're hopeless. My identity isn't very interesting."

Who are you? The narrative of John's Gospel refuses to resolve that question even as the priests' concern is transferred from John to Jesus. Throughout the Gospel Jesus is exposed to hostile questioning; again and again he struggles to bring to light the suspicion and unbelief that arouses such interrogation. Jesus refuses to fit easily within existing categories. Every time Jesus resists the question, "Who are you?" he compels his examiners to redefine who *they* are and where *they* stand. The people who consciously identify themselves as the ones who really believe, or the ones who are truly "in the know," are also those who cannot bear "the true light that enlightens everyone," which is "coming into the world" (Jn 1:9). This theme plays out near the end of John's Gospel when Pilate questions Jesus. In the exchange we see Jesus continue to slip through the categories others impose upon him:

> Pilate . . . asked him, "Are you the King of the Jews?" Jesus answered, "Do you ask this on your own, or did others tell you about me?" . . . Pilate asked him, "So you are a king?" Jesus answered, "You say that I am a king. For this I was born, and for this I came into the world, to testify to the truth. Everyone who belongs to the truth listens to my voice." Pilate asked him, "What is truth?" (John 18:33-34, 37-38)

Instead of getting a clear answer from Jesus, Pilate ends up in a position of wondering about truthfulness. After this exchange the narrator jumps to another scene, and we're left with Pilate's question hanging in the air: "What is truth?" Like John, Jesus also seems to evade interrogation. In the conversation we watch how misunderstanding causes frustration at disappointed expectations, and exasperation at the limits of the power to name and understand. Yet—and this is the risk John and Jesus both court with hope—misunderstanding and incomprehension can themselves be providential because misinterpretation provides the context for clarification. To put it another way, you have to risk getting it wrong sometimes in order to get it right. Understanding is a path, and conversation shows us the way. We wouldn't have our New Testament if it weren't for such misunderstandings, which necessitated correction, balance, and sometimes reprimand. And these discussions recorded in our Scriptures have elicited further elaborations throughout the history of the church, which have invited us into a holy conversation that continues even now.

The heart of our faith returns us again and again to this conversation, for the incarnation is an invitation to misunderstand God. Traditionally, "incarnation" is not a word that Mennonites have appreciated. For one thing, it's Latin, which means it sounds too Roman Catholic. A more important concern is that it is abstract, creedal language that risks turning faith into something we do with only our thoughts instead of our lives; Mennonites would rather talk about the faith expressed in our ethics and through the history of God's faithfulness. However, I think these concerns are also the result of a misconception, one in which we are tempted to abandon our conversation partners in other Christian traditions. Nevertheless, the language of incarnation leads us into this misunderstanding about the mysteries of God becoming flesh and offers a helpful way into the message of the Gospel of John. Incarnation and the theme of misunderstanding in John's Gospel go hand in hand for two reasons. First, because God acts in a fully human way in Jesus, getting the gospel wrong is an expected result. That's just what happens in human communication. Second, because God acts in a fully human way in Jesus, getting it wrong doesn't have to be the end of the story. Misunderstanding surely frustrates those who try to understand the identity of Jesus, yet it is also the occasion for growth.

There are at least two misunderstandings at the outset of John's Gospel that create opportunities for John's readers to grow in "the true light," as it says in the prologue, instead of being condemned for the darkness of "getting it wrong." First, there is a misunderstanding about who John is, and second, there is a misunderstanding about what kind of Messiah to which John's witness points. Since these two are interrelated, we will treat them together.

Clearly the author of the Gospel thought that talking about John the Baptist's role in the advent of the Messiah presented a risk of misunderstanding. The second half of the first chapter is almost entirely devoted to a series of brief stories, each taking place at different times and in different places, each involving different characters, but all agreeing that John, when approached by people who wanted to know about his mission, regularly told them to look past him to Jesus. John made sure that people knew that Jesus was the one they should be waiting for. Even in the prologue to the Gospel, the author thinks it is important enough to interrupt the poetic structure twice in order to clear the air about John's status as merely a harbinger: "There was a man sent from God, whose name was John. He came as a witness to testify to the light, so that all might believe through him. He himself was not the light, but he came to testify to the light" (1:6-8). Several verses later we find this repeated: "John testified to him and cried out, 'This was he of whom I said, "He who comes after me ranks ahead of me because he was before me""" (v. 15).

Why was all of that needed? Why did the author have to tell the readers over and over that John was not the light but only one of the witnesses to the Messiah? What was the risk of misunderstanding that required such careful clarification? That people might take John to be the true prophet, not Jesus? That people might fail to see Jesus as the fulfiller of John's promises? If these were indeed the concerns, why might they have had doubts about Jesus? To wonder about these doubts requires that we enter imaginatively into the shoes (or sandals, as it were) of the crowds who heard John preach, who saw in him the hope they'd longed for. In this task we're aided by what we know about John the Baptist's message from the other Gospels. He proclaimed that the kingdom of God was at hand, he promised judgment, and he preached repentance, all of which are themes Jesus affirmed and built upon. When John found himself in prison and the kingdom he proclaimed had not yet come, he sent messengers to see whether Jesus really was the promised savior John thought was supposed to be coming (see Matt 11:2ff, Lk 7:18ff). His expectations of the mission of the Messiah were not yet fulfilled. Apparently, Jesus' kingdom was not powerful enough to set the captives free from the Roman prisons. The Messiah's kingdom wasn't as sure a reality as John had hoped it would be. How might the kingdom be happening through the work of Jesus if the Romans were still in charge?

We can understand John's hesitation and doubt, can't we? If we believed that the promises of the kingdom of God were true, then we would have difficulty settling for anything less than what we had hoped for. I can imagine John the Baptist wondering what happened to the hope of the kingdom as he rots in a dungeon for preaching about how everything would change with the advent of the Messiah. In response to John's doubts, Jesus tells the Baptist's messengers to return and report to him that "the blind receive their sight and the lame walk, lepers are cleansed and the deaf hear, and the dead are raised up, and the poor have good news preached to them." (Matt 11:2; Luke 7:22). Jesus' language is reminiscent of our Old Testament text for today:

> The spirit the Lord YHWH has been given to me,
> for YHWH has anointed me.
> He has sent me to bring good news to the poor,
> to bind up hearts that are broken;
> to proclaim liberty to captives,
> freedom to those in prison;
> to proclaim a year of favor from YHWH,
> a day of vengeance for our God. (Isa 61:1–2)

From this promise in Isaiah, it is only a short step to the giddy happiness and blurry joy of our Psalm for today: "When Yahweh brought Zion's captives home, at first it seemed like a dream; then our mouths filled with laughter and our lips with song" (Ps 126:1–2).

With these texts from Isaiah and Psalms in the background, John the Baptist and his disciples seem to be right to question Jesus' messianic claims. It would be wrong to settle for anything less than God's promises. Yet herein lies the occasion for misunderstanding. John's expectation, Isaiah's prophecy, and the Psalmist's exultation all use the language of political liberation. To dull the revolutionary edge of these Old Testament texts would be to dishonor the Word of God. Given the promise of a conquering hero, were they still to believe that Jesus was this Messiah? Although the story does not reveal how John and his disciples processed Jesus' response, I bet they discussed whether or not there was a misunderstanding regarding the nature of the Messiah's kingdom.

When Jesus later suffered the "defeat" of his crucifixion, there was all the more reason for John's disciples to conclude that Jesus was not the awaited one. People do not easily let their hopes die. Isn't it better to keep waiting than to lower expectations? Isn't it better to believe that God really will bring justice, just not as soon as we thought, than to be satisfied with something less than divine victory? The situation of John's disciples is not very different from our own. It's hard to see how Jesus' resurrection is a victory over death as we continue to hear stories of wars overseas and gun violence in our cities. And if the church is supposed to be the community of Christ's resurrection, why do our worship and congregational life seem so modest, considering the problems of our world? Shouldn't our victory in Christ resolve our disagreements and frustrations with one another? Like John and his disciples, don't we have good reason to expect something more from Jesus, something more successful and less ambiguous, something more evident and less dependent on faith? Why isn't the resurrected life of Jesus among us an unmistakable victory? Misunderstanding causes frustration and despair, the sense that we may never be able to give voice to our hopes.

However, at the beginning of John's Gospel, the writer affirms that what came in Jesus really was what John the Baptist expected. But the writer's declaration about Jesus is by no means a conviction that is easy to believe. Are we really to believe that the baby lying in a pile of forage feed will grow up and set fire to the whole world? At the end of the story, as we watch Jesus hang on an instrument of capital punishment, how are we to believe that this one is at the heart of the world, sustaining all things with his undying love? As the body of Jesus becomes limp on the cross, we join John's disciples in their great disappointment.

So far nearly all of what I've said about the central question of our text today—this plea for understanding, "Who are you?" (1:22)—has focused on struggle, on the riskiness of misunderstanding that John the Baptist courts in refusing to satisfy his questioners. This initial misunderstanding about John sets the stage for the subsequent struggle with the identity of Jesus as the Messiah. Through these stories of confusion and unanswered questions, John's Gospel invites us into the uncontrollable reality of the incarnation, into the precarious situation of waiting for the truly human one who is fully God to make himself known to us on his own terms, which may not satisfy our desires for a secure victory and a definite understanding of Jesus. Yet, the frustration we may feel is part of what I mentioned at the beginning of my sermon: that misunderstanding may be providential. If, through misunderstanding, God makes room in our lives for the advent of Christ, then we discover that the "true light that enlightens everyone" is not something we can manufacture, not something to be possessed and protected, not a product of our own choices and willpower, and not a projection of our egos' desires, but a person who meets us. *He meets us*; for all our preparations, we don't meet him. He meets us, not in spite of our frustrations, not in spite of our misunderstandings of what he's all about, not in spite of our mangled attempts to "get it right." He meets us when we are at the brink of despair, when all of our strategies for making the world more just—our strategies for making our lives turn out the way we always wanted them to be, for imagining the savior we've always wanted—have failed.

Perhaps this is why the Psalmist's joy at seeing Zion restored is mixed with confusion, why he's at a loss to describe salvation in a way other than as a "dream." Perhaps this is why the silence with which John the Baptist meets the question, "Who are you?" is not obstinate, and not just a failure of communication, but also an invitation to stand where he stands and point beyond himself. John points not to an imagined future—not to a fantasy unmarked by tension, not to a life that denies or escapes the present moment—but to a light that has come into our world as a challenge to all of our expectations, a light that asks us to change and grow. This light is Jesus, who shows us that the only answer to the question—"Who are you?"—comes in the patience of a life lived in the difficult and divided world we actually inhabit, the same world in which his light enlightens everyone.

The Risen Body

John 20:19–31

As Christ hung on the cross, he told his disciples that the end had come: "Jesus said, 'It is finished.' Then he bowed his head and gave up his spirit" (John 19:30). Two days later the disciples gather in the evening behind locked doors, crouched in fear, as darkness descends upon the world. As if the events of three days before hadn't been sufficiently devastating and disturbing, news continues to trickle in. For one thing, two of them found that the tomb where Jesus was supposed to be buried was now empty. For another, Mary Magdalene reported that she had just seen Jesus in the garden where he had been buried. Yet all of this news seems far too strange. None of it can sink in. The disciples have been stretched to the mind's limits, and if they are numb to the core of their souls they are nevertheless wholly occupied with the destruction that has been inflicted on their group. As they huddle together, with their minds overwhelmed with shock and the trauma of loss, Jesus comes into the locked room and stands among them.

I've often wondered about this moment when Jesus first appears to the disciples—the moment before he says anything, before they respond to his presence in any way. What are those few seconds like? Elsewhere in the Gospels when the resurrected Jesus appears, people always fail to recognize him. Mary Magdalene mistook him for the gardener, and the disciples on the road to Emmaus encounter him as a stranger. I suspect that we can get our heads around something of this strangeness, if we imagine for a moment how we'd react if we came face to face with a friend whom we knew died a public death just a few days earlier. My initial inclination is to say that I'd be startled by my friend's presence, but that I'd have no trouble recognizing her or him. But, I wonder if that would really be the case.

David Hume, the great evidentialist philosopher of the Scottish Enlightenment, gave what I think remains a powerful argument against belief in miracles, and, of course, what Hume had principally in mind when he was criticizing the belief in miracles was Christ's resurrection. A miracle, Hume suggested, is when an event occurs that disrupts our sense of what is natural and regular. Water doesn't regularly or naturally turn into wine. Blind people don't regularly or naturally become able to see. Five loaves and fish are not regularly or naturally enough to satisfy five thousand growling stomachs. People don't on a regular or natural basis get up after being dead. Moreover, Hume says—and this is where his argument is most compelling—in any encounter you have with a potential miracle you will always be more justified in believing that a miracle has not occurred than that it has. There is and can be no evidence for a miracle, because evidence arises in the context of a natural and regular process, which is precisely what miracles disrupt. So, if you encounter water that has become wine, it will be better for you to assume that you are the victim of an elaborate hoax than it will be to assume that a miracle has occurred. The reason being, you can't produce evidence that the water has actually become wine. If you meet someone after she or he has died, it will be better for you to believe that she or he never really died, or that you've got a case of mistaken identity, or that you are hallucinating, than it will be to assume that this is really an encounter with your friend who was dead. The reason being, you can't produce evidence for resurrections. Even if you could, the counter-evidence would remain overwhelming. For this case, the counter-evidence would be cemeteries.

I should say that there are a lot of problems with Hume's argument. Nevertheless, he can help us highlight the strange and disorienting nature of the resurrection as it was for the disciples, especially Thomas. Unlike for Mary Magdalene or the disciples on the road to Emmaus, the Gospel of John does not speak of a failure to recognize Jesus when he appears in the room. The narrator gives us only a moment of silence after Jesus stands among the disciples and before he speaks words of peace to them. That moment of silence between his appearance and his words is a kind of literary therapy for people like you and me. As

Christians, we naturalize the experience of Easter. Over two thousand years of celebration, Christ's resurrection has become quite ordinary and expected. So we often read passages like our Gospel text for this morning without so much as batting an eye. We are rarely startled by this good news, even though the first disciples who experienced Christ's resurrected body were electrified, and stunned at the same time, by the shock of unbelievable newness.

That is the moment of Easter: in the breathtaking void opened up by the strangeness of Jesus' presence after his death. "Easter," writes Rowan Williams, "occurs when we find in Jesus not a dead friend, but a living stranger" (Williams, 74). But, you might be thinking, this can't be right. Doesn't John devote the final two chapters of his Gospel to convincing us that the risen Jesus is the same Jesus as the one who was baptized in the Jordan, who walked around Galilee with his disciples, who healed the sick, who taught in synagogues, who made his way toward Jerusalem, and who was crucified and buried? If that is the case, how can Easter depend on the experience of emptiness and loss? How can Easter be an encounter with a man who is not a dead friend but a living stranger? Those are the questions that ought to erupt for us in this moment when Jesus stands among his disciples on Easter. They are questions John keeps on our minds as he stretches out this moment of silence by telling the story of Jesus appearing again to the disciples, this time when Thomas is there. This subsequent scene with Thomas is not just a new piece of the story, but an intensification of the moment of encounter with a living stranger.

For whatever reason, Thomas was out when Jesus came and stood among the disciples; he wasn't present when Jesus extended his peace to them; he wasn't part of the moment when recognition flooded into the void of the disciples' minds as they rejoiced in having seen the Lord. When Thomas returns, the disciples confront him with their good news, just as Mary had confronted them earlier. Given the incredible news, it's hard to fault him for his response. If I were Thomas, this is what I would have told them: "You've been duped. You're clearly the victims of some hoax, or, if not a hoax, then a collective hallucination. Dear friends, don't misunderstand me. I sympathize with your desire to feel peace and joy. We're all grief-stricken; all of us long for the days when Jesus walked with us, when he taught us, when he ate and drank with us, when he showed us that we could be more than we'd ever asked or imagined. But all of that is over now." So, "Unless I see in his hands the mark of the nails, and place my finger in the mark of the nails and my hand in his side, I will not believe" (John 20:25).

Notice that Thomas does not ask for proof of the resurrection. He does not question his companions about how they recognized Jesus as alive. Instead, Thomas points toward the marks of Christ's death as his criteria for belief. In other words, Thomas describes the experience of emptiness in the face of Jesus' death, the traumatic void in which whatever God had meant to them was now meaningless. Thomas gives voice to the disciples' earlier posture, huddled together in fear as darkness descended on a hollow world. Despite his friends' hope, Thomas cannot dismiss the memory of his dead friend Jesus, and even that reminiscence, perhaps, is slipping away—a familiar experience for any of you who have lost a loved one. There is no indication that Thomas imagines the possibility of encountering anything other than a corpse, his dead friend Jesus. His condition for belief is death, or perhaps we might say, the condition of his belief is dead.

There is an interesting textual connection here that helps to flesh out some of this, for the Greek text of John 20:25–27 echoes a Greek version of Exod 27:7. In Exodus, God gives Moses instructions for how the altar of burnt offering is to be carried: rings are to be attached to the altar, through which poles will be put so that the altar might be carried with the people. Those rings are described as *daktulious* ("finger-holes") which, when you think about it, is precisely what rings are. Moreover, the rings are to be attached to the side of the altar. In John, Thomas demands to stick his fingers in the holes that the nails left in Jesus' hands, and to place his hand in the hole left by the spear that pierced Jesus' side. These marks of Jesus' death are to be Thomas' way of carrying his memory forward, just as the finger holes attached to the side of the altar are to be Israel's way of carrying the altar of burnt offering.

A week after Jesus' first appearance, John recapitulates the scene of Easter discovery. The details of the story are virtually unchanged from the first time Jesus appears to his disciples. Jesus again comes and stands among the disciples. The doors are shut, and he greets them with peace. But Thomas is present this time, and Jesus singles him out and says, "Put your finger here and see my hands. Reach out your hand and put it in my side" (John 20:27). The most astounding thing about this exchange is that Jesus has addressed Thomas *as his dead friend*. Jesus has come to Thomas on Thomas' own terms, just as he came initially to his disciples in their fishing boats, just as he came to the crowds following him with their tired, sick, hungry, and poor. Jesus has encountered Thomas as no one else but his dead friend. But, dead people cannot address us; dead people cannot come to us. Only someone who is alive can speak; only someone who is alive can offer herself in friendship to others. Recognition occurs the moment when Thomas sees Jesus again as a dead friend, as well as a risen stranger. *That's* the moment of Easter: when the darkness, fear, anxiety, and doubt are peeled away, and Thomas can do nothing but gasp, "My Lord and my God!" (v. 28).

By the way, you might have noticed that Thomas' criteria for belief become meaningless when he is addressed by Jesus, when he is called back from the void of loss by the unexpected, new presence of his dead friend now strangely alive. There's no indication in the text that Thomas does indeed stick his fingers in the nail holes or place his hand in Jesus' side. Thomas' experience of Easter is not dependent on the proof he initially thought necessary, though I suppose Thomas could have had it if he needed it. What is at stake in this Easter moment is having the terror of a world without God broken open in the presence of a dead friend made strangely new: strange *and* new because Jesus now bears death in his life and invites us to believe that he is the same Lord and friend that he always was.

The risen body of Jesus brought Thomas into the light of Easter, and now this same Jesus brings us into the dawn of Easter's light. Our lives in Christ consist both in growing into Jesus' resurrected life and in displaying the power of Easter to the world. God is this friend, the risen stranger, who embodied in his earthly ministry all of our hopes for the healing of the world, who died and thus epitomized all our hopeless emptiness, and who lives again beyond hope, beyond expectation, and calls out to us, again and again, saying, "Do not doubt. Believe" (v. 27).

Conclusion

Voices

1 Samuel 3:1–20; John 1:43–51

In my soul I feel just that terrible pain of loss, of God not wanting me, of God not being God, of God not really existing.

If I ever become a saint, I will surely be one of darkness.

~ Mother Teresa

I want to tell you three stories about the voice of God. These stories may sound completely foreign to your experience. And that's okay. God doesn't speak to everyone in the same way. But God does speak, and sometimes the best we can do is overhear what God has said to someone else and take his or her word from God as our own. Christians are great at eavesdropping. That's what we do when we read the Bible. This holy text is a compilation of letters and writings to other people—some are history books for the Jews, some are stories for particular churches in the first century to help them remember Jesus, and some parts of the Bible are pieces of mail addressed to other people. And in all of it, we find God speaking to us as well. For example, in our passage from John's Gospel, we hear Jesus offering an invitation to Philip. He says, "Follow me" (John 1:43). This is the call of discipleship, the call to be a Christian. And we take it as an invitation for us, too. We overhear Jesus saying, "Follow me" to Philip and we take it as a word to us. The voice of God continually echoes through history, through others, and reaches us as personally as it was first spoken.

That's what I'm hoping for in telling you these stories today. Listen for echoes of God's voice through these three lives. Their biographies can become God's speech to us. You don't have to have shared their experience. All you need to do is overhear God's voice and take it as a message for you. Hear God's voice, God's invitation, resounding into you through these stories—we always hear the same voice, but with different accents: "Follow me."

Story # 1: MLK

Tomorrow is Martin Luther King Jr. Day, which is quite extraordinary. Pastors usually don't get national holidays in their honor. Presidents of the United States do, not clergy. So I figured I should make the best of it, for the sake of that class of people called "the pastor."

Martin King frequently said this about himself: "In the quiet recesses of my heart, I am fundamentally a clergyman, a Baptist preacher" (Lischer, 3). His pastoral identity came naturally to him. King really didn't have a choice one way or the other. He was born a Baptist preacher; it was in his lineage, written in stars. His father and his grandfather were both pastors. So, King grew up at the center of attention at Ebenezer Baptist Church in Atlanta, Georgia. The role of pastor was familiar to him. But he lacked one thing, a requirement for ministry in the Baptist church: a call from the Lord, the voice from heaven. Every Baptist minister has to have a call. You don't become a pastor because it's convenient or because it comes naturally to you or even because you demonstrate pastoral gifts. None of that is primary for the Baptist churches King wanted to serve. No, you do it because God tells you to; and you better have a good testimony ready for the congregation when they ask about your calling—something similar to the story of the young Samuel we heard in one of the Scripture readings tonight. King didn't have one of those experiences. Here's what he said: "My call to the ministry was not a miraculous or supernatural something, on the contrary it was an inner urge calling me to serve humanity" (27)—*an inner urge to serve humanity*. That sounds like a weak substitute for a voice from heaven. But it turned out to be good enough. He was ordained on February 25, 1948, without hearing a call like Samuel's call.

But *something*—a "supernatural something," to use King's language—happened in his kitchen in January of 1956. At the time he was the pastor of Dexter Avenue Baptist Church in Montgomery, Alabama. It was the middle of the Montgomery Bus Boycott, which had gone on much longer than anyone expected. The whole city was raging with anger—and King was the focus of their anger because he was the leader of the boycott. At one point he was receiving forty phone calls a day at his house, death threats for him and his family. One night after a boycott strategy session, Martin King got home around midnight. He was in despair. King realized he wasn't a very good leader. He had no idea what to do. He was in over his head. He was just a pastor who got pushed into a community leadership position and he didn't want to be there anymore. He couldn't sleep, so he sat at the kitchen table with a cup of coffee. Then the phone rang. He picked it up. Another death threat: *If you want to live,* the voice said, *if you want your family to live, you better leave Montgomery tonight.* Click.

That was the last straw. He couldn't handle it anymore. King slumped back into his chair and started to give up. Let me read one of his accounts of that night: "I was ready to give up. With my cup of coffee sitting untouched before me, I tried to think of a way to move out of the picture without appearing a coward . . . ." King was devastated and exhausted. Then a voice called out to him: "Martin Luther, stand up for righteousness. Stand up for justice. Stand up for Truth" (176). He heard the voice of God and finally received his call—"a miraculous or supernatural something."

But what happened after God visited him in the kitchen? Three days later he and his family woke up to a terrible explosion. Someone bombed their house. Miraculously, he and his family were not harmed. And exactly a year (to the day) after God spoke to him, King heard a noise outside. He opened the door and found a bundle of dynamite; the fuse was lit but went out. He was spared, at least for a few more years, so he could do a little more work.

Story # 2: Samuel

The story from our assigned passage from the book of 1 Samuel opens with a statement about God's voice. "The word of the Lord was rare in those days" (1 Sam 3:1). Some time had passed without a word from God. Years of silence. No one heard the voice of God in those days . . . until one night. The boy Samuel was sound asleep, lying in bed. "Then the Lord called, 'Samuel, Samuel!' and he [Samuel] said, 'Here I am!' and ran to Eli, and said, 'Here I am, for you called me.' But Eli said, 'I did not call; lie down again'" (vv. 4–5). This happens again and again, three times: Samuel hears a voice and thinks it's the priest Eli, but when he goes to Eli, Eli tells him to go back to sleep. Maybe it was a dream? Finally, Eli figures out that something strange is going on. Could it be God? Perhaps. No one knew what God's voice sounded like anymore. It had been far too long since someone heard the Lord. Eli wondered if God's voice might be heard again; for some reason, God may be speaking to this boy. Eli told Samuel what to say when he heard the voice again: "if he calls you again, you shall say: 'Speak Lord, for your servant is listening'" (v. 10). Samuel did what he was told. He returned to bed and heard God's voice one more time. Samuel let God know that he was ready to listen. And so he heard and received a word from the Lord—the voice of God returned to the people.

I don't want to say too much about this episode in Samuel's life because I want you to make connections for yourself among these three stories. But I can't help but make a couple observations. First, the young Samuel hears God's voice but doesn't know it until the wise, old Eli tells him what to do. The old teach the young how to hear what God says. We don't know how to listen to God on our own. Someone must teach us. Second, the most important detail in this story is that God speaks. But it's also important to listen for what exactly God says—this isn't revelation in the abstract, not some generalized word from the Lord. God's word brings terrible news: God will punish Eli and his sons. It is a word of judgment. I'm sure Samuel wished God didn't end up speaking to him.

If you hear God's voice, beware! The road may be difficult after that. And it's probably because you're walking in the way of Jesus, which leads to the cross, as Martin Luther King showed us with his life.

Story # 3: Mother Teresa

In an interview many years ago, Dan Rather asked Mother Teresa about her prayer life. He asked, "Mother Teresa, you are a woman of prayer; what is it that you say to God when you pray?" She answered: "Well, I don't say anything; I just listen." Dan Rather followed with another question: "What is it that God says to you during prayer?" Mother Teresa thought for a moment, then responded: "He doesn't say anything. He just listens."

Teresa and God, sitting together in silence, enjoying each other's presence . . . a beautiful image.

In 2007 one of Mother Teresa's spiritual directors published a book of her personal and confidential letters. The book caused quite a controversy because in the letters Mother Teresa wrestles with God's silence. Who knew that such a holy person didn't hear God's voice for so long? Fifty years of silence, fifty years of doubt, fifty years of feeling abandoned by God. But she did hear God's voice . . . once: September 10, 1946, on a train in Calcutta. Jesus spoke to her. Teresa tells us what God's voice said: "I want Indian nuns, Missionaries of Charity, who would be my fire of love amongst the poor, the sick, the dying, and the little children . . . Wouldst thou not help?" She said yes and spent the rest of her life in the slums of Calcutta—*a fire of God's love amongst the poor, the sick, the dying, and the little children*. Teresa was that fire for love. She obeyed the voice of God until she died in 1997. And over those fifty years God offered her only silence in return. "The word of the Lord was rare in those days," as it says in our passage from 1 Samuel.

How did she do it? How could she go on with such difficult work without the voice of God continually speaking life in the midst of so much death? Half a century without reassurance: no second word to confirm the first, to keep it fresh, to convince her that it really was God who spoke to her. It's a miracle that she never gave up. We call that miracle *faith*—the God-given ability to press on in the midst of an experience of abandonment. She continued to have faith, despite the reality of death all around. Mother Teresa never let go of her faith, despite her fifty-year experience of doubt. She never abandoned the God who seemed to have abandoned her. Instead, she abandoned herself *to* God all the more. Even though she never again heard the voice of God, Teresa knew God's presence, even when her feelings said that God was absent. Feelings aren't always trustworthy; experience can be deceptive. She knew that. But that's where faith kicks in. Faith is a journey, a life-long abandonment *to God*. And that was exactly what Mother Teresa did.

We like to turn Teresa of Calcutta into an example of someone who knew how to serve the poor. She embodied selfless sacrifice and giving. But that's not how Teresa saw her own life. She didn't talk about the pressing need to do good. She didn't manipulate us, she didn't play with our sense of guilt, she didn't use statistics to get us to serve the poor with her. Instead, Mother Teresa testified to the mysteries of Eucharistic Adoration. This language is foreign to us because we are Mennonites. But if we want to understand Teresa's witness, if we want to overhear the voice of God in her life, then we have to pay attention to this practice that fueled her life. No one knows exactly when the church started meditating on the consecrated bread on the Eucharistic altar. But there are plenty of accounts and descriptions through the ages of people spending hours in the presence of Christ's body in the consecrated host. They contemplated the mysteries of the Eucharist and received Christ's gracious presence through their silent gaze. The Roman Catholic Church now calls it, "The Adoration of the Blessed Sacrament."

Teresa urged her fellow sisters of Charity to engage in this contemplative practice: "We begin our day with the Holy Mass and Communion, and we finish the day with an hour of adoration" (Teresa, *Essential Writings*, 103). But she also said that their presence with the dying lepers—as they washed them and cared for them—was also their Adoration of the Blessed Sacrament. "[I]n the Mass we have Jesus in the appearance of bread, while in the slums we see Christ and touch him in the broken bodies" (Teresa, *Gift for God*, 76). Teresa's sisters of Charity didn't take care of the dying and the poor because they felt the need to serve the less fortunate. No, Teresa and her sisters tended to the poor of Calcutta's slums because that was their Adoration of Christ, that was how they received Christ's gracious presence. With the dying, they sat with God. And sometimes, with contemplative patience, they were able to hear God's voice, sometimes just a whisper, sometimes in the silence of a breath without words—God's voice echoing in a sigh. That was where Teresa sat in the presence of God. That was where she heard God's silent voice. *The adoration of Christ.*

A Last Word

"The word of the Lord was rare in those days." Maybe so. Perhaps that's true today, for you and for me. But we can still hear echoes. We've heard echoes of God's voice in these three stories. Perhaps the word of God is *rare*, but that also means it is *precious*—something to hold onto, to remember, and to follow. "Follow me," says the Voice.

What Is This?

Exodus 16:2–16; Psalm 105:1–6, 37–45; Jonah 3:10–
4:11; Philippians 1:21–30; Matthew 20:1–16

Manna. *What is it?* The Israelites fear their death, their annihilation in the wilderness. They fear the possibility of dissolving into the desert sands. So they look back to Egypt, where life was somewhat stable, predictable, controllable. This isn't the first time their fear turns to grumbling and turns them back towards those warm meals in their Egyptian slave quarters. Remember back when they found themselves between the Red Sea on one side and Pharaoh's approaching army on the other. Listen to what they said to Moses then: "Was it because there were no graves in Egypt that you brought us to the desert to die? What have you done to us by bringing us out of Egypt? Didn't we say to you in Egypt, 'Leave us alone; let us serve the Egyptians'? It would have been better for us to serve the Egyptians than to die in the desert!" (Exod 14:11–12). At that moment—the moment when death seemed imminent—that's when their lack of trust was exposed. But God saved them anyway. God's gracious care for God's people exceeds our imaginations, God reaches beyond our ideas about what is possible and impossible.

Now again in our Scripture reading today, Israel remembers Egypt and complains in the wilderness. They say to Moses and Aaron, "Why did you take us away from those warm meals and bring us to the desert to starve to death?" (16:3). Despite their lack of trust, their constant grumbling against God's promised care, God graciously provides. God sends quail and bread from heaven. In the wilderness God sends abundant provision: heavenly bread, the bread of life. And this is where the story gets quite interesting. When they see the bread, they somehow don't recognize it. Even though Moses tells them God will provide bread from heaven in the morning, when they see it they ask, "What is this?" (v. 15). It comes, and they don't know what it is. It's morning, God promised them a hearty breakfast, and they don't see how this white stuff on the ground could be it. Maybe they want Oatmeal, not this dew-looking bread that tastes like honey wafers (v. 31). Somehow their expectations blind them from the heavenly bread right before their eyes. "*What is this?*" they asked.

What is this?

The shock, the completely foreign, the unimaginable, the unrecognizable. God's gift arrives so mysteriously that it doesn't fit into how we think gifts are supposed to be given, and what they are supposed to look like. This heavenly gift is so new that it's unnamable: they call it *Manna*, which is a Hebrew word that literally means, *"what is it"* (v. 31). They name it the same phrase they used as their question when they first saw it. *Manna: What is this?* They don't yet know how to name it, but they do the best they can with the words they have.

In our passage from the Gospel of Matthew, Peter asks Jesus the same sort of question. In many ways he repeats Israel's question in the wilderness: "What is this?" *What is this kingdom of heaven?* Peter asks Jesus, "We have left everything to follow you! What then will there be for us?" (Matt 19:27). Jesus tells Peter that he and the rest of the twelve disciples will "sit on twelve thrones, judging the twelve tribes of Israel" (v. 28). But Jesus goes on to say that the way they will rule from their heavenly thrones will not look like they expect. He unsettles their images of sitting on heavenly thrones by adding, "But many who are first will be last, and many who are last will be first" (v. 30). And we, along with the confused disciples ask, *What is this?*

Jesus says it's like this: "the kingdom of heaven is like a landowner who went out early in the morning to hire men to work in his vineyard" (20:1). In the morning he hires some guys and says he's going to pay them a *denarius*. Then he goes out again around lunchtime, and again in the afternoon, then in the evening, and every time he goes out the landowner hires new people. At the end of the day he starts with the last people he hired and pays them the same as the first. The folks who worked the longest grumble and ask, *What is this?*

Jesus has an answer. It's called generosity, grace. Jesus names it "the kingdom of heaven." This parable is what it looks like with heaven falls into the world. Everyone gets the same wage, a living wage—that's the way Jesus practices "trickle-down economics" from heaven. The kingdom comes down from heaven, and people wonder what is going on. It's just like that Manna in the wilderness: it's hard to name, to conceptualize, to fit into the world we know. We struggle with all the words we have to come up with some description, something to say, some way to tell others this good news—to say, "hey, this is how God's generosity works. I've seen it." And when we think we have a grasp on God's grace—the way God's generosity flows in the world, in our church, among our friends and enemies, among our co-workers—right when we approach the level of confidence required to say something, the voice of God descends from heaven and says, *"The last shall be first and the first shall be last."*

What is this?

We can't help but say to ourselves, "We've been here longer, we've been working on this discipleship business and know the ins and outs and that one—yeah, her over there—she's definitely out. That is *not* the way of the cross." We are like Jonah who says that the people of Nineveh do not belong. *They* shouldn't get God's generosity. Bread from heaven shouldn't fall in *that* desert. But the voice of the Lord says to Jonah, "Have you any right to be angry?" (Jonah 4:4). It's the same word that Jesus speaks in Matthew: "Are you jealous because I am generous?" (Matt 20:15). At such a word, all we can do is say, "What is this?" The news of God's new world shocks us; it scrambles our sense of direction. We lose our bearings: *this isn't the way reality is organized; something is changing, but we can't quite take hold of it.* "What is this?" That's all we can say. *How, O God, can you do this and expect order in our world?*

As I wander with you through these assigned Bible passages, it seems like we are coming to a familiar message. I can hear a familiar lesson sneaking its way into my sermon, so I want to register a suspicion. I'm suspicious of my own reading of these texts. I am suspicious because somehow, no matter what Scriptures are assigned, I seem to come up with a message I am quite comfortable with. I can name it. It goes something like this: the way into the eternal life God offers us is found as we break through our conceptions of God, as we reach with our imaginations into new territory, as we humble ourselves and see how God is speaking to us through our neighbor—the stranger sitting next to you right now, and the one tomorrow at work, and the one you thought you knew so well that you closed yourself off from how God wants to say something new to you through her or him. This all too familiar sermon is about how the Father's gift of the Son, and continuing presence through the Holy Spirit, wants to explode all of our jealousies, all of our selfish confidence, all of the ways we are like Jonah or the folks working in the vineyard since the early morning. This typical message is about all of the ways we try to control other people, and how little we dare to let other people see who we are, how we pigeon-hole others in ways that prevent us from looking them in the face and waiting for the newness of God to shock us to a question: *What is this? Is this one the Manna, the bread of life from heaven? Is this stranger supposed to sustain my faith? Is this one sent from heaven?*

That's the part of the gospel I like to preach. Please don't misunderstand me. I still think all of this is the good news and I'm not about to change my mind. Yet I am acutely aware that it's very easy for me to preach that message. I think part of this ease has to do with how such a message fits my personality. To listen to others is a more comfortable position for me than thinking that I have something to say, that what I have to say is all that important. That's why it is still strange for me to get up here and preach to you. This practice doesn't feel like who I think I am. I'm always nervous and uncomfortable. Always sweating.

This is probably why the apostle Paul makes me so uncomfortable. I tense up when I read him sometimes. Listen to what he says in our passage from Philippians:

> I desire to depart and be with Christ, which is better by far; but it is more necessary for you that I remain in the body. Convinced of this, I know that I will remain, and I will continue with all of you for your progress and joy in the faith, so that through my being with you again your joy in Christ Jesus will overflow on account of me. (Phil 1:23–26)

There is nothing here about how important it is to listen to others, to make room for someone to reveal the strange wonder of God in our midst. There's nothing in this passage from Paul that asks a question. He doesn't say anything about how important it is to wait for God's word to emerge in strange and unexpected ways. Frankly, Paul sounds completely full of himself: "necessary for you . . . for your progress . . . that your joy may overflow because of me." How dare he! *What is this?*

I don't know what to do with Paul's confidence. I cringe. I have a hard time seeing how this word is bread of life, a heavenly gift. His confidence makes me feel threatened, like there's no room for my voice. But Paul has something to say; he has some fruit of the Spirit he has to share and nothing will stop him. He must speak. He's like that Psalmist we heard tonight, who can't keep quiet about all the wonderful ways God has sustained Israel. In Psalm 105 we hear how God delivered Israel from Egypt, how God traveled with Israel in a fiery cloud, how God sustained the people with quail and bread from heaven and gave the people water from a rock, and how God is forever faithful to the promises made to Abraham. The psalmist must speak. Paul must speak. And so, I speak . . . and so must you.

All of these speeches—Paul's, the Psalmist's, yours, and mine—may be the product of self-absorbed confidence. But to reduce Paul's, or the Psalmist's, or Moses', or Jesus' proclamation of the good news to some sort of posturing—an attempt to manipulate an audience—is to miss the point entirely. Sure, most of us have mixed motives. Yet we still speak the good news because we have to make sense of the bread from heaven. The Christian life is about figuring out how to make sense of what happened when the Holy Spirit descended from heaven and revealed to our eyes the bread of life—the Word made flesh, the Son of God, our crucified savior, our Manna.

Paul speaks because he can't help but speak. He has to share himself with us. And it's a risk. It takes vulnerability to say what we think, to risk a moment of confidence, to speak up and let yourself be known—to speak through all our masks, all our posturing, and risk the possibility that someone might see us for who we are. That's scary. After mustering up the confidence to share, to speak, to testify to the good news, your audience may look at you funny and say, "What is this?"

Perhaps that's what you are thinking right now. And all I can say is that I hope this is the bread of life, that somehow the Word from heaven has descended in our midst and that we have received our daily Manna. So, here I am, up here learning to speak about all of the ways our Scriptures make me uncomfortable, all of the ways I feel exposed as I stammer away trying to say something about what I saw as I squinted and cringed at these texts. But the good news is that some among us know what it means to suffer with Christ like Paul did, and some among us have something to say about how they are learning to see Manna—

that Word made new every morning, just enough for our daily bread. That's why after I'm done preaching, I will sit down and you will have a chance to speak. We call it a time for the "discernment of the Word." In the Mennonite tradition, it's called the *Zeugnis*—a German word for "conversation." We believe the Word comes to us through a conversation, a dialogue with Scripture and each other. The conversation opens us to the newness of Christ, the new light that the Holy Spirit shines in our lives.

I started my sermon by asking, with the Israelites in the wilderness, "What is this?" What is the voice of God saying to us? What does God's grace do to us? And in a few moments you will have a chance to give an answer and, perhaps, ask your own questions. The conversation is how we struggle together to name God's grace, to see Christ's face, to open our lives to the Holy Spirit. This is holy communication, our communion in the Word. This sacred process is how you and I are giving and receiving the presence of God, the bread of heaven, holy Manna. We trust that wherever two or more are gathered, Christ is present with us, in our midst, transfiguring our risky words with the true Word from God, and transforming our flesh into the One who is the Word made flesh.

Manna.

What is this?

The Word echoes in our words.

Notes

Introduction

Our language of "resting into God" comes from the work of Herbert McCabe, Sebastian Moore, and James Alison. Their theologies resound with a call for us to be with the God who is always already just there. Alison's essay, "Worship in a violent world," is one good place among many to find a discussion of what it means to rest into God. Alison writes, "True Worship presupposes that the crucified and risen Lord is *just there*.... So we can relax, because we know he's just there.... Because he is just there, our liturgy is an ordered and relaxed way of habitually making ourselves present, as worshipping group, to the one who is just there, already surrounded by festal angels and our predecessors in the faith" (42–43). James Alison, *Undergoing God: Dispatches from the Scene of a Break-in* (New York, NY: Continuum, 2006).

Sebastian Moore's short book, *The Inner Loneliness* (New York, NY: Crossroad, 1982) is a profound meditation on resting into God: "to relax all the way into a God who plays in this world" (106). And, of course, the great preacher Herbert McCabe: "All that [God] asks is that we relax and let ourselves be filled with his love, which eliminates our sins and makes us channels and bearers of his love and forgiveness to everyone." *God, Christ and Us* (London, UK: Continuum, 2003) 123.

Section 1: Hope

Lament and Repent

Isaac preached this Advent sermon at CHMF on December 9, 2007. For N. T. Wright's description of John the Baptist at a "counter-clerical prophet," see his *Jesus and the Victory of God*, (Minneapolis: Fortress, 1996) 161. For more information on Chris and Phileena Heuertz and Word Made Flesh, see their website: http://www.wordmadeflesh.org/. Scott A. Bessenecker also features Chris and Phileena, and their ministry, in his recent book, *The New Friars: The Emerging Movement Serving the World's Poor* (Downers Grove, IL: InterVarsity, 2006). Also, Chris Heuertz recently wrote a book that shares what he's learned from becoming friends with the poor: *Simple Spirituality: Learning to See God in a Broken World* (Downers Grove, IL: InterVarsity, 2008).

CRIES FROM THE DARKNESS

Isaac preached this sermon at CHMF on October 15, 2006. For another meditation on the moment in worship when Rebecca shared her prayers with tears, see Isaac Villegas, "Blessed are those who mourn," *The Mennonite* 11:7 (April 1, 2008) 2. The article is also available online: http://www.themennonite.org/issues/11-7/articles/Blessed_are_those_who_mourn

SILENT WITNESSES

Isaac preached this sermon at CHMF on July 16, 2006. For Karl Marx's famous line where he compares Christianity to a drug, see his essay, "Critique of Hegel's Philosophy of the Right." In his private collection of thought-fragments called "The Mystery of Jesus," Blaise Pascal makes his comment about the unceasing agony of Christ: "Jesus will be in agony until the end of the world. There must be no sleeping during that time" (*Pensée #* 919). Blaise Pascal, *Pensées*, trans. A. J. Krailsheimer (London: Penguin, 1995) 289.

WAITING FOR A PROMISE

Alex preached this Advent sermon at Grace Mennonite Church in Bluffton, Ohio, on December 2, 2007. In order to get a sense for how Ernst Käsemann talks about "the gospel as promise" in Hebrews, here are a few illustrative passages: "Christian hope is always encountered as bound to the revelation of God, thus as the reflection of the divine promise" (26). Salvation "is already present and perceptible in history, yet not other than as promise, that is, as orientation and direction toward a future still to come" (28). The promise "has a fixed content, a clearly outlined goal, a guaranteed realization, and is thus qualitatively superior to every earthly promise" (29). *The Wandering People of God: An Investigation of the Letter to the Hebrews*, trans. Roy A. Harrisville and Irving L. Sandberg (Minneapolis: Augsburg, 1984).

WAITING WITH MARY

Isaac preached this Advent sermon at CHMF on December 21, 2008. For Martin Luther talking about "all of life is baptism," see Stanley Cavell's comments in his essay "A Matter of Meaning It," in *Must We Mean What We Say? A Book of Essays* (Cambridge: Cambridge University Press, 2002) 229.

When Isaac compares our human experience to floating as bubbles of foam on a stormy sea, he is paraphrasing William James: "The bubbles on the foam which coats a stormy sea are floating episodes, made and unmade by the forces of the wind and water. Our private selves are like those bubbles,—epiphenomena, as Clifford, I believe, ingeniously called them; their destinies weigh nothing and determine nothing in the world's irremedial currents of events." Williams James, *Varieties of Religious Experience: A Study in Human Nature* (New York: Mentor, 1958) 408.

This sermon is indebted to a couple of sermons by Rowan Williams: "Waiting on God," and "Born of the Virgin Mary." Both are in *A Ray of Darkness: Sermons and Reflections* (Cambridge, MA: Cowley, 1995).

MATER ECCLESIA

Isaac preached this sermon at CHMF on September 24, 2006; this was the service for Isaac's licensing and installation as a pastor. For a full description of the Mennonite liturgy for calling a pastor, see the *Minister's Manual*, ed. John Rempel (Scottdale, PA: Herald, 1998) 166–69.

For an early church father who discusses the motherhood of the church, see St. Cyprian's *The Unity of the Church*: "You cannot have God for your Father if you have not the Church for your mother" (*De ecclesiae catholicae unitate* 6). Isaac also quotes St. Irenaeus of Lyons, who writes: "one must cling to the Church, be brought up within her womb, and feed there on the Lord's Scripture" (*Adversus Haereses* l.5, c. 20, n. 2.) This passage can be found in Henri de Lubac's important study, *The Motherhood of the Church: Followed by Particular Churches in the Universal Church* (San Francisco: Ignatius, 1983) 70. Also see Henri de Lubac, *The Splendor of the Church*, trans. Michael Mason (San Francisco: Ignatius, 1999), especially chapter 8: "Ecclesia Mater."

A Protest of Hope

Isaac preached this sermon at CHMF on March 20, 2008, for the Maundy Thursday footwashing service.

Section 2: Communion

Eucharist Means Gratitude

Isaac preached this sermon for Christ the King Sunday at CHMF on November 23, 2008. He quotes from Rowan Williams, *Tokens of Trust* (Louisville, KY: Westminster John Knox, 2007) 37. Williams provided the central insight of this sermon: as Williams writes, "the moment of creation is now. . . . It means that within every circumstance, every object, every person, God's action is going on, a sort of white heat at the centre of everything. It means that each one of us is already in a relationship with God before we've ever thought about it" (35).

Flesh and Blood

Alex preached this sermon at CHMF on August 17, 2003. For his reference to Dawkins' comments on transubstantiation, see Richard Dawkins, "Viruses of the Mind" (1991), in *Dennett and His Critics: Demystifying Mind*, ed. Bo Dahlbom (Cambridge, MA: Blackwell, 1993) 13–27.

Our Tortured King

Isaac first preached this sermon for Christ the King Sunday at CHMF on November 25, 2007; this revised version was preached on November 21, 2010. For his account of the socio-political meaning of Jesus' crucifixion, Isaac relies on N. T. Wright, who writes: "Crucifixion was a powerful symbol throughout the Roman world. It was not just a means of liquidating undesirables; it did so with the maximum degradation and humiliation. It said, loud and clear: we are in charge here; you are our property; we can do what we like with you. . . . It told an implicit story, of the uselessness of rebel recalcitrance and the ruthlessness of imperial power. It said, in particular: this is what happens to rebel leaders. . . . Jesus was executed as a rebel against Rome. . . . [W]hen Jesus was crucified, the general impression in Jerusalem that day must have been that he was one more in a long line of would-be, but failed, Messiahs." *Jesus and the Victory of God* (Minneapolis: Fortress, 1996) 543–44.

For a discussion of "a dangerous memory," see Johann Baptist Metz, *Faith in History and Society: Toward a Practical Fundamental Theology* (New York: Seabury, 1980). There is a "dangerous memory," writes Metz, "that threatens the present and calls it into question because it remembers a future that is still outstanding... This memory breaks through the grip of the prevailing consciousness. It claims unresolved conflicts that have been thrust into the background and unfulfilled hopes. It maintains earlier experiences in contrast to the prevailing insights and in this way makes the present unsafe" (200).

BODIES MATTER

Part 1 is the sermon Isaac preached on the property of a U.S. Immigration and Customs Enforcement regional detention center in Cary, North Carolina, hidden in a suburban business park next to the offices of Oxford University Press. The footwashing service took place on the morning of Holy Thursday, 2010 (April 1st). The local Raleigh-based newspaper covered the story: see Yonat Shimron, "Protestors hold demonstration outside Cary ICE office," *The News & Observer*, April 1, 2010. The article is available online: http://www.newsobserver.com/2010/04/01/417012/protesters-hold-demonstration.html.

Part 2 is the sermon Isaac preached that same day, but at the evening footwashing service for Chapel Hill Mennonite Fellowship. For the quotation Isaac uses from Sebastian Moore, see *God Is a New Language* (Westminster, MD: Newman, 1967) 141.

Section 3: Desire

HEART'S DESIRE

Alex preached this sermon at CHMF on June 18, 2006. For his reference to Richard Hays regarding the Greek of 2 Corinthians 5, see Richard B. Hays, *The Moral Vision of the New Testament: Community, Cross, New Creation: A Contemporary Introduction to New Testament Ethics* (San Francisco: HarperSanFrancisco, 1996) 20.

FAITH AND LOVE

Alex preached this sermon at CHMF on June 13, 2004. For more information on the historic ecumenical discussion between the Lutherans and Catholics on the doctrine of justification, see their recent publication: The Lutheran World Federation and the Roman Catholic Church, *The Joint Declaration on the Doctrine of Justification* (Grand Rapids: Eerdmans, 2000).

There are plenty of places to go for a discussion of the meaning of "Faith of Christ" in Galatians. J. Louis Martyn has a short and clear discussion of the issues: "The Apocalyptic Gospel in Galatians," *Interpretation* 54:3 (July, 2000) 246–66. For an in-depth study that also surveys the recent literature on Galatians, see Appendix 2 (272–97) at the back of Richard B. Hays' book, *The Faith of Jesus Christ: The Narrative Substructure of Galatians 3:1—4:11*, 2nd ed. (Grand Rapids: Eerdmans, 2002).

Alex depends on the work of Sebastian Moore for describing the voice of sin. The quote he uses comes from Sebastian Moore, *The Fire and the Rose Are One* (New York: Seabury, 1980) 69.

CLOSER

Isaac preached this sermon for Trinity Sunday at CHMF on June 7, 2009. For the passage from Augustine that Isaac quotes, see Augustine of Hippo, Sermon 169, 11, 13.

Much of this sermon was shaped by reading Eugene F. Rogers Jr. wonderful book about the Holy Spirit: *After the Spirit: A Constructive Pneumatology from Resources outside the Modern West* (Grand Rapids: Eerdmans, 2005). Rogers offers a helpful discussion of the Holy Spirit that refuses to let us draw an easy line between God's Spirit and our human spirit. Throughout Scripture, Rogers argues, the Holy Spirit befriends creation. God is always closer to us than we want to admit. Here's a passage from the end of his book: "The Spirit moves the heart *from the outside* and *most internally*, since it is a feature of God's transcendence of creatures to be more internal to them than they are to themselves" (219).

An insight from Sebastian Moore also stands in the background of this sermon. In Moore's book, *The Inner Loneliness* (New York: Crossroad, 1982), he shows how our desire to argue for God's transcendence over against us is rooted in a fear of intimacy, a fear of a God who gets to close—ultimately, a fear of the depths of Jesus' incarnation. For Moore, we can see how this fear develops from the Christological arguments in the fourth century, especially with those who follow Arius. Moore writes, "What Arius represents is a failure to relax all the way into a God who plays in this world. He represents a foreshortened theism in which the creature, in the last resort, is struggling towards God, not participating in God's play with himself" (106).

When Isaac argues that "the crucifixion kills our picture of a detached God," he is drawing from Rowan Williams' essay "Word and Spirit" where Williams shows how the event at Calvary dismantles our vision of God as a sovereign victor. Here's an important passage from his essay: "Father and Son are not to be set against each other at Calvary: the God who 'abandons' is the God of Caiaphas, the God whose relation to the world is that of master to slave. But Jesus is not a slave but child, and *eldest* child, and adult 'child', and his Father is not the castrating despot of infantile nightmare. 'God' vanishes on the cross: Father and Son remain, in the shared, consubstantial weakness of their compassion. And the Father will raise the Son in the power of the Spirit." Rowan Williams, *On Christian Theology*, Challenges in Contemporary Theology (Oxford: Blackwell, 2000) 121.

IF OUR HEARTS CONDEMN US

Alex preached this sermon at CHMF on May 7, 2006. His reading of the community of 1 John as one in conflict is dependent on Robert Kysar's commentary, *Augsburg Commentary on the New Testament: 1, 2, 3 John* (Minneapolis: Fortress, 1986). For Alex's quotations from Karl Barth, see Barth's *Church Dogmatics* 4/2, trans. G. W. Bromiley (Edinburgh: T. & T. Clark, 1958).

YOU SHALL NOT COVET

Alex preached this sermon at CHMF on March 19, 2006. He draws from a passage from C. S. Lewis' book, *The Weight of Glory* (San Francisco: HarperSanFrancisco, 2001): "Indeed, if we consider the unblushing promises of reward and the staggering nature of the rewards promised in the Gospels, it would seem that Our Lord finds our desires, not too strong, but too weak. We are half-hearted creatures, fooling about with drink and sex and ambition when infinite joy is offered us, like an ignorant child who wants to go on making mud pies in a slum because he cannot imagine what is meant by the offer of a holiday at the sea. We are far too easily pleased" (16).

For Alex's quotation of Martin Luther, see Luther's *The Large Catechism*, trans. Robert H. Fischer (Philadelphia: Fortress, 1959). For his use of Stanley Hauerwas and William H. Willimon, see their book *The Truth About God: The Ten Commandments in Christian Life* (Nashville: Abingdon, 1999). And, lastly, for the extended passage from Karl Barth, see his *Church Dogmatics* 4/2, trans. G. W. Bromiley (Edinburgh: T. & T. Clark, 1958).

Section 4: Power

ILLUSIONS OF PEACE

Alex preached this sermon at CHMF on June 19, 2005. For his quotation from Archbishop Williams, see Rowan Williams, *The Truce of God* (Grand Rapids: Eerdmans, 2005). In this sermon Alex engages with the thought of Sigmund Freud. For a good introduction on Sigmund Freud's conception of the death drive, see Jonathan Lear, *Freud* (London: Routledge, 2005) chapter 5: "Principles of mental functioning." And for Alex's reference to Karl Barth, see *Church Dogmatics* 1/2, trans. G. W. Bromiley, G. T. Thomson, and Harold Knight (Edinburgh: T. & T. Clark, 1956).

PAUL'S POLITICS

Isaac preached this sermon at CHMF on Jan 21, 2007. He refers to Jim Wallis, *God's Politics: Why the Right Gets It Wrong and the Left Doesn't Get it* (San Francisco: HarperSanFrancisco, 2006). For Isaac's references to McCabe, Bonhoeffer, Barth, McClendon, and Weber, see the following: Herbert McCabe, *The People of God: The Fullness of Life in the Church* (New York: Sheed & Ward, 1964); Dietrich Bonhoeffer, *Dietrich Bonhoeffer Works, Vol. 1: Sanctorum Communio*, trans. Reinhard Krauss and Nancy Lukens (Minneapolis: Fortress, 1998); Karl Barth, *Church Dogmatics* 4/2, trans. G. W. Bromiley (Edinburgh: T. & T. Clark, 1958); James Wm. McClendon, Jr., *Doctrine: Systematic Theology, Volume II* (Nashville: Abingdon, 1994); and Max Weber, "Politics as a Vocation," in *From Max Weber: Essays in Sociology*, trans. by H. H. Gerth and C. Wright Mills (London: Routledge, 1946) 77: "We wish to understand by politics only the leadership, or the influencing of the leadership, of a *political* association, hence today, of a *state*."

Isaac relies heavily on Dale Martin's account of Greco-Roman political rhetoric as a context for understanding Paul's correspondence with the Corinthian church. Dale B. Martin, *The Corinthian Body* (New Haven: Yale University Press, 1995).

For a description of the way Bible reading creates a political body, see John H. Yoder's essay, "Is Not His Word Like a Fire? The Bible and

Civil Turmoil," in *For the Nations: Essays Evangelical and Public* (Grand Rapids: Eerdmans, 1997) 79-93.

POWER IN WEAKNESS

Alex preached this sermon at CHMF on July 6, 2003.

PREPARING FOR PEACE

Alex preached this Advent sermon at CHMF on Dec 9, 2001. The church asked him to incorporate article 22 of the Mennonite Confession of faith into his sermon, as well as the assigned lectionary texts. To read article 22, see *Confession of Faith in a Mennonite Perspective* (Scottdale, PA: Herald, 1995). The title of article 22 is "Peace, Justice, and Nonresistance."

Alex refers to Dietrich Bonhoeffer's description of the Psalter as the "prayer book of the bible." Bonhoeffer wrote a small book for his community on praying the Psalms, which he titled, *Prayerbook of the Bible: An Introduction to the Psalms*. In *Life Together*, Bonhoeffer calls "The Psalter is the great school of prayer" (*Life Together*, 55). See Dietrich Bonhoeffer, *Dietrich Bonhoeffer Works, Volume 5: Life Together and Prayerbook of the Bible* (Minneapolis: Fortress, 1996).

For his discussion on "not being in charge," Alex is drawing on the work of John Howard Yoder. For an obvious place to start exploring Yoder's discussion of this mode of existence, see the essay "On Not Being in Charge" in *The Jewish-Christian Schism Revisited*, eds. Michael G. Cartwright and Peter Ochs (Grand Rapids: Eerdmans, 2003). But Yoder's most sustained and helpful discussion is found among the essays in *For the Nations: Essays Evangelical and Public* (Grand Rapids: Eerdmans, 1997).

REMEMBERING HOME

Isaac preached this sermon at CHMF on July 6, 2008. The church asked him to incorporate article 23 of the Mennonite Confession of faith into his sermon, as well as the assigned lectionary texts. To read article 23, see *Confession of Faith in a Mennonite Perspective* (Scottdale, PA: Herald, 1995). The title of article 23 is "The Church's Relation to Government and Society."

Isaac used Leon Kass as a guide through the story of Joseph. See Leon R. Kass, *The Beginning of Wisdom: Reading Genesis* (Chicago: University of Chicago Press, 2003), chapter 18: "Joseph the Egyptian."

Section 5: Money

Caesar's Coin

Alex preached this sermon at Raleigh Mennonite Church in Raleigh, North Carolina, on July 3, 2005.

Dirty Money

Isaac preached this sermon at CHMF on Sept 23, 2007, for the church's anniversary celebration. His reading of the story of the shrewd manager draws from William R. Herzog, *Parables as Subversive Speech: Jesus as Pedagogue of the Oppressed* (Louisville, KY: Westminster John Knox, 1994), especially chapter 13: "A Weapon of the Weak: The Parable of the Dishonest Steward (Luke 16:1–9).

In his sermon, Isaac quotes a line from T. W. Manson: "All money gets dirty at some stage in its history." See Manson, *The Sayings of Jesus* (London: SCM, 1961) 293.

For a discussion of the Anabaptist teaching in the sixteen-century regarding sharing all things in common ("Omnia sunt communia"), see James M. Stayer, *The German Peasants' War and the Anabaptist Community of Goods* (Montreal: McGill-Queen's University Press, 1991), especially chapter 5: "The Anti-Materialistic Piety of Thomas Müntzer and Its Anabaptist Expressions."

The quote from McCabe that Isaac frequently uses comes from Herbert McCabe, *The People of God: The Fullness of Life in the Church* (New York: Sheed & Ward, 1964).

Irresponsible Stewards

Isaac preached this sermon first at University Baptist Church in Chapel Hill, North Carolina, on February 4, 2007, and at Greensboro Mennonite Church in Greensboro, North Carolina, on August 12, 2007.

Human Enough

Alex preached this sermon at CHMF on September 14, 2008. For his reference to Hauerwas and Willimon, see Stanley Hauerwas and William Willimon, *Lord Teach Us: The Lord's Prayer & the Christian Life* (Nashville: Abingdon, 1996).

Section 6: Salvation

COMPANIONS WITHOUT PAYCHECKS

Isaac preached this sermon at CHMF on June 29, 2008. He depends on two sources: Ellen Davis, "Vulnerability, the Condition of the Covenant," in *The Art of Reading Scripture*, eds. Ellen Davis and Richard Hays (Grand Rapids: Eerdmans, 2003) 283–93; and Leon R. Kass, *The Beginning of Wisdom: Reading Genesis* (Chicago: University of Chicago Press, 2003) 333–48.

For Isaac's reference to a Rabbinic reading of God's "please" to Abraham, see *BT Sanhedrin* 39b.

LIFE ON THE VINE

Alex preached this sermon at CHMF on May 18, 2003.

DELIVERANCE FROM EGYPT

Isaac preached this sermon at CHMF on Sept 7, 2008. For his reference to the itinerant preacher of the Radical Reformation who proclaimed a message of freedom from slavery, see Thomas Müntzer, "A Highly Provoked Defense," in *The Radical Reformation*, ed. and trans. Michael G. Baylor (Cambridge: Cambridge University Press, 1991) 74–94.

Isaac draws from Stanley Hauerwas' discussion of Matthew 18. See Hauerwas, *Matthew*, Brazos Theological Commentary on the Bible (Grand Rapids: Brazos, 2006): "Failure to confront the brother or sister whom we think has sinned against us is not simply a recommendation of how we are to work out our disputes and disagreements, but rather an indication of the kind of community that Jesus has called into existence. This is a people who are to love one another so intensely that they refuse to risk the loss of the one who has gone astray—or the loss of ourselves in harboring resentments" (165).

In talking about love as protest, Isaac uses an insight from Barth's commentary on Romans: Karl Barth, *The Epistle to the Romans*, 6th ed., ed. Edwyn C. Hoskyns (London: Oxford University Press, 1933): "Love of one another ought to be undertaken as the protest against the course of this world. Love is that denial and demolition of the existing order which no revolt can bring about. In this lies the strange novelty of love. . . . Love . . . sets up no idol, is the demolition of every idol. Love is the destruction of everything that is—*like God*: the end of all hierarchies and authorities and intermediaries, because, in every particular man and also in the 'Many', it addresses itself, without fear of contradiction—to the One" (496).

SALVATION IS CREATED

Alex preached this sermon at CHMF on January 1, 2006. He refers to Pavel Tchesnokov's "Salvation is Created," (Choral Public Domain Library, ed. Rafael Ornes, March 19, 2002).

Throughout his sermon, Alex explores an insight from Augustine of Hippo: "The God who created us without us will not save us without us" (Epistle 73). For Alex's use of Karl Barth, see these two volumes: *Church Dogmatics* 1/2, trans. G. W. Bromiley, G. T. Thomson, and Harold Knight (Edinburgh: T. & T. Clark, 1956); and *Church Dogmatics* 4/2, trans. G. W. Bromiley (Edinburgh: T. & T. Clark, 1958). Lastly, as his quotations indicate, Alex develops some of his sermon from one by Rowan Williams, "Born of the Virgin Mary," in *Ray of Darkness: Sermons and Reflections* (Cambridge, MA: Cowley, 1995) 17–21.

Section 7: Strangers

STRANGERS

Alex preached this sermon at CHMF on August 14, 2005.

DO YOU SEE THIS WOMAN?

Isaac preached this sermon at CHMF on June 17, 2007. His exegesis is dependent on Barbara E. Reid's essay, "'Do You See This Woman?' A Liberative Look at Luke 7:36–50 and Strategies for Reading Other Lukan Stories against the Grain," in *A Feminist Companion to Luke*, ed. Amy-Jill Lavine (New York: Sheffield Academic Press, 2002). For Isaac's quotation from Green where exposed hair is likened to being topless, see Joel B. Green, *The Gospel of Luke*, New International Commentary on the New Testament (Grand Rapids: Eerdmans, 1997).

Isaac quotes from Alex's sermon, "Faith and Love," in this volume. On this point about sin, Alex and Isaac are indebted to Sebastian Moore (see the notes for Alex's sermon in section 2). Here is one significant line among many from Moore's corpus: "What we call sin is the enormous darkness everywhere, the worldwide conspiracy to turn our back on what we most deeply know about ourselves. Jesus had a name for society as he dreamed it, society ruled by our real desire. He called it the Kingdom of God." *The Contagion of Jesus: Doing Theology as if it Mattered* (Maryknoll, NY: Orbis, 2007) 121.

WHO ARE YOU?

Alex preached this Advent sermon at CHMF on December 15, 2002.

THE RISEN BODY

Alex preached this sermon at First Mennonite Church in Bluffton, Ohio, on March 30, 2008. He draws from Rowan Williams, *Resurrection: Interpreting the Easter Gospel*, rev. ed. (Cleveland: Pilgrim, 2002). Here is the extended passage from which Alex quotes: "Easter occurs, again and again, in this opening-up of a void, the sense of absence which questions our egocentric aspirations and our longing for 'tidy drama'; it occurs when we find in Jesus not a dead friend but a living stranger" (74).

Section 8: Conclusion

VOICES

Isaac preached this sermon at CHMF on January 18, 2009. The two epigraphs from Mother Teresa come from James Martin, "A Saint's Dark Night," *The New York Times* (August 29, 2007). I also found helpful an essay by Carol Zaleski, "The Dark Night of Mother Teresa," *First Things* (May 2003). This line from Zaleski's essay especially stuck out to me: "And it gave her access to the deepest poverty of the modern world: the poverty of meaninglessness and loneliness."

For the life of Martin Luther King Jr., Isaac relies of Richard Lischer, *The Preacher King: Martin Luther King, Jr. and The Word That Moved America* (New York: Oxford University Press, 1995).

The quotations in the sermon from Teresa are taken from two sources: Mother Teresa, *Essential Writings*, ed. Jean Maalouf (Maryknoll, NY: Orbis, 2001), and *A Gift for God: Prayers and Meditations* (San Francisco: HarperSanFrancisco, 1996).

WHAT IS THIS?

Isaac preached this sermon at CHMF on September 18, 2005.

www.ingramcontent.com/pod-product-compliance
Lightning Source LLC
Chambersburg PA
CBHW020837160426
43192CB00007B/685